Museum Marketing: Competing in
the Global Marketplace

Museum Marketing
Competing in the Global Marketplace

Edited by

Ruth Rentschler
and
Anne-Marie Hede

Routledge
Taylor & Francis Group

LONDON AND NEW YORK

First published by Butterworth-Heinemann

This edition published 2011 by Routledge
2 Park Square, Milton Park, Abingdon, Oxon, OX14 4RN
711 Third Avenue, New York, NY 10017, USA

Routledge is an imprint of the Taylor & Francis Group, an informa business

Copyright © 2007, Ruth Rentschler and Anne-Marie Hede.
All rights reserved

The right of Ruth Rentschler and Anne-Marie Hede to be identified as the
authors of this work has been asserted in accordance with the Copyright,
Designs and Patents Act 1988

Notice
No responsibility is assumed by the publisher for any injury and/or damage
to persons or property as a matter of products liability, negligence or otherwise,
or from any use or operation of any methods, products, instructions or ideas
contained in the material herein.

British Library Cataloguing in Publication Data
A catalogue record for this book is available from the British Library

Library of Congress Cataloguing in Publication Data
A catalogue record for this book is available from the Library of Congress

ISBN: 978-0-7506-8065-3

Typeset by Charon Tec Ltd (A Macmillan Company), Chennai, India

Contents

Figures

Tables

Contributors

Amelia Bartak, Deakin University, a.bartak@deakin.edu.au
John Byrom, John.Byrom@utas.edu.au
Megan Cardamone, Deakin University, megan.cardamone@deakin.edu.au
Derrick Chong, Royal Holloway School of Management, University of London, d.chong@ruhl.ac.uk
Stuart Davies, University of Greenwich, a.slater@lcc.arts.ac.uk
Anne-Marie Hede, Deakin University, anne-marie.hede@deakin.edu.au
Pamm Kellett, Deakin University, pamm.kellett@deakin.edu.au
Volker Kirchberg, University of Lueneburg, Germany, kirchberg @uni-lueneburg.de
Huong T.K. Le, University of Sydney, t.le@usyd.edu.au
Kim Lehman, University of Tasmania, Kim.Lehman@utas.edu.au
Wee Wen Liew, Singapore Art Museum, Liew_wee_wen@nhb.gov.sg
Leonie Lockstone, Victoria University, Leonie.Lockstone@vu.edu.au
Michelle Loh, National University of Singapore, cfalwhm@nus.edu.sg
Fiona McLean, Glasgow Caledonian University, Fiona.McLean@gcal.ac.uk
Suzette Major, University of Waikato and Tamarisk Sutherland, suzi@waikato.ac.nz
Sandra Mottner, Western Washington University, USA, Sandra.Mottner @wwu.edu
Mark O'Neill, Head of Glasgow Museums, mark.o'neill@cls.glasgow.gov.uk
Daragh O'Reilly, Leeds University Business School, UK, dor@lubs.leeds.ac.uk
Martha Phillips, Leads University Business School, UK, martha.phillips@ hotmail.co.uk
Ruth Rentschler, Deakin University, ruth.rentschler@deakin.edu.au
Carol Scott, Powerhouse Museum, Carols@PHM.GOV.AU
Alix Slater, University of Greenwich, a.slater@lcc.arts.ac.uk
Jonathan Sweet, Deakin University, jonathan.sweet@deakin.edu.au
Stefan Toepler, George Mason University, USA, stoepler@gmu.edu
Annette Van den Bosch, Deakin University, annette.bosch@deakin.edu.au
Dirk Vom Lehn, Kings College University, London, dirk.vom_lehn@kcl.ac.uk
Linda Young, Deakin University, lindy.young@deakin.edu.au

Preface

Museum marketing is a field growing in importance for museum professionals and audiences alike. The idiosyncratic nature of existing material and its lack of attention to the needs of the information age highlighted the need for a book such as this. This book presents a collection of museum marketing themed analyses and case studies, useful to students and practitioners. The edited readings will enable them to keep abreast of developments in the field of museum marketing. The editors were careful to include contributions from those working in museums as well as academics familiar with the range of research which is taking place on museum marketing. Collaboration of academics and practitioners as co-authors of chapters makes for a rich combination of experiences, skills and knowledge. The authors of the chapters are experts in their fields, with a keen understanding of both marketing and museums, and write in a non-technical manner in order to make their contributions accessible to the widest possible audience.

Ruth Rentschler from Deakin University was approached by Anna Fabrizio from Elsevier Butterworth-Heinemann as she had identified a need for a single text containing a comprehensive analysis of the changes which have occurred globally in museum marketing. The authors would like to thank Anna for her support and enthusiasm for the book. She offered valuable advice at all stages of its implementation. They would also like to thank Tim Goodfellow and Julie Trinder from publishing, Claire Hutchins from production and Liz Burton from marketing for their intelligent advice, incisive comments on draft material and professional approach to the project. We would like to thank the team for their organisational skills and work on the manuscript which kept the project on track over many months of hard work.

Our greatest debt is to the practitioners in the organisations who gave generously of their time and their knowledge of their organisations and industry. Their dedication to museums and museum practice was always evident and provided a rich setting for the investigations in this book. Their energies built innovative museum marketing into the organisations studied and enabled the book to be completed. Without their co-operation, the story could not have been told. All the chapters in this book have been researched and written by experts who hold key positions in the academic or museum field and they have a deep knowledge of museums and marketing. Their contributions reveal a high level of dedication to their work and practice, to their organisations and their staff. They also reveal an affinity to the social mission, indicating the significance of museums to the communities they serve.

Ruth Rentschler and Anne-Marie Hede

Introduction

The last few decades have seen a considerable debate about the significant changes that have taken place in the museum sector. One of the chief forces for these changes was the legitimization of the creative industries by governments. The potential corollaries of these changes are feelings of discontent in some quarters that things will never be the same again, and excitement for the possibilities of globalization from other quarters. Globalization is characterized by a rapid diffusion of concepts, services and products around the world with social-structural and cultural consequences (McGuigan 2005). The globalized marketplace is proliferated with new media. New media includes the use of digital media and computer technology (such as software websites, mobile devices, CD-Roms), which emerged less than 20 years ago. New media, however, has had a profound impact on museum marketing as it is one of the most widely available innovations relevant to both management and cultural practitioners. The pressures caused by these changes have triggered a re-examination of the role of museum marketing. Museums now compete for the leisure dollar, and in an increasingly competitive, globalized marketplace.

DiMaggio (1985) identified the paradoxical situation in which museums operate. His argument, which still has currency in the twenty-first century, was that on the one hand, museums are sheltered from the broader market by governmental policies which offer incentives for them to adopt a non-profit framework, but, on the other hand, they exist in a free market economy and are expected to compete with other businesses in a supply and demand framework. Additionally, notions of the self-regulating market can distort discourse about public policy towards cultural organizations. This split view of operation and purpose lends additional complexity to the task of marketing in within the context of the museum sector in the twenty-first century.

Kotler and Andreasen (1996) define marketing strategy for non-profit organizations, including museums, as positioning so that it is customer focused, with appropriate orientation towards the marketplace. The advantages of successful strategic museum marketing include the achievement of clear organizational purpose, sound organizational structure and improved managerial practice. Within this conceptual environment museums can flourish, how-ever, there is a need to assess the notion of marketing within the context of globalization and the era of new media while simultaneously acknowledging the social mission of museums. The approach to museum marketing in this book attempts to strike a balance between the current global economic realities and the need to cultivate innovation. It sees the recipe for flourishing cultural organizations as recognition of the dual aims of them meeting the social edification and cultural preservation requirements and establishing and meeting audience needs, asserting that better museum marketing is not an end in itself.

This book is a collection of themed analyses and case studies from around the world, on topics of importance to museum marketing within a global framework. The book is an extension of work undertaken by Rentschler (1999) which firmly placed the concept of marketing in the context of museums. The explosion of interest in the cultural sector, the expansion of new media and the internet, and reduced funding for some museums have generated a distinctive environment for strategic transformation in museums. Marketing in the museum sector requires a change in focus to respond to these global trends of twenty-first century museum.

This book comprises three major sections with underlying themes. Each of the sections contains chapters that elucidate the chapter theme. Case studies have been prepared that highlight theory in practice. The case studies and analyses within this book afford an insight into how marketing in museums is developing in the sector.

In the first section of the book, Museums: marketing in the global marketplace, Ruth Rentschler provides a synopsis of the history of museum marketing to set the scene for the chapters in this book. In their case study, Michelle Loh and Wee Wen Liew examine the challenges associated with e-marketing and communicating with international tourists. Amelia Bartak provides insights into how museums can take advantage of the opportunities that arise from on-line marketing. Indeed, she argues that it is imperative for museums to develop an on-line presence in the twenty-first century. Two case studies are presented in this section of the book that highlight the challenges and responses museums and audiences have had in relation to the approaches taken by museums to marketing in the global market place. The two case studies, one of the Quai Branly Museum in Paris by Annette Van den Bosch and the other of the Vietnam of Museum of Ethnology by Huong Le, provide insights into the how the new media phenomenon can impact museum marketing.

The next section of the book focuses on the audiences and their experiences in a leisure context. Kim Lehman and John Byrom have undertaken an interesting analysis of the Boags Centre for Beer Lovers in Tasmania, Australia. They explore the ways in which the themed corporate museum can build relationships with their audiences by building brand loyalty. In a similar vein, Pamm Kellett examines the ways in which tennis organizations can engage spectators of tennis in the sport at an emotional level through visitation to a tennis museum. Dirk Vom Lehn unpacks the audience's response to their attendance at museums and galleries by using a video-based methodological approach. 'The genie in the lamp: realizing the potential of UK museums' by Alix Slater and Stuart Davies is a chapter that segments museum audiences, and Daragh O'Reilly demonstrates that museum collections can be curated in such a way as to have resonance with the younger and more diverse audiences. He examines the exhibition of the New Model Army's 25 Years of Punk/Rock Culture. In her case study, Leonie Lockstone examines the role of and function of modern museums, and Pamm Kellett poses the question that many a curator faces, that is *'how can this collection of great significance best be used for interpretation and audiences?'* in a case study of a international tennis collection.

The third section of the book focuses on marketing, revenue and retailing within the context of museums. Sandra Mottner examines the role of retailing in museums. She argues that new forms of museum retailing haven't dented the power base of museum super-stores, such as The Met in New York, but have expanded their bases for operation. Stefan Toepfler and Volker Kirchberg highlight the ways in which museums can use merchandising and marketing to create revenue to enable the delivery of the core product. Anne-Marie Hede and Carol Scott have each prepared chapters on the role of branding in the museum sector considering the philosophical, theoretical and practical perspectives. Martha Phillips and Daragh O'Reilly examine the role of branding in the museum sector and 'rethink' the Tate Modern as an Art Museum Brand. Linda Young has developed a case study set within the context of house museums. She poses a number of strategies to satisfy the house museum visitor considering the constraints that are often placed on the management of house museums.

In the final section, which is focussed on the culture of museum marketing, Derrick Chong discusses the incremental rise of museum marketing discourse. Fiona McLean and Mark O'Neill examine the implications of the social museum and for marketing. 'Museum architecture and the visitor experience' by Jonathan Sweet examines the ways in which both the museum exteriors and their internal spaces influence visitor perceptions and outcomes for them. Three case studies, one prepared by Megan Cardamone, another prepared by Suzette Major and Tamarisk Sutherland, and another by Sandra Mottner, provide insights as to how aspects of collaboration can be developed to facilitate the enhancement of knowledge about heritage and respect among diverse global communities.

The authors of the chapters and the case studies have drawn on a number of sources to create a comprehensive analysis of the marketing in the museum sector, including web sites, government instrumentalities, private museums, organizations and individuals who can help museum marketers find resources for the future. A selection of contacts for these organizations is provided as tools for the museum marketer at the end of the book. The authors have referred to a wide range of research, and references to these works are provided at the end of each chapter or case study.

This book illustrates that marketing has become a vital component of museum activity. Globalization plays a major role in directing the energies and focus of museum marketers as is clearly demonstrated by the case studies and analyses found in this volume. The book reinforces the notion that the cultural context in which museums operate is unique, partly due to the particular blend of social responsibility and cultural preservation that it espouses. What is required in the museum sector is a combination of a production and marketing orientation, with something innovative which captures audiences' attention. New media provides an opportunity for innovation, and is a salient, yet powerful theme in this book. The museums in this collection offer guidelines, ideas and insights into how museums around the globe are responding to the challenges of incorporating marketing into their activities in the global marketplace in the twenty-first century.

References

DiMaggio, P. (1985). 'When the profit is quality: cultural institutions in the marketplace'. *Museum News*, pp. 28–35.

Kotler, P. and Andreasen, A. R. (1996). *Strategic Marketing for Nonprofit Organizations* (Fifth edition). Prentice Hall, Englewood Cliffs, NJ.

McGuigan, J. (2005). 'Neo-liberalism, culture and policy'. *International Journal of Cultural Policy*, 11(3), 229–41.

Rentschler, R. (ed) (1999). *Innovative Arts Marketing*. Allen and Unwin, Sydney.

Abbreviations

AAM	American Association of museums
AAMD	Association of Art Museum Directors
ABS	Australian Bureau of Statistics
ACORN	A classification of residential neighbourhoods
ACT	Australian Capital Territory
AFL	Australian Football League
AGNSW	Art Gallery of New South Wales
AMNH	American Museum of Natural History
ASDM	Arizona-Sonora Desert Museum
ASDP	Alice Springs Desert Park
CILR	Council on Library and Information Systems
DCMS	Department of Culture, Media and Sport (UK)
FMCG	Fast moving consumer goods
GMRC	Glasgow Museums Resource Centre
GNMA	Greenland National Museum and Archives
HMG	Hillwood Museum and Gardens
IMLS	Institute of Museum and Library Services
IPAM	International Partnerships Among Museums
MOMA, MoMA	Museum of Modern Art (New York)
MMS	Multimedia messaging systems
NHL	National Hockey League
NMA	New Model Army
NMGs	National Museums and Galleries
PDA	Personal digital assistant
PMAM	Peary-MacMillan Arctic Museum
POS	Point of sale
RSS	Really Simple Syndication
SFMOMA	San Francisco Museum of Modern Art
SKU	Stock keeping unit
SMS	Short message service
SRM	State Russian Museum

SWOT	strengths, weaknesses, opportunities, threats
V&A	Victoria and Albert Museum
VME	Vietnam Museum of Ethnology
www	World Wide Web

Tools for further research

Museums and Libraries

American Museum Association, http://aam-us.org/
Association of Art Museum Directors, http://www.aamd.org/
Bangkok National Museum, http://www.thailandmuseum.com/
thaimuseum_eng/bangkok/main.htm
British Museums Association, http://www.museumsassociation.org/
British Natural History Museum, http://www.nhm.ac.uk/
Canada Museums, http://www.museums.ca/
Council of Library and Information Resources, http://www.clir.org/
Guggenheim Museum, http://www.guggenheim.org/
Kyoto National Museum, http://www.kyohaku.go.jp/eng/index_top.
html
Museums Australia, http://www.museumsaustralia.org.au/
Museums Libraries and Archives Council, http://www.mla.gov.uk/
Museum of Modern Art, New York, http://www.moma.org/
National Museum Indonesia, http://www.museumnasional.org/
National Museum of Australia, http://www.nma.gov.au/index.html
National Sports Museum, http://www.mcc.org.au/default.
asp?pg=museumsmuseum
New York Public Library, http://www.nypl.org/
Rock and Roll Hall of Fame, http://www.rockhall.com/
Singapore Museum, http://www.singart.com
State Russian Museum, http://www.rusmuseum.ru
Tate Online, http://www.tate.org.uk/
Te Papa Museum, http://www.tepapa.govt.nz/Tepapa/
Vietnam Museum of Ethnology, http://www.vme.org.vn/
vietnam/

Statistical organisations
Australian Bureau of Statistics, http://www.abs.gov.au
UK Office of Statistics, http://www.statistics.gov.uk/
US Statistics Agency, http://www.fedstats.gov/
Singapore Statistics, http://www.singstat.gov.sg/
Hong Kong Statistics, http://www.censtatd.gov.hk/hong_kong_
statistics/index.jsp
Statistics New Zealand, http://www.stats.govt.nz/default.htm

Arts bodies
Australia Council, http://www.ozco.gov.au
British Council, http://www.britishcouncil.org/arts
Jibaozhai China Arts, http://www.cnarts.net/
Singapore Heritage Board, http://www.nhb.gov.sg/MCC
US National Endowment for the Arts, http://www.nea.gov/

Part A

Museums: marketing in the global marketplace

1

Major case study: cultural memory re-presented at the Quai Branly Museum

Annette Van den Bosch

A strategic commission

The Quai Branly Museum was designed and built by Jean Nouvel. The architect's commission from President Chirac of France was to build a museum bridge to promote dialogue between cultures and civilizations. The new cultural institution houses the collection of the Musée Nationale des arts d'Afrique et d'Oceanie, and those of the Musée de l'Homme Ethnology Laboratory. The challenge for Stephane Martin, the new Managing Director, and the Ministers for Culture, Higher Education and Research, was to promote the museum to the domestic and international audience as a destination which was contemporary and exciting. The choice of eight Australian Aboriginal artists, to design and paint the ceilings and the facade for the research wing on the Rue de l'Université, was a strategic commission, given current world record prices for Australian Aboriginal art and the difficulties of representing a collection with colonial associations in a new museum dedicated to cultural dialogue.

The enthusiastic and generous support of the Federal Government of Australia and the Harold Mitchell Foundation, for the commission and promotion of Aboriginal art was also strategic, given the dismal failure of government policies to improve the social, economic and health status of their indigenous population.

Cultural memory re-presented at Musée du Quai Branly

France, Germany and Britain established collections which represented the ideologies of the emerging disciplines of archaeology and anthropology in the nineteenth century. Bernice Murphy and others pointed out that the discourse of memory, which contests the role of history and the Western concept of time, poses significant challenges for the re-presentation of the museum collection (Murphy, 2005, p. 73). 'The fragmentation of objects, detached and recomposed as "collections", entailed a radical de-socialization of once-lived connections and meaning through the de-contextualizing logic of ethnography' (Murphy, 2005, p. 72). Ivan Karp, in a seminar at the Smithsonian, pointed out as early as 1988 that museums needed to change in three areas: they needed to give populations a chance to exert control over the way they are presented; they needed to improve their expertise in the presentation of non-Western and minority cultures; and their exhibition design should offer multiple perspectives on the objects and cultures represented (Karp in Murphy, 2005, pp. 72–3). The new museum needs to demonstrate that it has absorbed these critiques.

The Australian Aboriginal art collection at the Musée du Quai Branly includes 250 paintings from the collection of Karel Kupka who made four trips to Arnhem Land before publishing his book, *Dawn of Art: Painting and Sculpture of Australian Aborigines* (1965). 'The title of Kupka's book refers to the mistaken belief that Aboriginal people were living "survivors of the stone age" and that Aboriginal art was a way of discovering the reasons for the existence of art at the earliest stages of human civilization' (Naumann, 2006, p. 586). In addition, the museum collection has 230 bark paintings, some 1500 artefacts, including boomerangs, weapons, tools, sculpture, jewellery and burial poles, and 40 acrylic paintings (Naumann, 2006, p. 586). Apart from its collection of contemporary photography, the Australian Aboriginal material is the museum's only collection of contemporary art.

The design, display and marketing of the Musée du Quai Branly were aimed at presenting a new concept of the museum, in a building that was purpose-built to establish modern museum facilities. The emphasis in the mission statement on accessibility, research and education, public programmes and live performance needed to be packaged in a visual form that created a more contemporary, artistic and lively image in the media. The request to the Australian Government to include Aboriginal Australian artists in the design and fabric of the museum building was central to the marketing of the museum. It highlighted the museum's main collection of contemporary indigenous art with the intention that its new policies and strategies to develop a wider audience would be conveyed by the world's media. The director and staff must have also been aware of the growing visibility of Australian Aboriginal art in contemporary art museums in Europe that guaranteed the viability of their campaign (Naumann, 2006, p. 599).

The marketing campaign in Australia and France

'Dotted pathways from the outback to the stars' was the evocative title of the article by *Sydney Morning Herald* correspondent James Button (2006). The *Sydney Morning Herald* leader was followed by an image of Nyakul Dawson gazing at the painting by his friend Tommy Watson on the stainless steel ceiling of the museum with the caption, 'A building swallowed by art'. Later, Gulumbu Yunupingu is quoted as saying, 'My father sang to me about the stars. They tell our stories', while gazing up to the ceiling on which thousands of her stars are painted in white, black and red ochre. The impact of the presence of five Australian Aboriginal artists painting on site on the building was probably far greater than the impact that their paintings and their culture will have on the museum audience. The media releases in Britain (*artdaily.com*, 2006; *The Economist*, 2006) depicted the press kit images of the museum model, but the media in Australia and France emphasized the presence of artists, influenced no doubt by the joint media release by the museum and the Federal Government, entitled *L'art Aborigene Australien au Courer du Projet Architectural du Musée du Quai Branly*. Even New Zealand, whose relations with France have been cool since the blowing up of the Rainbow Warrior in Auckland Harbour, welcomed the visit of the Director, Stephane Martin, and his curator for Oceania, Yves le Fer, in 2005 (ambafrance, 2006). New Zealand's Te Papa Museum is the museum which exhibits more Oceanic, especially Polynesian, culture than any other, making collaboration and exchange between them essential.

The key media releases in Australia and France were official statements. At a doorstop interview on 20 June 2006, Mr Downer, the Australian Foreign Minister, said how excited he was by the request by Stephane Martin for an Australian contribution to the new museum. He assumed that Australian Aboriginal art was to be represented because it was the world's oldest continuous culture, and that its presence at the new museum was significant because Paris was important in intellectual debate and international relations (Downer, 2006). He went on to say that France was also the world's major tourist destination so that it was important to emblazon an Australian Aboriginal presence at the Musée du Quai Branly. To coincide with the opening of the museum, the Australian Embassy in Paris (itself a notable architectural site by Harry Seidler) presented the collection of Gabrielle Pizzi, who was a leader in the collection, exhibition and marketing of Aboriginal art (Australian Embassy, Paris, 2006). The exhibition *Mythology and Reality: Contemporary Australian Aboriginal Desert Art* marked the culmination of six exhibitions at the embassy, cited as an attempt 'to cultivate a strong appreciation and awareness of Australian Indigenous art in France and, more broadly, in Europe'. The last three of these exhibitions generated major positive reviews in *Le Figaro*, promoting media awareness of Australian Aboriginal art. The success of this campaign resulted in a number of galleries in Paris specializing in Australian Aboriginal art and an increase in its display by other commercial galleries.

The Musée du Quai Branly was opened by President Jacques Chirac with a speech that articulated his vision of 'a moment of great cultural, political and moral significance'. His speech, interview and the press release were widely covered.

> In 1998 I decided to create this museum, in full agreement with the Prime Minister Lionel Jospin. France wanted to pay rightful homage to peoples to whom, throughout the ages, history has all too often done violence. People injured and exterminated by the greed and brutality of conquerors. People humiliated and scorned, denied even their own history. Peoples still now often marginalized, weakened and endangered by the inexorable advance of modernity. Peoples who nevertheless want their dignity restored and acknowledged.
>
> (Chirac, 2006a)

The Secretary-General of the United Nations, Kofi Annan, was a guest at the opening, and Chirac mentioned the declaration of the rights of indigenous peoples which is being drafted for the United Nations. The tone of Chirac's speech, however, was quintessentially French in its invocation of the role of Claude Levi-Strauss in promoting cultural understanding and in its ideal of universal acceptance of diversity and creativity. Chirac emphasized 'the vitality of cultures reflected in the superb Australian Aboriginal ceiling paintings, and the dynamism and generosity of the Australian Government towards France' (Chirac, 2006b). In Chirac's view, this contemporary vitality was harnessed in support of a museum that rejected ethnocentrism, and the hierarchy of cultures and peoples, and promoted the equal dignity of all cultures.

The impact of the campaign in Australia

The initial marketing of the Musée du Quai Branly in Australia focused on the positive response of the government and the curators to the opportunity to showcase Australian Aboriginal art in Paris. On an *ABC Sunday Arts Review* (2 July 2006) interview with Virginia Trioli, the two curators from the Art Gallery of NSW and the National Gallery of Australia, Brenda Croft and Hettie Perkins, talked up their role in developing the original idea to a larger commission for four men and four women from different regions: Paddy Nyunkuny Bedford (East Kimberly); John Mawurndjul (West Arnhem Land); Ningura Napurrulu (Gibson Desert); Leni Nyadbi (East Kimberly); Michael Riley (Dubbo); Judy Watson (Brisbane); Tommy Watson (Gibson Desert) and Gulumbu Yunupingu (Arnhem Land). The aim of the indigenous curators was to establish the largest and most significant permanent display of their art outside Australia. The aim of the architect, Jean Nouvel, was to integrate architecture and art in the building design. John McDonald in the *Sydney Morning Herald* agreed that 'the architecture was crucial, because the building itself had to symbolize the new-found cultural sensitivity of the former colonialists' (McDonald, 2006). McDonald understood, however, that the Australia Council, who were commissioned by the Federal Government to market the commission, had overdone their claims for significance in a publicity blitz. 'They have done [the publicity] with such zeal that anyone who knows the project only from the press conferences and press releases in Sydney would believe that the museum had been transformed into a shrine to Aboriginal art' (McDonald, 2006).

Critics in Australia questioned why more than A\$1.3 million of taxpayers' money was spent to decorate the museum's administrative and curatorial offices and the bookshop (Hudson, 2006). Jayne Tuttle in *The Age* ran with the leader, 'The house that Jacques built' (Tuttle, 2006). She pointed out that although the collection of Aboriginal bark paintings, carved shields and spears, and a range of contemporary paintings were displayed in the museum's exhibition galleries, it would have been more interesting for people to read about the symbolism, the artists' painting methods and the history of the objects. She added that she could understand the controversy surrounding Musée du Quai Branly's objectification of indigenous cultures and culturally specific works. Other curators and art historians I spoke to were less generous, they criticized the hanging of the bark paintings in rows, on top of each other, and the ignorance and insensitivity evident in the display of contemporary Aboriginal painting in the exhibition area. Patrick Hutchings, a former Melbourne Professor of Aesthetics and a critic, pointed out that the complex light filters in the museum, the black ceilings and the tiny lights like stars work against the current Australian Aboriginal paintings in the collection which were made in bright outback light and in this setting become illegible (Hutchings, 2006). To add insult to injury, the exhibition of African art and objects, which are by far the largest collection in the museum, were displayed like art: individual objects highlighted and displayed to their full advantage.

The limits of the Australian Aboriginal presence at Quai Branly

The majority of paintings in the collection of Australian Aboriginal art in the museum were bought by the Paris-based Czech artist, Karel Kupka, in Arnhem Land in the 1960s. There are far fewer works in the collection that represent the explosion of Aboriginal creativity in the last three decades which is why the Australian Indigenous Art Commission (AIAC) was so important in projecting the new image that the Musée du Quai Branly aims to convey (Press release, 2006). Australian Indigenous art is only one part of the wider Oceania collection which includes collections from the French Polynesian territory of Tahiti, and the Melanesian territory of Niue Caledonie, as well as Insulindia, South East Asia, which includes Vietnam and Cambodia, also former French colonies.

The innovative aspect of the commission (AIAC) is that it represents some of the leading artists in the current art scene and showcases their work prominently: on the facade; through the large glass windows of the left wing of the museum, which is open to view from the street; walking away from the Seine; and left into Rue De L Université. The grey building tones into the area's fin de siècle landscape, until you register Leni Nyadbi's spearhead designs sandblasted onto the building's facade, and observe Gulumbu Yunupingu's painted ceiling stars through the windows. The audience, especially a European audience, will be amazed at the scale of the designs in the building. Paddy Bedford's *Thoowoonggoonarin* is painted on the left of the doorway of the building in tones of blue-black and pinky-white set in a glass installation. In the foyer are the large-scale photos of Michael Riley, and adjacent to this is the 11-metre long glass ceiling designed by Judy Watson, based on her painting in the National Gallery of Australia, *Two halves with bailer shell* (2002). Judy Watson's work, *Museum piece*, is also acid-etched across the front window: a direct challenge to the British Museum which still holds Aboriginal remains, against the wishes of their descendants. The work of John Mawurndjul, who has transformed bark painting by adopting the cross-hatching technique of body painting known as *rarrk*, was painted on a 150 square metre ceiling in the bookshop with the help of Aboriginal and French assistants.

The president, the architect and destination architecture in the global museum age

The erection of the Musée du Quai Branly as a monument to President Jacques Chirac, who retires in 2007, follows the tradition set by Francois Mitterand who commissioned the IM Pei carousel pavilion at the Louvre and the new opera building at the Place de la Bastille, and also that of Georges Pompidou, who commissioned the Pompidou Centre. In his speech, Chirac emphasized that the museum was founded on the belief in the equal dignity of all cultures (Chirac, 2006a). In a subsequent interview, he mentions that the new museum together with the renovation of the Musée Guimet (Asian Art) explains why France has become the world's leading tourist destination.

> All museums are affected by the growth of cultural tourism but some cities and countries are better placed to capitalize on its potential. The key role of the museum in urban development and tourism is recognized in cities as far apart as Bilbao and Bendigo. The Frank Gehry designed Guggenheim Museum in Bilbao has become an international icon, a logo for the marketing of the city similar to that of the Sydney Opera House.
>
> (Van den Bosch, 2005, p. 82)

The Musée du Quai Branly is situated on the banks of the Seine amidst Hausman's nineteenth century apartments in the fashionable, wealthy seventh arrondissement. The lights of the Eiffel Tower reflect in the windows of the museum at night. The main exhibition building is elevated on 10-metre curved supporting pillars and set back from the street in a landscape garden. There is an extraordinary 800-metre long vegetation wall of suspended plantings, and public access to the roof which commands splendid views. Jean Nouvel, the architect, was quoted as saying that he wanted to create space organized around 'the symbols of the forest, the river and the obsessions of death and oblivion' (Nouvel in *The Economist*, 2006). The architect understood the concept of 'destination architecture' that is required to attract contemporary audiences. Quai Branly displays 3500 indigenous artefacts and artworks, as well as housing and conserving 280,000 objects from around the world in an innovative building, but Australia's contribution is unique. Through an ingenious system of mirrors, and by extending the paintings onto the exterior window frames, all bar one of the works on three storeys can be seen through glass from the Rue de l'Université. Lit up at night, they make a 24-hour exhibition of Aboriginal art in Paris. The Musée du Quai Branly building design, including the visibility of its contemporary Australian art installations, is central to its audience appeal. Visitors must want to go inside.

The challenge for social marketing and public programmes at Quai Branly

A close reading of the official press release for the Musée du Quai Branly demonstrates that the new museum building provides the staff with the opportunities necessary to reach contemporary audiences, opportunities which are hard to organize in a nineteenth century building. The museum has published its museographic commitment to the accessibility of its collections through the use of new media technologies for display and research (Press release, 2006, pp. 3–13, 16). Its focus on the strength or themes of a particular continent, such as Asian textiles, enables the audience to appreciate and enjoy a particular gallery without suffering from 'museum overload'. Its commitment to temporary exhibitions and the rotation of the permanent collection is designed to encourage repeat visits. It has already scheduled international exhibitions. The museum includes a theatre to enable the performance of theatre, poetry, dance and music, so that the living artists of indigenous cultures can transform prejudices about 'dead' cultures that have been overwhelmed by modernity (Press release, 2006, pp. 23–8).

The challenge for Quai Branly is to encourage visitors who may previously not have visited an ethnographic museum, or those who view all museums as elitist institutions designed for the dominant French majority, to make their first visit. Curiosity and fashion will play a big part in attracting the domestic audience, especially the immigrant audience. In October 2005, France was the scene of serious riots by its immigrant minorities who feel that in education and employment they are subjects of discrimination (CNN, 2005). Social marketing of exhibitions of contemporary art, such as those of the British-Nigerian artist, Yinka Shonibare, and the Vietnamese-American multimedia artist, Trinh T Minh-ha, will need to attract French immigrant communities. In the art market, major research publications, exhibitions and new museums generally encourage collectors. The place to start for new middle-class collectors is often at the museum. Alison Dalbis, the Director of Dad Gallerie which represents 200 indigenous artists in Paris, is showing John Mawurndjul and Ningura Napurrulu to coincide with the opening. Her comment: 'installing it in the university building will bring it to the forefront, eventually take it out of the ethnographic category and towards high art. But it won't happen overnight it will take a great deal of education' (Dalbis in Owens, 2006, p. 44). Laure Churchette, who founded Espace Aborigine in 2004 and sells works from her home in Paris, is selling Utopia artists prior to opening a permanent gallery space in December 2006. She is optimistic 'there's a new museum, a new interestin the art; one person buys it and so everyone wants it. That's the French way. Never underestimate fashion' (Churchette in Owens, 2006, p. 44). Indigenous Australian art undoubtedly has cross-cultural appeal, but even if this commission promotes the fashion for collecting contemporary Aboriginal art, more needs to be done to educate the audiences at Musée du Quai Branly about the meanings, values and cultural significance of Aboriginal Australian art.

Conclusion

Quai Branly Museum has begun to face the challenges set by President Chirac, specifically to build a museum bridge to promote dialogue between cultures and civilizations. The challenge for new Managing Director, Stephane Martin, and the Ministers for Culture, Higher Education and Research, is to promote the museum to domestic and international audiences as a destination which is contemporary, exciting and relevant to a globalizing world. The choice of eight Australian Aboriginal artists, to design and paint the ceilings and the facade for the research wing on the Rue de l'Université, was a strategic beginning, given current world record prices for Australian Aboriginal art, and the interest in living indigenous cultures demonstrated by the growth of cultural tourism.

The museum faces significant marketing challenges as it re-presents a collection with essentially colonial associations as a new museum—dedicated to cultural dialogue. In particular, the indigenous peoples to whom the cultural material belongs need to be re-connected with their material heritage in tangible ways, such as employment, the exhibition of contemporary cultural forms, travelling exhibitions, research opportunities and scholarships. In this way, indigenous people can be brought into the museum as professional contributors and consultants. Most importantly, the existing museum staff should improve their expertise in presenting non-Western and minority cultures. Australian curators have significantly greater expertise in the exhibition of Aboriginal art, than the expertise demonstrated in the museum's exhibition of the Karel Kupka collection. In best practice, the exhibition design should offer multiple perspectives on the objects and cultures represented so that the museum is not dominated by a European aesthetic. The key challenge for marketing the museum is to attract a diverse audience. The marketing of current exhibitions, events and education programmes at Musée Quai Branly will only be as good as the changes in thinking and practices brought about by inter-cultural dialogue between museum staff and indigenous peoples, as contributors and as audience.

References

ambafrance(2006).<http://www.ambafrance-nz.org/article-imprim.php3?id_article=543> (accessed 5 July 2006).

Artdaily.com. (2006). Quai Branly Museum Inaugurated by Jacques Chirac. <http://www.artdaily.com/section/news/index.asp?int_sec=2&int_new =15995&b=musee%20du%20quai%20branly> (accessed 5 July 2006).

Australian Embassy, Paris (2006). <http://www.france.embassy.gov.au/pari/Pizzi> (accessed 6 July 2006).

Button, J. (2006). Dotted pathways from the outback to the stars. *Sydney Morning Herald*, 20 June, p. 5.

Chirac, J. (2006a). Speech by M. Jacques Chirac at the Opening of the Quai Branly Museum. <http://www.ambafrance-uk.org/article7357> (accessed 5 July 2006).

Chirac, J. (2006b). Foreword. Musée du Quai Branly (press release).

CNN (2005). Fiery riots spread beyond Paris. CNN.com World. <http://www.cnn.com/2005/WORLD/europe/11/04/france.riots/index.html> (accessed 7 July 2006).

Downer, A. (2006). <http://www.foreignminister.gov.au/transcripts/2006/060620> (accessed 5 July 2006).

Hudson, F. (2006). Art of the controversial. *The Courier Mail*, 22 June, p. MO7.

Hutchings, P. (2006). At the roots of art. *The Age Review A2*, 8 July, p. 5.

Kupka, K. (1965). *Dawn of Art: Painting and Sculpture of Australian Aborigines.* London, Viking Press.

McDonald, J. (2006). Voila, the art of reconciliation. *Sydney Morning Herald*, 1 July, p. 16.

Murphy, B. (2005). Memory, history and museums. *Museum International Quarterly Review*, 57(3), 70–6.

Naumann, P. (2006). Aboriginal art in faraway places: The Musée du Quai Branly and new thinking about Aboriginal art in Europe. *Art and Australia*, 43(4), 586–8.

Owens, S. (2006). Dreamtime assault on Paris fashions. *Australian Financial Review*, 8 June, p. 44.

Press release (2006). *L'art Aborigene Australien au Coeur du Projet Architectural du Musée du Quai Branly.* Ministry of Research and Higher Education and Ministry of Culture and Communication.

The Economist (2006). Gallic Grandeur. <http://www.economist.com/books/displaystory.cfm?story_id=7055766> (accessed 6 July 2006).

Tuttle, J. (2006). The house that Jacques built. *The Age*, Travel, 1 July, p. 3.

Van den Bosch, A. (2005). Museums: constructing a public culture in the Global Age. *Third Text Critical Perspectives on Contemporary Art and Culture*, 19(1), 81–9.

Museum marketing: no longer a dirty word

Ruth Rentschler

Although most arts organizations are non-profit institutions, they are not non-market institutions.

(DiMaggio, 1985)

Introduction

Marketing is still a dirty word to some in museums. With the term comes images of used car salesmen and the 'Disneyfication' of culture. Is it possible to market your product successfully without 'dumbing' it down? This brief history of museum marketing, the changes it has undergone, and the approaches taken in many museums, shows that it is.

It would be nice if museums did not have to worry about marketing. It would be nice if the money just rolled in by itself. Sadly, new economic realities mean that cash-strapped museums cannot afford to be complacent about attracting visitors through the doors to exhibitions. To stay afloat, they need to attract new audiences as well as keep established ones. Marketing is no longer an option: it's a survival tool rather than a dirty word.

What many in museums fear, however, is that in pursuing a larger market they will be forced to tamper with their product in a way that compromises its artistic integrity. They are worried their art will suffer at the hands of the market. Finding the middle ground between complacency and Mickey Mouse is the tricky part, and the challenge.

Background

Marketing in museums is in a period of major reassessment. This change in the purpose and priorities of museums has impacted on the nature of museum marketing. The recognition of new museum roles and the need to appeal to differentiated audiences has created new challenges for previously traditional, custodial directors (Gombault, 2002; Rentschler, 2002). This chapter explores the role of marketing in museums over 30 years, from the mid-1970s. It briefly overviews some of the changes which museums have undergone that have led to an increased focus on marketing. It contextualizes the change in marketing approaches and roles within the different management styles for museum directors. In doing so, it shows how these different styles illustrate the changes in professional perspective from the traditional focus on custodial preservation to the more current focus on educating and entertaining the public.

Museums: changing roles, changing context

Since the early 1900s, not-for-profit museums have been subjected to accelerated change, due to a refocusing of government policy; a well-educated community with higher expectations of museums and a more diverse community which desires a better reflection of contemporary issues in museums (Griffin, 1987; Ames, 1989). At the same time, the level of funding to museums has come under increased pressure, arguably forcing directors of museums to become entrepreneurial, particularly when devising strategies to meet the needs of their creative mission (Rentschler and Geursen, 2003). Museums are fulfilling a role of tellers of a sacred story and sometimes on a sacred site.

Museums are therefore combining the traditional, functional role with their new purposive role (Weil, 1990; Thompson, 1998), using a range of approaches including online technologies. Functional definitions relate to activities performed in the museum and are object-based: to collect, preserve and display objects. More recently, the shift in definitions relates purpose to the intent, vision or mission of the museum where the focus is on leadership and visitor services: to serve society and its development by means of study, education and enjoyment (Besterman, 1998). These definitions are illustrated in Table 1.1.

Table 1.1 Shift in museum definitions.

Functional	Museums acquire, conserve, communicate and exhibit art for study and education	Object based
Purposive	Museums are for people to enjoy and to learn from collections which are held in trust for society	People based

As museums themselves are changing to meet the needs of a changing world, so too important concepts change. Change has led to an increased interest in marketing in museums and to a reappraisal of their purpose, evident in the changing definition of the word 'museum'. The change in definition has been gradual and has been influenced by prevailing social and philosophical attitudes. The change in purpose affects not only the stories museums tell, but also the method of telling those stories, the corollary of which is a greater role for marketing—the focus of this chapter.

Museums contribute not only to social and cultural development, but also to the spiritual and emotional sense of national self through telling stories. In the UK, government is responsible for roughly 60 per cent of museum funding

(Matty, 2005). In the USA, museums receive a median figure of 24 per cent of their funding from government sources (AAM, 2006). The Australian museum sector alone reached 1329 museum locations in June 2004, with income of $919.4 million. While most museum income was derived from government funding, 9.7 per cent came from fundraising, 6.1 per cent from admissions and 5.4 per cent from sales of goods (Australian Bureau of Statistics, 2005). The museum sector faces more competition from new venues and leisure attractions for visitors who have less and less free time (Burton and Scott, 2003). Contemporary approaches, using marketing, to tell legendary stories are appropriate for museums.

The cultural industry, a growth industry in which museums play a central part, contributes $19 billion to the Australian economy annually, emphasizing also the economic contribution museums make. This is mirrored in the UK where museums contribute £3 billion to the economy (BBC, 2004). Museums closely follow popular music as the most frequently attended cultural activity, both in terms of number of people attending and number of visits (Australian Bureau of Statistics, 2005). The Australian Bureau of Statistics conducted a survey of attendance at selected cultural venues in March 1995. It revealed that a total of 3.1 million people (22.3% of the Australian population aged 15 years and over) had visited a museum in the period studied and museums were considered to be either very important or important by 71.5 per cent of the Australian community. This support was evident across all states and territories, irrespective of whether the reporting individuals were users of the facilities. US museums receive 600 million visits annually (AAM, 2006). In the UK, museums attract upwards of 100 million visits per year (BBC, 2004), this number is steadily increasing, being up from 59 million in 2000 (Wright et al., 2001). By marketing museums, their role can be improved, which is of national benefit in times of change and funding scarcity.

Museums: managers and marketers

Museums may differ in the types of collections they hold, but they do not differ in their principal aim: education (Griffin and Abraham, 1999). How then do museums and their directors implement effective marketing practice, without compromising the needs of their educational mission. Indeed, a rational economic approach to museum marketing often dilutes the effectiveness of the educational mission.

In this chapter, by taking a historical perspective, it can clearly be seen that both directors and marketing styles have evolved to meet the changing needs found within the museum sector. The style of the director impacts on the performance of the museum, given that there may be a gap between the desired performance and actual performance, due to the nature of museums as professional bureaucracies (Griffin and Abraham, 1999). In professional bureaucracies, individuals are influential in setting the agenda of the organization, often by appealing to colleagues outside the organization rather than those within.

As such, directors' styles and managerial preferences may not be applied evenly across the museum.

Traditionally the prime function of museums has been to gather, preserve and study objects. The director was perceived as the keeper of objects, as one who performed the custodial role for the cultural capital of the institution: its creative works. Today, managing museums entails understanding both the custodial role and the need to attract visitors. As museums are part of the not-for-profit sector and depend on government for up to 70 per cent of their income, they must be seen to offer value to government by attracting increasing visitor numbers. Government funders are asking for greater accountability for money granted. One way accountability can be documented is by sound marketing approaches (Laczniak and Murphy, 1977).

Marketing approaches have been used to increase visitor numbers and to encourage, change and expand the museum role from one of custodial emphasis to one of audience attraction and increased participation. Hence, museums are developing marketing techniques to help them become more successful in meeting these challenges.

These transitional changes have impacted on the internal cultural organizational factors such as museum structure, complexity and diversity of services (Gombault, 2002). Together with the drive towards formal accountability, these changes have increased the need for museum directors to have the orientation and skills of marketers, in addition to their custodial skills. Rentschler (2001) identifies four types of museum director, two of which are relevant to this discussion. These are the 'entrepreneur' and the 'custodian'. Each type brings a different emphasis to aspects of museum service. For example, the entrepreneur focuses on the furtherance of the organization through creative programming. The generation of funds—through changing exhibitions, identifying donors, personally contacting major donors, developing efficiency measures, using consultants strategically and preparing market analyses—is a consequence of this outlook. The entrepreneur also uses relationship-marketing programmes to encourage visitors to become members and then donors. In contrast, the custodial manager focuses on the traditional activities of research and collections. Custodians are less involved in business activities. For example, they do not use consultants or prepare market analyses, survey non-visitors, or encourage visitors to become members and donors. Today's museum managers are required to use the skills and approaches of both the entrepreneur and the custodian in order to fulfil the changed mission found in today's museum sector.

Changes in museum marketing reflect the changing directorial role. Museum marketing has been academically conceptualized as falling into three main periods, each building on the previous—the foundation period, the professionalization period and the entrepreneurial period (Rentschler, 1998).

Research on the foundation period (1975–1983) has found that articles on museum marketing were dominated by issues of educating visitors; raising staff awareness of the benefits of visitor studies; and, occasionally, the economic impact of the arts on the community. The articles in the first two groups have a data-collection focus rather than a strategic action-oriented focus. The modus operandi operating during this time was beginning to be challenged from a number of sources that herald the beginning of a more professional period, in which cultural change occurred in museums.

Museums became more democratized in the professionalization period (1988–1993). These changes forced the recognition of the applicability of marketing to non-profit arts organizations (Andreasen, 1985) and marketing departments were added to museums (Ames, 1989). Restructuring of the public sector also had an impact: evidenced by a shift in power and authority from producer to consumer, funders demanding greater accountability and the contracting out of services occurring at the local level. All of these elements empowered 'a new managerial elite', less focused on 'cultural gate keeping' and more engaged with the 'celebration of entrepreneurship' (Volkerling, 1996). It is assumed that professionalization will draw closer to achieving the twin aims of increasing and diversifying audiences (Rentschler, 2002).

Marketing in museums is in transition, heralding the beginning of an entrepreneurial period (1994–present). Recently, collaborative marketing models and a new view of visitors are evident, which diversify revenue sources by obtaining new audiences, products, venues and multi-art experiences (Radbourne, 1997). In tandem with this shift, has been increased focus on identifying the nature of the relationship between the visitor, the museum and the market (McLean, 1997).

Different perspectives on museum marketing: then and now

The identified periods impacting on marketing in museums are discussed in this section. The distribution of academic articles reflects the wider history of museum marketing. Two comments can be made about the distribution and focus of articles. First, the USA dominates in both volume of articles and in thrust of articles. There are approximately three times as many articles in the USA published 'Museum News' as the 'British Museum Management and Curatorship' on the subject of marketing. Second, even when the North American journals do not dominate in volume or articles (e.g., 'Muse'), these journals reassert their dominance with special issues on marketing.

The number of articles focusing on marketing as 'tactic' has remained steady over the years, while the number of articles which focus on marketing as 'culture' and marketing as 'strategy' has altered significantly. Prior to 1994, articles in industry journals which discuss marketing as strategy accounted for 10 per cent of the total number of articles. After 1994, this percentage jumps to 60 per cent (Rentschler, 2002). This rise reflects the shift that has occurred in museums with respect to the use and role of marketing within the organization, which is, in turn, indicative of the change in museums' perception of audiences. As museums are now much more reliant on philanthropic and corporate support, the relationship has been transformed from a hierarchically based one-to-one of service (Rentschler, 2002), thus marketing now plays a very significant role.

The focus of the articles in marketing as culture is quite different from those which locate marketing within the fields of strategy and tactics. Articles which address marketing as culture often show no awareness of, or interest in, the marketing implications of the study. As DiMaggio et al. (1978) found many such studies are for internal or external political purposes, didactic purposes or to argue for more resources by citing the economic impact of the arts on the community. In contrast, articles which locate marketing as strategy and marketing as tactical are action oriented rather than data-gathering oriented.

A wider interest in the methodologies of the behavioural and social sciences is suggested by the focus of more recent articles. McManus and Miles (1993) visitor studies article entitled 'United Kingdom: focusing of the market' chronicles this shift in attitude. A market-driven approach to exhibition planning and design has resulted in an increasing use of preliminary assessments of visitors' opinions on contents and topics for new exhibitions.

Recognition of the multi-dimensional nature of the museum experience, and consideration of the value of both purposive and functional roles, is vital in any organizational analysis. Adoption of appropriate and current marketing practices keeps museums culturally relevant and ensures their place as loci of cultural importance, particularly in the context of changing consumer practices. The Internet has enabled audiences to visit museums located far outside their physical region, frequently offering new and different kinds of experiences with which to engage on a vast array on topics traditionally explored within museums. It is vital therefore that museum managers adopt such marketing practices as will ensure their continued attraction of audiences and other stakeholders. Links within online exhibitions can direct the visitor to engage in other museum activities, thus utilizing the potential for audience engagement. In an age where income revenue is of high importance it would behove museums to explore all avenues to their full capacity. Philanthropic opportunities to support their preferred institutions can be offered to visitors as they navigate their way through exhibitions without compromising the quality of the content, providing a thoughtful and informed process is designed and adhered to (Burnette and Spann, 2006). Sponsorship opportunities are likewise abundant, harnessing the marketing capacity of the Internet.

A new economic reality is emerging where financial viability is more dependent on 'success in the commercial marketplace' (Williams and Rubenstein, 1992). Museums continue the trend by targeting and segmenting the marketplace, and recognizing the variety of audiences to whom they are marketing their services—the funders, the public and the organizations' staff and volunteers, whether board members, curators or artistic directors (Tweedy, 1991; Scaltsa, 1992; Mclean, 1997). Kotler and Andreasen (2003) cite the importance of these constituencies in not-for-profit marketing. The marketer needs to be sure to whom they are marketing—whether to funders to make them feel confident and therefore a source of funds to the museum, or to the visitors to whom the service is delivered. Different strategies are needed for each audience.

Conclusion

This chapter has provided a framework within which the development and history of marketing in museums can be analysed. This chapter has looked at the role of marketing in museums since the mid-1970s. It briefly overviews how increased focus on marketing has been underpinned by changes in museums' appreciation of the role of marketing, as also their mission has changed. It contextualizes the alteration in marketing approaches and roles within the different management styles for museum directors. It has shown how different styles exemplify the transformation in professional perspective from the traditional focus on custodial conservation to the more contemporary focus on educating and entertaining the public.

Awareness of the concurrent responsibilities of the director to attract new audiences through appropriate marketing is essential if museums are to remain culturally salient institutions. Successful museum marketing may require a combination of different management styles. However, this needs careful consideration in relation to how each aspect should be managed. The custodial style works well with education, the core dimension of the museum service. All staff need to know the value, history and context of education as it forms the core part of the service delivery. The more augmented dimensions of service delivery such as interaction, interpretation, communications and accessibility need to be addressed, particularly in relation to complex and interactive, social exchange service queries. This requires a greater marketing emphasis. Diversity, degree of variability and complexity of individual customer service requirements are valid experiences in museums. This is an inherent characteristic of the multi-dimensional museum service and the varying degrees of customer needs, requirements, perceptions, experience and ability to comprehend instructions and directions. Therefore, recognizing the importance of the augmented aspects of the museum service is vital. A key purpose of museum directors is to continually develop and improve all dimensions of service to visitors. This requires staff commitment, as well as staff development and the need for guidelines and measures for both core and augmented service dimensions.

The implication for museum directors is that they become more 'hands on', outwardly focused managers as well as efficient managers of a 'collection', in all aspects of museum management. The use and recognition of informal networks are important if internal performance in terms of communication and cooperation are to be successful. The thinking and behaviour of managers are also particularly important within museums. The willingness and ability of individual managers to adapt and develop their internal communication and cooperation, underpins successful development of the service marketing offering. Often, any change in the nature of management decision-making will necessitate a change in managerial structure and have an impact on the individual staff roles and competencies required. Custodial and entrepreneurial skills will assist the effective manager to form a cohesive entity which is meeting its service delivery requirements to all its stakeholders.

By recognizing the multi-dimensional nature of service delivery, museum managers can ensure that the benefits of both custodial and entrepreneurial marketing, management styles are used to achieve cohesion. All the aspects of service quality require attention and, as each interacts with the other, unity is vital for staff. Participation and involvement contribute to the commitment and cooperation of staff in the evolving work environment. In this context, the continual development of service quality in which marketing plays a central role can become the museum ethos.

The implications that are emerging from this shift in attitude to museum marketing since the mid-1970s, can be speculated: the strategic focus will continue to develop, along with the tactical focus, and visitor analysis studies will be integrated into mainstream decision-making for marketing and general management purposes. Given indications since the mid-1990s, marketing will continue to be a crucial issue as it is a proven method of positioning museums in times of change.

References

American Association of Museums (AAM) (2006). Survey—financial snapshot for the field. Press Release. <http://www.aam-us.org/pressreleases.cfm?mode=list&id=116> (accessed 24 November 2006).

Ames, P. (1989). Marketing museums: means or master of the mission. Curator, 32(1), 5–15.

Andreasen, A. R. (1985). Marketing or selling the arts: an orientational dilemma. Journal of Arts Management and Law, Spring, 15(1), 9–20.

Australian Bureau of Statistics (2005). Museums, Australia, 2003–2004. Cat. no. 8560.0. <http://www.abs.gov.au/Ausstats/abs@.nsf/Lookup/E49AC1246 6062415CA256A80007FB6AF> (accessed 18 August 2006).

BBC (2004). Museum funding appeal. BBC News. <http://news.bbc.co.uk/1/hi/entertainment/arts/3545715.stm> (accessed 24 November 2006).

Besterman, T. (1998). Saying what museums are for – and why it matters. Museums Journal, April, 37.

Burnette, A. and Spann, L. (2006). MoMA.org and MoMAstore.org: the crossover. In Museums and the Web 2006: Proceedings (J. Trant and D. Bearman, eds.) Archives & Museum Informatics. <http://www.archimuse.com/mw2006/papers/burnette/burnette.html> (accessed 8 November 2006).

Burton, C. and Scott, C. (2003). Leisure and Change. International Journal of Arts Management, Winter, 56–68.

DiMaggio, P. (1985). When the profit is quality. Museum News, June, 63(5), 28–35.

DiMaggio, P., Useem, M. and Brown, P. (1978). Audience Studies of the Performing Arts and Museums: A Critical Review. National Endowment for the Arts, Washington, DC.

Gombault, A. (2002). Organizational saga of a superstar museum: the Louvre. International Journal of Arts Management, 4(3), 72–84.

Griffin, D. (1987). Managing in the Museum Organisation: leadership and communication. *The International Journal of Museum Management and Curatorship*, 6, 387–98.

Griffin, D. J. G. and Abraham, M. (1999). Management of museums in the 1990s. In *Management in Museums* (K. Moore, ed.), The Athlone Presa, London.

Kotler, P. and Andreasen, A. R. (2003). Strategic Marketing for Nonprofit Organizations (Sixth edition), Prentice-Hall, Upper Saddle River, NJ.

Laczniak, G. and Murphy, P. (1977). Marketing the performing arts. *Atlanta Economic Review*, November–December, 4–9.

Matty, S. (2005). Museum Statistics in England. Report to the Expert Meeting on Statistics and Performance Indicators for European Museums, 13–14 October, Museums Libraries, Archives.

McLean, F. (1997). *Marketing the Museum*. Routledge, London: New York.

McManus, P. and Miles, R. (1993) United Kingdom: focusing on the market. *Museum International*, 14(2), 26–32.

Radbourne, J. (1997). Creative Nation: A policy for leaders or followers? An evaluation of Australia's 1994 cultural policy statement. *Journal of Arts Management, Law and Society*, 26(4), 271–83.

Rentschler, R. (1998). Museum and performing arts marketing: a climate of change. *Journal of Arts Management, Law and Society*, 28, 83–96.

Rentschler, R. (2001). Is creativity a matter for cultural leaders? *International Journal of Arts Management*, Spring, 3(3), 13–24.

Rentschler, R. (2002). Museum and Performing Arts Marketing: The Age of Discovery. *Journal of Arts Management, Law and Society*, 32(1), 7–15.

Rentschler, R. and Geursen, G. (2003). Entrepreneurial Leadership in Non-profit Performing Arts Organisations. AIMAC, *7th International Conference on Arts & Cultural Management Proceedings*, University Bocconi, Milan, pp. 1–12.

Scaltsa, M. (1992). Defending sponsorship and defining the responsibility of governments towards the visual arts. *Museum Management and Curatorship*, 11(2), 171–84.

Thompson, G. D. (1998). Performance measurement in museums and New Zealand's service performance reporting model. Paper presented at the *Accounting Association of Australia and New Zealand Conference, Adelaide*, 6–8 July.

Tweedy, C. (1991). Sponsorship of the arts: an outdated fashion or the model of the future? *Museum Management and Curatorship*, June, 10(2), 161–6.

Volkerling, M. (1996). Deconstructing the difference engine: a theory of cultural policy. *European Journal of Cultural Policy*, 2(2), 189–213.

Weil, S. E. (1990). *Rethinking the Museum and Other Meditations*. Smithsonian Institution Press, Washington, DC.

Williams, R. and Rubenstein, R. (1992). Visitor studies: committed to change. *Muse*, Spring, 12(1), 41–5.

Wright, M., Selwood, S., Creaser, C. and Davies, J. E. (2001). *UK Museums Retrospective Statistics Project*. Library and Information Statistics Unit, Leicestershire.

The departing train: on-line museum marketing in the age of engagement

Amelia Bartak

Introduction

In this chapter, we consider how museums can effectively use the on-line, virtual environment to interact with audiences and importantly, why they should. On-line, a museum can provide programs, market to and educate audiences—possibly generate revenue—all the while communicating and building relationships with those audiences, the essence of audience development. The museum website is a critical platform from which to launch these activities. Audiences range widely in their experience, encompassing new users through to extant regular users of websites. They may be global—thousands of miles away and never likely to set foot inside the museum's walls—or they may be local, regular visitors to the museum. When we read the reports of the ever-increasing, enormous number of visitors to flagship museum websites compared to the physical museum, such as Tate Online, London's Natural History Museum, New York's Museum of Modern Art (MOMA) and the Louvre, we get a sense of the importance of museums developing their on-line capabilities. By the close of 2005, 1.08 billion people worldwide had Internet usage (Computer Industry Almanac, 2006), offering massive audience potential to museums. Rapidly changing on-line technologies have become pivotal to marketing in the ongoing redefinition of the relationship between museums and audiences. Using technology, museums are liberating the physical experience from the constrictions of time and space, bringing the museum to audiences, anywhere and at any time. All museums, regardless of size, need to consider the strategic advantage of on-line technologies now—the age of engagement is upon us, and the train *is* departing.

Developing audiences using the on-line environment

Hill et al. (2003) describe audience development as building audiences by encouraging repeat visits (physical or virtual) from existing audience members, and generating new attendees and participants (diversification). It requires adoption of long- and short-term approaches that seek to attract and engage audiences. The three key methods to achieve this are education, marketing and programming. An effective development program should be a collaborative, strategic effort across these three activities (Hill et al., 2003). Hence utilizing inter-departmental teams, particularly relevant for the museum sector where departments often work independently, will capitalize on the integrative potential of 'on-line' strategies for audience development purposes.

Most of us are familiar with some notion of on-line marketing, in the form of communication tools such as e-mail, websites, podcasts and multimedia messaging systems (MMS) (see <http://www.matisse.net/files/glossary.html> for definitions of unfamiliar terms). For some time now, museums have been developing on-line content and programming to engage with a greater variety of audiences. These endeavours, combined with recent and significant technological advances, have greatly increased the scope of what can now be achieved. Highly interactive marketing and educational materials as well as 'digital-only' projects (i.e., no physical manifestation) are becoming prevalent. Rather than merely supporting the museum's physical offerings, the website is augmenting, enriching and, for some visitors, replacing the visit (Hamma, 2004; Barry, 2006; Rellie, 2006a). Stimulating experiences that are refreshed regularly, combined with successful marketing, encourage audiences to visit the museum repeatedly—whether this be virtually or physically.

The virtual museum visit doesn't replicate the physical experience, rather it represents a valid alternative. Evaluation of user behaviour of Tate Online reveals that average 'virtual' visits are usually between 3 and 10 minutes (Rellie, 2006a, c) as compared to physical visits of 2 hours or more. By shifting emphasis from 'object' value to 'information' value, audiences take away a rich information experience that has its own advantages (Varisco and Cates, 2005). Digital access to collections enables far more of the collection to be seen by many more people than can be physically contained at any museum site. Indeed, this is an ideal way for objects and artefacts too delicate for public access or viewing to be displayed (Varisco and Cates, 2005). When complementary interpretative materials are linked to specific items, a richer, dynamic and multi-levelled experience is developed that is potentially accessible from inside or outside museums. Museums can now add recently available interactive features that facilitate individual content creation (one-to-many) and many-to-many communication, enabling a supporting virtual community. These experiences, driven by individual users, work to break down more traditional barriers to engagement with museums.

Technology is both catalyst and support. Computers and the Internet are both getting faster and more ubiquitous. Web-based software and tools are proliferating, as are converged personal devices and wireless networks, allowing for 'continuous computing' using the World Wide Web (Roush, 2005). As a result, people are spending increased time on-line and engaged with screen-based activity. The average American 21-year-old is reported to have played 5000 hours of video games, spent 3500 hours on-line and exchanged 250,000 messages via e-mail or cell-phone messaging systems (Rainie, 2006). This is driving museums to take advantage of digital technologies or potentially lose relevance. They are developing a wide array of activities that fulfil the core museum missions of education, research, cultural engagement and enrichment, *and* meet user needs.

Technology enables a dialogue with audiences to take place, paramount for relationship building. The ability to monitor audience behaviour on-line builds insight and facilitates greater understanding of users. Relationships are further cultivated when museums link in other resources such as permission-based e-mail newsletters, functional and unique sales and retail options (such as on-line shops, ticket sales) as part of a distinct on-line marketing strategy. It is imperative that the 'on-line' approach be holistic and integrated with all marketing, educational and programming strategies to maximize outcomes.

New societal roles for museums

On-line activities and their evaluation, through measurement of outcomes, are vital for museum accountability and viability (Rentschler and Gilmore, 2002). In the UK, the government is including strategic audience development through diversification and increased accessibility (social inclusion) as funding criteria, and requesting on-line performance figures in annual reporting. It is believed that a positive impact on society can be achieved by its citizens participating in, and engaging with, culture in richer and more meaningful ways (Harcup and Nesbitt, 2006). Multi-dimensional and multi-functional websites can now facilitate and importantly, quantify achievement of these goals. When museums work to build iterative processes between audiences, the museum and websites—a 'virtuous circle' in content creation and consumption, and between physical and virtual museum experiences—relationships are continually strengthened (Barry, 2006; Harcup and Nesbitt, 2006). Museums can offer both education and entertainment through on-line programming and digitization of content, while marketing the museum and its services in the same instance to millions, thus accomplishing audience development objectives and fulfilling government accountability measures.

National Gallery, London <www.nationalgallery.org.uk>

By Tim Roberts

As part of its stated goal to constantly seek ways to improve access to, and understanding of its collection, which comprises 2,300 paintings, the National Gallery in London had digitized its entire collection by 2000. The Gallery has been a leader in the application of on-line technology, utilizing this digital resource in a variety of ways. Innovative campaigns have been inspired by and applied digital images of the art, ranging from e-postcards and MMS messages, to personalized calendars and greeting cards comprising works from the collection, to animated promotional e-mails and much more.

Some other service offerings that help extend the reach and revenue potential of this asset in the digital realm are as follows.

Zoomable Pictures

'The Zoomable Pictures facility enables you to discover fabulous details in the paintings—sometimes even features which you can't easily notice while in front of the original,' Charles Saumarez Smith, Director of the National Gallery.

Launched in 2003, Zoomable Pictures, the gallery's on-line facility for viewing paintings in incredible detail, won a Museums and Heritage Award for Excellence in May 2004. A winner in the 'Use of Technology' category, over 4 million visitors used the facility in its first year. Digitized using a 100 megapixel camera, on-line visitors may explore nearly 300 works of art in the gallery's collection in detail. The aim is to eventually make every painting in the permanent collection available. All such images carry a discreet logo embedded within the image, to deter copyright infringement.

Print On Demand

This service enables people to buy prints of any painting from the Gallery's permanent collection in their desired size and format. The shop carries no inventory of prints, only blank paper. Using touch screens in the gift shop, visitors browse, choose size and format and then watch their poster being printed in around 7 minutes. The facility won the award for 'Best Use of Technology in an Emerging Business' at the 2004 European Retail Solutions Awards.

Take One Picture

The website <www.takeonepicture.org.uk> is an on-line resource for UK primary school teachers. It was developed in response to the success of the 'Take One Picture' scheme. Teachers were invited to attend a one-day course, and then embark upon a range of classroom projects based around a painting chosen each year from the Gallery's collection. The website seeks to expand the scheme's reach, to inspire teachers nationwide and make art accessible to the widest possible audience. Teachers access on-line educational resources that support National Curriculum objectives in subjects from literacy, science and history. The site also offers examples of work from previous years, teachers' notes and on-line forums for the exchange of ideas.

ArtStart

In 2005, the National Gallery launched ArtStart, a multimedia centre providing access to its entire collection of paintings via touch-screen technology. The objective of ArtStart is to enhance the visitor's experience by offering an alternative way to discover the National Gallery's collection of paintings, regardless of their knowledge of art or technical skills. The entire collection has been catalogued and can be easily searched and sorted by key words, artists, themes, schools, years, mediums and more. Visitors can even plan and print their own tailor-made tours according to their interests.

Globally, the sociopolitical context and role of museums is also changing. While the primary role of museums is as collecting institutions, the emphasis is shifting from preservation to include facilitation of cultural exchanges, and becoming a *social* site for debate (Martin, 2003; Ellis, 2006; Rellie, 2006a). Recognition that learning is a complex activity that continues throughout our lives is growing. Learning takes place in a variety of interrelated personal, social, and physical contexts and this is impacting on the ways in which museums—where these contexts are converged—design visitors' experiences, whether physical or virtual (Walker Art Centre, 2004; Varisco and Cates, 2005). Museums are accruing greater value to society as a result of their increased capacity to facilitate positive social impact through culture and education.

Technology extends the reach of museums. It allows museums to create new kinds of access for new kinds of audiences, changing perceptions of the institution of 'museum' and affecting the nature of curatorial practice and interpretation in the process (Smith in CLIR, 2001). This is clearly evident in an educational context, where schools can use on-line museum resources for teaching purposes without visiting. But this is also now evident in a social context; partly due to the way the on-line medium now enables participation and allows users to generate and post their own content, creating value and independence in the way audiences interact with museums (Schwartz, 2005). A significant challenge is for museums to find balance between what is possible using these technologies while maintaining its authoritative position (Dietz, 2000; Soren, 2004; Cooper, 2006; Ellis, 2006; Rellie, 2006a). Museums own and manage an incredible diversity of rich, cultural content and hold a trusted position and brand (Burton and Scott, 2003; Bawa, 2006) within our society. By creating interactive spaces for visitors, and opening up their content for use in a myriad of ways, museums are potentially ceding control of 'culture' to unknown voices and in unknown (digital) realms.

The virtual gallery quandary

An ongoing quandary for many museum professionals and curators is the professional implications of allowing people external to organizations, to 'curate' shows using on-line collections for others to view via interactive on-line features. Does it trivialize, devalue and denigrate the specialist expertise, research and training required to develop these professional skills, as well as the value of museums to society?

Jonathan Cooper (Cooper, 2006), from the Art Gallery of New South Wales (AGNSW) in Australia, confronted some fundamental questions about the role of museums when developing myVirtualGallery <www.artgallery.nsw.gov.au/ed/myvirtualgallery>. The internal debate between the gallery's curators, educators and marketing people revealed a spectrum of opinion on questions such as:

● Who has the right to comment on art?
● Can there be only one interpretation of an artwork?
● Who protects the reputations of artists and the art?

There was also division on the potential for public criticism through such forums. The final design—including interpretative materials, wording and location of the entry page for this interactive feature—differentiates it from AGNSW's other 'expert' on-line resources. Yet it still fulfils the aim of increasing access and a more active, reciprocal, personal engagement between users and the museum.

The age of engagement

As many writers on museums and the web have recently noted, there is a palpable excitement connected with the rapid development of the Internet, of continuous computing and increased mobility, of the proliferation of web-based software and tools that some (but not all) commentators are calling Web 2.0. Fundamentally social, and specifically built to enable participation and social interaction, Web 2.0 harnesses the collective intelligence of users (Roush, 2005; Hinchcliffe, 2006). The new web-based software enables personal publishing such as blogging, podcasting, wikis, RSS (really simple syndication), sharing photos and videos, and so on. Individual users consume, organize and create their own content, then publish it via the Internet. The software is usually available free on-line; part of the democratization of the web and an underlying principle of Web 2.0. In addition, people are combining content and software from other diverse sources to create 'mash-ups' which may transform or subvert the original utility. Jon Pratty from UK's 24 Hour Museum noted that Web 2.0 is being 'embraced by the public with real mania'

(Pratty, 2006). This is compelling while causing some concern for museums as content owners.

Important to grasp is the 'profound shift in emphasis' from information seeking to active participation and engagement in the way the Internet is being used (Carey and Jeffrey, 2006). Hence, as Carey and Jeffrey note, the era and its form has already been called various names, from 'age of engagement' (Meeker, 2005) to 'age of participation (Schwarz, 2005) and 'authorship society' (Rushkoff in Carey and Jeffrey, 2006). This is particularly apparent in sites such as *flickr* (photo sharing <http://www.flickr.com/>), *youtube* (video sharing <http://www.youtube.com>), *myspace* (social interaction and networking <http://www.myspace.com>) and *del.icio.us* (social tagging <http://del.icio.us>) where global visitors are in the millions—daily. These sites rely on people contributing and consuming content and then sharing it by e-mailing friends and colleagues of their experiences. A push–pull effect is created that is integral to Web 2.0. It utilizes an 'architecture of participation' (O'Reilly, 2004) and viral messaging to develop ever larger numbers of participants. The challenge for museums lies in finding ways to capture and work with the growing momentum and energy of on-line users, as is evident in these sites, while remaining mission appropriate.

Alongside the development of the Web as a platform for engagement, other factors are also important to highlight. Firstly, Internet access is becoming faster and less expensive for the majority, as more people use it. Secondly, the accelerated development of wireless computing devices—from wireless laptop computers to smaller devices, such as personal digital assistants (PDAs), iPods and other MP3 players, digital cameras, mobile phones and converged appliances (phone, camera, MP3 player, PDA, etc. in one)—is changing the mode of access. Hence, Internet access in some form is becoming increasingly mobile and, combined with the range of web-based software and services, continuous in the way it integrates with our lifestyle (Bannister, 2006; Meeker et al., 2006) We are no longer tied to desks, computers or network connections in order to avail ourselves of the Internet.

Developing on-line interactions

> Is there a way … that museums can use the digital realm to negotiate a hybrid third way, in between classification and wonder, in between facts and stories, in between teleological narratives and hyperventilating sampling?
>
> (Dietz, 2000)

Many museums are already engaging with audiences via on-line technologies and the Internet in unique and innovative ways. However, early adopters note that better results are obtained when museums develop content and functions specifically for this platform, with the end user in mind, rather than just translating existing materials to digital formats (Hamma, 2004; Sayre, 2005). Web 2.0 publishing tactics, like podcasting and blogs, facilitate new methods of interpretation and interaction that museums can use to great advantage.

San Francisco's Museum of Modern Art (SFMOMA) has developed a successful monthly podcasting program, 'Artcasts' <http://www.sfmoma.org/education/edu_podcasts.html>, which invites artists, musicians, writers and the general public to develop the audio-based files, bringing multiple insights to the art on display (Samis and Pau, 2006). While SFMOMA was already providing rich, multimedia interpretative options on PDAs, the buzz created in May 2005 by guerilla podcast audio tours of New York's MOMA drew the attention of many museums to the interpretive potential of podcasting. Developed by communications students from Marymount Manhattan College, the 'Art Mobs' project was designed to 'hack the gallery experience' or 'remix MOMA' (Kennedy, 2005). Podcasts can be downloaded to digital audio players such as iPods or MP3 players before a museum visit, or listened to on personal computers.

Minneapolis's Walker Art Centre <www.walkerart.org> has used blogs very successfully and now has six different blogs on different disciplines (Spadaccini, 2006; Walker Art Centre, 2006). This allows for a multiplicity of voices in dialogue about art in a sanctioned on-line facility, safely chaperoning while relinquishing 'curatorial authority'. In addition, Walker Art Centre has developed 'Art on Call' <http://newmedia.walkerart.org/aoc/index.wac>, which offers a range of data and interpretive audio files, integrating education with event listings and booking options in a flexible, interactive system that works across different platforms. Visitors access the program via their own phone (mobile or landline) by calling one number. They use interactive voice response technology, linked to chosen options, and are then prompted to select further content and activities. This is also accessible via the website and via RSS feed (podcast) for MP3 players.

At the J. Paul Getty Museum, the 'Gettyguide' has been developed; a multimedia system that links hand-held devices at its museums with its website. Hamma notes that it 'puts everything each visitor needs to know literally in their hands' (Hamma, 2004). 'Gettyguide' is a mobile audio tour, interactive, information kiosk and bookmarking device in one. It interfaces with the visitor's experience of the museum and the collections, and can be continued from home—a 'virtuous circle' (Harcup and Nesbitt, 2006).

As demonstrated by these and earlier examples, the increasing capability of particular technologies and platforms like the web, opens up the ways audiences access and interpret museum collections, while offering promotional and revenue generation opportunities.

Audience potential

The sheer scope and diversity of on-line projects occurring at museums around the world is striking. User numbers are similarly impressive. Websites for Tate Online, the Getty, New York's MOMA, Natural History Museum in the UK, for example, each attract 1 million or more visitors per month (Barry, 2006; Rellie, 2006a), far greater than numbers for physical visits. But this is small compared to other market figures. As already noted, by the close of 2005, over a billion people worldwide had access to the Internet (Computer Industry Almanac, 2006).

Mobile phone ownership is reaching saturation point in many countries and is fast becoming the dominant platform to access the Internet, overtaking at-home personal computers (Ipsos, 2006a). This is particularly important in developing countries where previously, little infrastructure existed to obtain Internet access via PCs (Watson et al., 2002). In some countries, mobile Internet surfing is becoming mainstream, particularly as speed increases and for reasons of convenience (Ipsos, 2006a).

Research from USA revealed that 1 in 5 people over the age of 12 years own a portable MP3 player and 1 in 20 own more than one device, of which over 75 per cent are Apple iPods (Ipsos, 2006b) and ownership rate increases as age decreases. Clearly, audience development opportunities lie in developing wireless services and applications that link personalized services across multiple Internet platforms, and are accessed through multiple personal devices (Ipsos, 2006a). It is imperative that museums keep the user in mind however, and develop offerings for targeted groups using appropriate delivery mechanisms. These should clearly fulfil desired strategies and objectives, to meet defined audience needs.

Considering museum capability

> Digital technology enables the full range of holdings in our museums, libraries, and archives—audio, video, print, photographs, artworks, artifacts, and other resources—to be catalogued, organized, combined, and made accessible to audiences in new ways. It provides the public with new pathways to access museum and library collections and brings them 'face-to-face' electronically with librarians, curators, scientists, artists, and scholars. By using technology, rich scientific, historical, aesthetic, and cultural resources can be presented with contextual information that enhances educational value.
>
> (IMLS, 2006, p. 4)

While most museums have some kind of website, there is considerable variation in what is offered on-line. Variability, due to differences in size, ownership, structure and funding arrangements, render generalized conclusions impossible. Worth noting is that all museums appear similar to audiences because of the one screen size used to visit them on-line. A report from the Institute of Museum and Library Services (IMLS), 'Status of Technology and Digitization in the Nation's Museums and Libraries' (January, 2006) provides insight into digital capability and highlights key issues for American museums. Digitization of collections has been the significant thrust of digital activities for some years now beyond brochure type materials. Over 50 per cent of museums make some or all of their collection available via the web and nearly 40 per cent provide on-site access to digital collections. Nearly 90 per cent of museums have websites. It is principally 'early adopters'—museums with sufficient scope and resources (human and financial), and more importantly, the entrepreneurial initiative to drive technology projects—that have developed innovative digital knowledge management in their organizations. The biggest issue affecting smaller museums' ability to effectively participate on-line is insufficient funding and staff time. Only 23.4 per cent of museums have the right amount of staff to accomplish their technology activities. While almost 55 per cent of all museums have the technological capacity to meet or almost meet their missions, over 60 per cent reported that a majority of their technology needs are not met with current funding, and all agreed that their ability to introduce new technologies is marginal (IMLS, 2006, p.17).

Critical issues for museums

Our analysis of the most recent proceedings of five major conferences[1] on museums, their digital practices and the web, and other research papers, highlighted common issues of which all museums clearly need to be aware. These include:

- developing an integrated approach between virtual and physical activity,
- sustainability,
- supportive managerial policies and appropriate resources,
- copyright,
- marketing the on-line museum offer,
- effective content design including useability and functionality,
- evaluating what they are doing.

As mentioned earlier in this chapter, any on-line marketing activity needs to be fully integrated with all other facets of the museum's management, including its program, to maximize its potential value. As well, it needs to be

[1] Conferences included:
- Museums and the Web (2000–2006); see <http://www.archimuse.com/conferences/mw.html>.
- American Association of Museums Conference; see <http://www.mediaand-technology.org/panels/2006.html>.
- UK Museums on the Web 2006; see <http://mcg.man.ac.uk/meetings/2-2006-abs.shtml#dphillips>.
- Virtueel Platform 'Take Away Museum' 2006; see <http://www.virtueelplatform.nl/article-2751-en.html>.
- Institute of Museum and Library Services Web-Wise conferences: selected papers available from *First Monday* (Internet Journal); see <http://www.firstmonday.org>.

sustainable. The digital resources being built today have to be adaptable to multiple platforms, and to continue to be deliverable to users and audiences well into the future. This means developing policies that guide on-line activities that are adopted throughout the organization and signed off at the highest level. Resources to maintain and develop on-line programs of any kind were a universal concern.

Another issue is copyright. Current laws are often unable to be enforced in the digital realm, particularly relevant as more users generate their own content using others' intellectual property (including museums') to do so. Museum websites must be marketed as a destination in their own right, in order to capture digital market share. One way to circumvent some of these issues is for museums to form partnerships and work collaboratively with new partners—across media, locations and platforms.

Central to the discourse surrounding on-line activity is the need to clearly define the user and their behaviour, including purpose of on-line visit. It is imperative to involve test groups of targeted users when developing sites, to ensure any activity delivers desired benefits and value to the museum and constituents. While the body of research on users is growing, the percentage of museums that conduct user needs assessment relating to any technology-supported experience remains very low; only 12 per cent of museums in USA are doing so (IMLS, 2006). Hence the issues of effective content design, including useability, functionality and maintaining user interest, create the greatest challenge (Hamma, 2004; Marty and Twidale, 2004; Sayre, 2005; Varisco and Cates, 2005; Hecht, 2006; Rellie, 2006a, b). Research and evaluation at every stage of program development are vital to these efforts.

Snapshot: developing projects through global partnerships

UK Government-commissioned projects like 'Every Object Tells a Story' <www.everyobject.net>, 'Plant Cultures' <www.plantcultures.org.uk> and 'ORIGINATION:INSITE' <www.channel4.com/insite> are heralded as capturing the public imagination, engaging non-traditional audiences and encouraging participation. These sites are showcased as examples of unique partnerships and collaborations between diverse organizations (Greenwood and Streten, 2006; Harcup and Nesbitt, 2006; Streten et al., 2006). How can these principles be applied in smaller museums where resources are often stretched?

An important source of seed funding for some organizations is coming from the International Partnerships Among Museums (IPAM) program, administered by the American Association of Museums <www.aam-us.org> and funded by Department of State's Bureau of Educational and Cultural Affairs <http://exchanges.state.gov/education/>. This program provides money for travel to facilitate international educational exchange residencies. The goal is to seed the development of long-term linkages and collaborative projects between participating institutions (AAM, 2005). Three recipients of this project funding are developing collaborative web-based exhibitions and resources to come on-line in 2007–2008, in order to reach new and existing target audiences that may never visit those museums.

An exchange between Alice Springs Desert Park (ASDP) in Australia <www.alicespringsdesertpark.com.au> and the Arizona-Sonora Desert Museum (ASDM), USA <www.desertmuseum.org> is looking to foster recognition of cultural similarities in diverse regions. An interactive web-site for children and teenagers, linked to teacher resources, will consider survival strategies used by native animals, plants and people in two distinct desert locations. Cultural information past and present, obtained directly from Arrernte Aboriginal elders and children, can be compared and contrasted with similar information from the Tohono O'odham and Patayan peoples of Arizona (ASDM and ASDP, 2005).

The Greenland National Museum and Archives (GNMA) <www.natmus.gl> is working with the Peary-MacMillan Arctic Museum (PMAM), based at Bowdoin College, USA, <http://academic.bowdoin.edu/arcticmuseum> to develop a bilingual website (English and Greenlandic) that explores the different perspectives of Euro-American and Greenlandic societies in their shared history of exploration of the North. It aims to specifically target the remote, regional communities that are the focus of each muse-um's collection, who rarely get to visit the museum. Internet connection for people who live in these small communities is by satellite only, mak-ing the design and architecture of the site a prime consideration. Also targeted are the existing audiences for each institution, comprising locals and tourists, which are very different. Audience development and engage-ment via the site is a primary motivation. Curators intend that the site include some interactivity, allowing users to create their own portfolios of images from the collections and possibly submit identification or other information about selected photos, as individuals are often not named (PMAM and GNMA, 2005).

Finally, the Art Libraries at Hillwood Museum and Gardens (HMG), USA <www.hillwoodmuseum.org> and the State Russian Museum (SRM) <www.rusmuseum.ru> in St Petersburg, Russia, are collaborating to develop content for a web-based exhibition on the traditions, history and techniques of imperial Russian illustrated art books and journals. Curators are also exploring the collections of these museums to source content for the exhibition:

USA
- The Library of Congress, Washington, DC
- New York Public Library, New York City, NY
- Harvard University, Boston, MA

Russia
- The State National Library, St Petersburg
- The State Hermitage, St Petersburg
- Pushkin Museum on Moika River Embankment, St Petersburg
- The Museum-reserves: the Pavlovsk Palace, Tsarskoe Selo and Peterhof

The site will cater to the research community as well as general visitors, and provides deeper interpretation and access to materials that are often remote to these audiences. A further anticipated outcome is a hard publication on the traditions of pre-Revolutionary Russian illustrated arts books (SRM and HMG, 2005).

Summary

Museums now have a vast array of technology at their disposal that can be used to reach expanded audiences in numbers unheard of in the not so distant past. All museums are the same size on the screen we use to visit these cultural gatekeepers—regardless of size and scope of the institution. The rapid development of communication hardware and software, including the development of Web 2.0, is facilitating increased levels of interactivity and participation. This provides enormous opportunities to improve access to museum collections, for strategic audience development and to potentially generate revenue, appropriate to mission. As has continued to be demonstrated over the short life of the Internet in the last decade or so, 'content is king' (Gates, 1996) and museums are potentially 'rich' in this regard. However, the train is departing and the opportunity to adopt a competitive position on-line is becoming marginal. Museums must consider their own potential within the new realm of technological possibility. There is an urgent need for museums to develop a holistic and integrated approach to on-line marketing activities in order to generate maximum exposure, engagement and value for their constituents, even if they never physically visit.

Points for discussion and activities

- What are the main opportunities for museums in developing an on-line presence?
- What is significant about recent developments in technology?
- Explore the websites of five large museums and five small museums. You may also like to consider five non-museum sites of your own choice (such as other culture and heritage, sports, web-based business, corporate, fashion or university sites).
  - What features do each offer?
  - Can you develop a rating system that considers level of engagement, useability and functionality of design?

- What purpose do these features fulfil?
- Suggest what the underlying museum objectives might be that are attached to features on museum sites.
- Can you identify features that could be adopted from non-museum sites by museums?

Acknowledgement

The author wishes to acknowledge the invaluable support of Tim Roberts during the writing of this chapter through comments and editing, as well as his contribution of the vignette on National Gallery in London.

References

American Association of Museums (AAM) (2005). *About International Partnership among Museums (IPAM)*, <http://www.aam-us.org/getinvolved/ipam/about.cfm> (accessed 14 March 2006.

Arizona-Sonora Desert Museum (ASDM) and Alice Springs Desert Park (ASDP) (2005). *IPAM Project Proposal*. ASDM, ASDP.

Bannister, L. (2006). User generated content: power to the people. TMC Net. <http://www.tmcnet.com/usubmit/2006/08/25/1830743.htm> (accessed 11 September 2006).

Barry, A. (2006). Creating a virtuous circle between a museum's on-line and physical spaces. In *Museums and the Web 2006: Proceedings* (J. Trant and D. Bearman, eds.). Archives & Museum Informatics. <http://www.archimuse.com/mw2006/papers/barry/barry.html> (accessed 2 May 2006).

Bawa, M. (2006). How people find museum collection content online. *UK Museums on the Web Conference*. <http://mcg.man.ac.uk/meetings/2-2006-abs.shtml#dphillips> (accessed 11 July 2006).

Burton, C. and Scott, C. (2003). Museums: challenges for the 21st century. *International Journal of Arts Management*, 5(2), 56–68.

Carey, S. and Jeffrey, R. (2006). Audience analysis in the age of engagement. In *Museums and the Web 2006: Proceedings* (J. Trant and D. Bearman, eds.). Archives & Museum Informatics. <http://www.archimuse.com/mw2006/papers/carey/carey> (accessed 2 May 2006).

Computer Industry Almanac (2006). Worldwide Internet users Top 1 billion in 2005. Press release, 4 January. <http://www.c-i-a.com/pr0106.htm> (accessed 21 August 2006).

Cooper, J. (2006). Beyond the on-line museum: participatory virtual exhibitions. In *Museums and the Web 2006: Proceedings* (J. Trant and D. Bearman, eds.). Archives & Museum Informatics. <http://www.archimuse.com/mw2006/papers/cooper/cooper.html> (accessed 2 May 2006).

Council on Library and Information Sources (CLIR) (2001). *Building and Sustaining Digital Collections: Models for Libraries and Museums*. Council on Library and Information Resources. <http://www.clir.org/pubs/reports/pub100/pub100.pdf> (accessed 22 August 2006).

Dietz, S. (2000). The online museum-archive-library of wonder-curiosity-art. <http://gallery9.walkerart.org/midtext.html?id=157> (accessed 10 September 2006).

Ellis, M. (2006). Web 2.0: why museums are excited and scared all at the same time. *UK Museums on the Web Conference*. <http://mcg.man.ac.uk/meetings/2-2006-abs.shtml#dphillips> (accessed 11 July 2006).

Gates, B. (1996). *Content is King*. Essay. Microsoft, 3 January 1996. <http://www.microsoft.com/billgates/columns/1996essay/essay960103.asp> (accessed 11 September 2006).

Greenwood, M. and Streten, K. (2006). How do audiences discover museums online? Culture online: partnerships, participation, outreach. *UK Museums on the Web Conference*. <http://mcg.man.ac.uk/meetings/2-2006-abs.shtml#dphillips> (accessed 11 July 2006).

Hamma, K. (2004). The role of museums in online teaching, learning, and research. *First Monday*, 9(5). <http://firstmonday.org/issues/issue9_5/hamma/index.html> (accessed 9 May 2006).

Harcup, C. and Nesbitt, M. (2006). Attaining the holy grail: how to encourage wider engagement with museum collections through participation in new media projects. In *Museums and the Web 2006: Proceedings* (J. Trant and D. Bearman, eds.). Archives & Museum Informatics. <http://www.archimuse.com/mw2006/papers/harcup/harcup.html> (accessed 2 May 2006).

Hecht, P. (2006). Evaluating the NGA web site: focusing on the user. *AAM 2006 Media and Technology conference*. <http://www.mediaandtechnology.org/panels/AAM06handouts/Millions-Hecht.ppt> (accessed 30 August 2006).

Hill, L., O'Sullivan, C. and O'Sullivan, T. (2003). *Creative Arts Marketing*. Elsevier Butterworth-Heinemann.

Hinchcliffe, D. (2006). Architectures of participation: the next big thing. On Dion Hinchcliffe's Web 2.0 Blog. 1 August. <http://web2.wsj2.com/architectures_of_participation_the_next_big_thing.htm> (accessed 9 October 2006).

Institute of Museum and Library Services (IMLS) (2006). Status of Technology and Digitization in the Nation's Museums and Libraries. <http://www.imls.gov/publications/TechDig05/index.htm> (accessed 24 March 2006).

Ipsos (2006a). Mobile phones could soon rival the PC as world's dominant Internet platform. Press release, 18 April. <http://www.ipsos-na.com/news/pressrelease.cfm?id=3049> (accessed 11 September 2006).

Ipsos (2006b). Portable MP3 Player Ownership Reaches New High. Press release, 29 June. <http://www.ipsos-na.com/news/pressrelease.cfm?id=3124> (accessed 11 September 2006).

Kennedy, R. (2005). *With Irreverence and an iPod, Recreating the Museum Tour*. New York Times, 28 May, <http://query.nytimes.com/search/restricted/article?res=F0061FFA3A5D0C7B8EDDAC0894DD404482> (accessed 11 September 2006).

Martin, R. (2003). Cooperation and change: archives, libraries and museums in the United States. Conference presentation at *World Library and Information Congress: 69th IFLA General Conference and Council*, Berlin. <www.ifla.org/IV/ifla69/papers/066e-Martin.pdf> (accessed 21 August 2006).

Marty, P. F. and Twidale, M. B. (2004). Lost in gallery space: a conceptual framework for analyzing the usability of museum web sites. *First Monday*, 9(9). <http://firstmonday.org/issues/issue9_9/marty/index.html> (accessed 9 May 2006).

Meeker, M. (2005). The Age of Engagement. Conference presentation at *Ad: Tech 2005*. <http://www.morganstanley.com/institutional/techresearch/age_of_engagement.html?page=research> (accessed 5 July 2006).

Meeker, M., Pitz, B., Fitzgerald, B. and Ji, R. (2006). *Global Internet Trends*. Research Report, <http://www.morganstanley.com/institutional/techresearch/Trends040106.html?page=research> (accessed 5 July 2006).

O'Reilly, T. (2004). Open source paradigm shift. <http://tim.oreilly.com/articles/paradigmshift_0504.html> (accessed 11 September 2006).

Pratty, J. (2006). The digital museum turned inside out. *UK Museums on the Web Conference*. <http://mcg.man.ac.uk/meetings/2-2006-abs.shtml#dphillips> (accessed 11 July 2006).

Rainie, L. (2006). Digital 'Natives' Invade the Workplace. Young people may be newcomers to the world of work, but it's their bosses who are immigrants into the digital world. *Pew Internet and American Life Project*, September 28. <http://pewresearch.org/obdeck/?ObDeckID=70> (accessed 31 October 2006).

Rellie, J. (2006a). 10 years on: hopes, fears, predictions and gambles for UK Museums On-line. In *Museums and the Web 2006: Proceedings* (J. Trant and D. Bearman, eds.). Archives & Museum Informatics. <http://www.archimuse.com/mw2006/papers/rellie/rellie.1.html> (accessed 2 May 2006).

Rellie, J. (2006b). Digitising Delivery at Tate Online: the challenges faced programming an art gallery in 21st century. University College London, Lecture slides, 10 May. <http://www.publishing.ucl.ac.uk/news-200605101900/img0.html> (accessed 10 August 2006).

Rellie, J. (2006c). Comparing Tate Online: quantitative data across sites and borders. *AAM 2006 Media and Technology conference*. <www.mediaand-technology.org/ panels/AAM06handouts/Millions-Rellie.ppt> (accessed 22 April 2006).

Rentschler, R. and Gilmore, A. (2002). Museums: discovering services marketing. *International Journal of Arts Management*. Montréal, Fall, 5(1) (11 pages).

Roush, W. (2005). Social machines: computing means connecting. Technologyreview.com, August. <http://www.technologyreview.com/read_article.aspx?id=16236&ch=&sc=&pg=1> (accessed 9 May 2006).

Samis, P. and Pau, S. (2006). 'Artcasting' at SFMOMA: First-Year Lessons, Future Challenges for Museum Podcasters broad audience of use. In *Museums and the Web 2006: Proceedings* (J. Trant and D. Bearman, eds.). Archives & Museum Informatics. <http://www.archimuse.com/mw2006/papers/samis.html> (accessed 2 May 2006).

Sayre, S. (2005). Multimedia that matters: Gallery-based technology and the museum visitor. *First Monday*, 10(5). <http://firstmonday.org/issues/issue10_5/sayre/index.html> (accessed 9 May 2006).

Schwartz, J. (2005). The participation age. <http://blogs.sun.com/roller/page/jonathan/20050404>. (accessed 30 August 2006).

Soren, B. J. (2004). *Research on 'Quality' in Online Experiences for Museum Users*. Canadian Heritage Information Network (CHIN), Canada. <http://www.chin.gc.ca/English/Pdf/Digital_Content/Research_Quality/research_quality.pdf> (accessed 9 May 2006).

Spadaccini, J. (2006). Museums 2.0: A Survey of Museum Blogs & Community-Based Sites. <http://www.ideum.com/blog/wp-content/uploads/2006/03/museumblogs3-6-06.pdf> (accessed 11 September 2006).

State Russian Museum (SRM) and Hillwood Museum and Gardens (HMG) (2005). *IPAM 2005–2007 Project Proposal*. SRM, St Petersburg Russia and HMG.

Streten, K., Burnett, T. and Hand, M. (2006). Linking minority communities through the web. In *Museums and the Web 2006: Proceedings* (J. Trant and D. Bearman, eds.). Archives & Museum Informatics. <http://www.archimuse.com/mw2006/papers/streten/streten.html> (accessed 2 May 2006).

The National Gallery (2003). *Zoomable Pictures: An Exciting Way To Explore The National Gallery's World Class Painting Collection Online*. Press release. National Gallery.

The Peary-MacMillan Arctic Museum (PMAM) and Greenland National Museum and Archives (GNMA) (2005). *IPAM Phase II Project Proposal*. PMAM, Brunswick, Maine and GNMA, Nuk.

Varisco, R. A. and Cates, M.W. (2005). Survey of web-based educational resources in selected U.S. art museums. *First Monday*, 10(7). <http://firstmonday.org/issues/issue10_7/varisco/index.html> (accessed 26 July 2006).

Walker Art Centre (2004). Art on Call (AoC): project narrative. <http://newmedia.walkerart.org/downloads/aoc/Walker_AOC_IMLS_final.rtf> (accessed 19 July 2006).

Walker Art Centre (2006). About art on call. <http://newmedia.walkerart.org/aoc/about.wac> (accessed 19 July 2006).

Watson, R., Pitt, L., Berthon, P. and Zinkhan, G. (2002). U-Commerce: Expanding the Universe of Marketing. Journal of the Academy of Marketing Science, 30(4), 333–47.

E-marketing, communications and the international tourist

Wee Wen Liew and Michelle Loh

Overview of e-marcom and the international tourist

Real-time podcasts, mobile instant messaging, blogs and e-newsletters. Such terms were virtually unheard of until a few years ago. The impact of technology has influenced all aspects of our economy including the arts and cultural sector. Since the late 1990s, many museums have entered the age of digital information technology with great vigour. Websites are more than information providers; they are port keys for virtual users into reality. Personal digital assistants (PDAs) allow users to be inter-connected to the world regardless of where they are. Information technology has since expanded the conventional definition of marketing.

There are now no boundaries or barriers to art appreciation and the museum. Technological readiness has further increased the potential for the effectiveness and efficiency of the traditional marketing strategy. The uses of e-marketing and communications have endowed the modern-day visitor and the museum with tangible and intangible benefits.

This chapter will refer to a sample of 26 Asian national museums and art galleries, looking at their websites, e-marketing and communication tools. With reference to Table 1.2, the sample is selected based on two simple criteria: English as the main language medium on the website and on-line accessibility.

E-marketing and communications

No earlier literature has been published on the definition of e-marketing in the cultural context. According to the business and commerce sector, 'e-marketing is the use of information technology in the process of creating, communicating, and delivering value to customers, and for managing customer relationships in ways that benefit the organization and its stakeholders' (Strauss in Strauss et al., 2006, p. 3). Strauss also states that e-marketing is basically the

Table 1.2 Sample of 26 museums in Asia.

S/N	Museum/gallery and website address	Country
1	Museum of Contemporary Art, Shanghai www.mocashanghai.org	China
2	National Art Museum of China www.namoc.org	China
3	Shanghai Art Museum www.cnarts.net/shanghaiart/INDEX_C.ASP	China
4	Hong Kong Heritage Museum http://www.heritagemuseum.gov.hk/english/main.asp	Hong Kong
5	Hong Kong Museum of Art http://www.lcsd.gov.hk/CE/Museum/Arts/english/intro/ eintro.html	Hong Kong
6	Museum Nasional Indonesia http://www.museumnasional.org	Indonesia
7	21st Century Museum of Contemporary Art Kanazawa www.kanazawa21.jp/en/index.html	Japan
8	Fukuoka Asian Art Museum http://faam.city.fukuoka.jp/eng/home.html	Japan
9	Kyoto National Museum http://www.kyohaku.go.jp/eng/index_top.html	Japan
10	The National Museum of Art, Osaka http://www.nmao.go.jp/english/home.html	Japan
11	Islamic Arts Museum Malaysia http://www.iamm.org.my	Malaysia
12	Muzium Negara Malaysia http://www.museum.gov.my/english/home.htm	Malaysia
13	National Art Gallery http://artgallery.gov.my/mod_com/index.php	Malaysia
14	National Museum (Arts Div.) http://members.tripod.com/philmuseum/index	Philippines
15	The Metropolitan Museum of Manila www.metmuseum.ph/events.htm	Philippines
16	Asian Civilisations Museum http://www.acm.org.sg/home/home.asp	Singapore
17	Singapore Art Museum www.singart.com	Singapore
18	National Museum of Contemporary Art, Korea http://www.moca.go.kr/Modern/eng/main.html	South Korea
19	National Museum of Korea http://www.museum.go.kr/eng/	South Korea
20	Bangkok National Museum http://www.thailandmuseum.com/thaimuseum_eng/bangkok/ main.htm	Thailand
21	The National Gallery in Bangkok www.thailandmuseum.com/thaimuseum_eng/artgallery/ main.htm	Thailand
22	Kaohsiung Museum of Fine Art www.kmfa.gov.tw	Taiwan
23	Museum of Contemporary Art Taipei www.mocataipei.org.tw/	Taiwan
24	National Palace Museum www.npm.gov.tw	Taiwan
25	Taipei Fine Arts Museum www.tfam.gov.tw	Taiwan
26	Taiwan Museum of Art http://www.tmoa.gov.tw/english/home.php	Taiwan

'result of information technology applied to traditional marketing'. This refers to three main types:

1. Internet—including the intranet, extranet and web.
2. Non-web Internet communication—e-mail and newsgroups.
3. Other information-receiving appliances besides the PC—PDAs, mobile phones, digital cameras, televisions and radios.

E-marketing and communications in the cultural context is the use of information technology to achieve the aims and objectives as part of the overall marketing strategy of the cultural organization.

A conventional piece of marketing strategy typically involves, but is not restricted to, the five 'P's (price, product, place, position, people), SWOT (strengths–weaknesses–opportunities–threats) analysis, the marketing mix, market segmentation and segregation. Communications 'hardware' has long included the printed media, newspapers, word-of-mouth, television and radio broadcasts. The museum has grown to envelope important technologies such as text and multimedia messages via the Internet and e-mail as well as a generous proportion of information-receiving appliances. This is also known as new media. 'New' media in 1999 includes touch-screen information and booking points around different parts of town (Runyard and French, 1999, p. 105). In 2006, this has expanded to SMS marketing, audio guides and even PDA guides that deliver full explanatory notes by just beaming the device to a small electronic beacon next to an exhibited painting. It even comes with language selection for the user to choose an appropriate language.

Combining both the conventional and modern, the overall marketing strategy could help the museum achieve its goals of, for example, outreach, access, visitorship, education, research and funding.

Marketing executives have increasing problems managing unplanned messages between the museum and its visitors, since visitors now have more control over information from the Internet. 'Firms have to concentrate on creating positive product experiences so that unplanned messages will be positive' (Strauss et al., 2006, p. 317). The website should not simply be a replica of the organization's brochure; however, consistent branding and image should be ensured in all marketing tools.

The international tourist

Tourism marketing and cultural tourism has proved itself to be an economic generator in the UK (Runyard and French, 1999, p. 93). Museums form an integral part of the tourism chain, generating income for other related services such as the amenities around the museum building. 'Museums are increasingly working with travel and tourist agencies and the hospitality industry to develop plans, promotions and programmes to attract tourism' (Kotler and Kotler, 1998, p. 105). The tourism aspect is factored into many UK museums' marketing strategies in order to tap into the enlarging pool of both overseas and domestic holiday-makers. According to Kotler and Kotler, tourists or holiday-makers have the following characteristics:

- Provide a source of income for museums.
- Are first-time visitors.
- Plan their visits and site destinations.
- Seek particular kinds of experiences.
- Have high expectations of visits and experiences.

The international tourist has all of the above characteristics and is much more than the average holiday-maker or local tourist. The international tourist has in mind certain aims and objectives to fulfil during their visit. They have control over their overall museum experience which begins right from the moment they visit the website or receive an e-alert. Technology advancements have resulted in enhanced visitor control over Internet communications (Strauss et al., 2006, p. 317).

In this cultural context, the international tourist refers to a person who adopts assistance from any type of information-receiving appliance to access information as an enhancement to an overall museum or gallery experience. They could be staying in a hotel in Australia and watching the latest news of the Singapore Art Museum on TV. They could be a holiday-maker using audio guides in the art gallery. In their own country, they could also be travelling on the train and using a mobile phone to receive Short Message Service (SMS) on upcoming exhibitions and late night events. They could also be at the comfort of their home, planning the next family visit to the museum. As long as an information-receiving appliance is available, the virtual world is an enhancement to the overall museum experience, providing a borderless reality for the modern international tourist.

An international tourist's museum experience is tangible, sensory and deeply personal. With access to a virtual bank of information at all stages of the visit, the international tourist has more control over the museum experience and may form a customized menu of what to see, do, buy and eat in the museum.

Tangible and intangible benefits

Implementations of e-marcom bring about a variety of benefits for both the international tourist and the museum, such as infinite virtual shelf life, enhanced access from home for the physically impaired, increased visitorship in terms of demographic and geographical profiles. The use of e-marketing has also expanded opportunities for funding and museum support from a wider variety of sources.

Figure 1.1 displays the various components of e-marketing implemented by the 26 museums, but not confined to the following: ticket promotions,

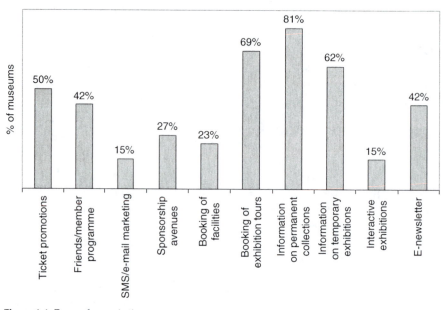

Figure 1.1 Types of e-marketing

members' programme, SMS/e-mail marketing, sponsorship avenues, booking of facilities, exhibition tours, information on permanent and temporary collections, interactive exhibitions on-line, and e-newsletters. The international tourist could easily obtain such information through the Internet or e-mail via personal computers, mobile phones and PDAs. Other types of e-marcom include those retrievable at the museum itself, such as handheld PDA guides, touch-screen installations, audio guides and interactive exhibitions at the museum.

Outreach and visitorship

The most frequently and best used form for all the museums and galleries is the Internet via the museum's website. On-line access to websites has widened the museum's visitorship profiles not just geographically but also demographically. There are no age restrictions, no entrance fees and no closing times. Domestic visitors have a higher rate of returning to the museum. Both local and overseas visitors could be sustained through the friends' or members' programmes on-line. Applicants at home can sign up for annual memberships with physical benefits such as ticket promotions, discounts at services and facilities, regular updates on programmes and events, or private viewings. Applicants in other countries can sign up for regular e-newsletters and free on-line access to more than one museum.

Singapore Art Museum has a shared membership programme with six other museums under the National Heritage Board. The latest events, programmes and membership discounts at Singapore Art Museum, Asian Civilisations Museum, Heritage Conservation Centre, National Archives of Singapore, Reflections at Bukit Chandu and Singapore Philatelic Museum will be available to subscribers of the e-Museum Card. Joint partnership and marketing collaborations between museums and other cultural organizations can attract more attention from audiences and the media and maximize costs at the same time (Kotler and Kotler, 1998, p. 352). The Friends of the Hong Kong Museum of Art, a not-for-profit organization, is set up to promote the activities of Hong Kong museums and the Hong Kong community's interest in the visual arts. The membership benefits extend to the Hong Kong Art Museum, Art Promotion Office, Hong Kong Visual Arts Centre and Flaghouse Museum of Teaware.

Audience profiles are changing with changing technologies. The majority of the young who visit actual museums are fervent users of art museum websites, undoubtedly due to the enthusiasm the young have for the Internet, unlike older adults who visit the actual museums (Desmarteau, 2003). Audience development has always been a significant objective of any museum. Once the target audience and respective visitor groups are identified, marketing executives then position proactive techniques to reach out to the respective segments. Singapore's Asian Civilisations Museum actively promotes its public programmes to three groups of targeted visitors. Programmes are specially tailored to the specific preferences of adults, children and families. The museum communicates to its younger audience through schools where it fosters a sustainable relationship with the teachers which is more cost- and time-effective.

In a new 'multi-lingual e-audio guide' project, under way at the Singapore Art Museum, traditional audio guide content on the museum's exhibits and architecture is uploaded into PDAs for museum visitors. Upon project completion, a personalized tour route will be indicated at the beginning of a visit, when museum visitors input their interest and preferred duration of visit into the PDA. At any time, strategically placed beacons throughout the museum can be activated wirelessly by the visitor, providing audio and visual information. Topics of interest, with links to related websites and on-line information, can be bookmarked and the bookmarks sent to e-mail addresses input by the visitor. In terms of sustainability, it is also foreseeable that the e-audio guide's bookmark function will encourage visitors to explore the museum's displays, collections and architecture on-line. This increased research interest should translate into repeat visits to the Singapore Art Museum's physical location.

From the international tourists' perspective, they now have access to smaller galleries where such information may not previously have been readily accessible. Websites are easily affordable for even a small art museum to maintain (Kotler and Kotler, 1998, p. 18).

Museums can attract a diverse set of international tourists who are otherwise uncaptured on site. Technology currently allows computer programmers to survey the profile of the international tourists but designing of such software requires programming expertise, investment and time.

Access

Museums and galleries have a history of being an environment that 'provoked awe and intimidation rather than learning' with 'no immediate right of entry' (Mclean, 1997, p. 11). Digital advancements may greatly change the image of museums as ivory towers. Like experiencing the prelude before exposing to the full sonata, visitors can learn more about a museum before entering it. Some museums even prompt visitors to prepare their visit with three simple steps: plan your visit, go through the proposed routes; select the one that suits you best and choose the restaurants in which you'll rest. Visitors need no longer be deterred by expected or unexpected behavioural patterns. If still unsure, visitors can attend regular evening events or family programmes where the atmosphere is relaxed and less confronting. At Taipei Fine Arts Museum, Saturday night and family night programmes are uploaded 2 months before the events for visitors to plan their late night visits.

Some websites even offer a detailed staff organization chart and contact list of the museum's curators, marketers and managers. Museum, NUS Centre for the Arts has an organization chart that offers on-line visitors direct access to whomever they want to contact, from the director to the operations officer. Visitors can feed back to the person-in-charge directly instead of being diverted all over the place. The museum can also react to public feedback and suggestions with an immediate response via e-mail. Barriers between the management and audience are narrowed thus improving the museum's overall public image, relations and communication effectiveness.

Funding and museum support

Successful sponsorship and corporate funding are dependent on a proactive management with knowledge in marketing. At the Singapore Art Museum, the website acts as an additional avenue for sponsorship and is creatively crafted to respective tiers in the society. Users can choose how they would like to support the museum—through corporate sponsorship, donation (cash or artefact) or a long-term loan. Marketing executives continue reaching out to potential sponsors through traditional marketing methods for particular programme grants or long-term corporate partnerships. Only a surprising 27 per cent of the museums surveyed have considered sponsorship avenues as part of their e-marketing strategy.

Other income generating activity, such as the booking of facilities, is also at an unexpected 23 per cent. The museums with sponsorship avenues and booking of facilities include some in Malaysia, Manila, Shanghai, Singapore and Taiwan. On-line museum and retail shops are almost non-existent, while sale of publications is few and far between. This trend could be a reflection on the country or city's economy as well as the characteristics of the people. On-line transactions are usually dependent on credit cards. To take full advantage of the convenience and ease of transactions, museums may consider investing in secured sites for on-line purchases.

Another form of museum support is volunteering. Most museums are increasing their reliance on volunteers, docents and interns. As well as being the lifeblood of many museums, 'volunteer involvement and volunteer enthusiasm have the potential to improve every aspect of museums, provide opportunities to pilot new projects and encourage strong links between the museum and the community' (Report in Office of Arts and Libraries, 1991, p. 176).

Museums use both passive and active e-marketing to recruit volunteers. Some use more active e-marketing such as forwarding e-mails to potential graduates in the required areas. Most prefer to use the website as a passive marketing tactic to select candidates who are committed, passionate and have the right attitude. A volunteering policy should 'integrate into the marketing strategy and consequently reflect the museum's mission' (Mclean, 1997, p. 177). At the Museum of Contemporary Art in Shanghai, the website provides potential candidates with museum details such as the different departments, duration of internship and the type of candidate the museum is seeking. Such insightful details equip potential candidates with full knowledge of what is expected of them and vice versa. This in turn helps the museum to sift out the ideal candidate from the mixture. At the Museum, NUS Centre for the Arts, docents have to be recommended first, then interviewed before they are finally selected and engaged on a more regular basis.

Education and research

Websites are also evolving from an information medium to a learning medium (Desmarteau, 2003). For most, the visit to the actual museum promotes equally the acquisition of new knowledge as well as a modest learning.

Museums can prolong the shelf life of temporary exhibitions through on-line portals. Eighty-three per cent of the survey sample has on-line information on temporary exhibits. National Palace Museum dedicates an on-line exhibition section to three segments: current, future and past exhibits. Any permanent or temporary exhibits can be found under any of these three segments. By clicking further, the website will launch users to another realm of informative pages related to the particular exhibition. On-line visitors can continue to view past exhibitions even after these installations or paintings have been removed from the museum.

Information on conservation techniques, art installations, paintings and curatorial expertise add value to education and research. Research at the National Art Museum in China is classified under five on-line categories: museum publication, academic activities, research analysis, research topics and academic publications. Researchers from around the globe can retrieve information related to the museum's exhibitions. Visits and revisits to the website to search for a particular piece of information are highly sustainable.

In other instances, website revisits may extend beyond research to the other types of visitor. Schools, families and working adults may check the website regularly for museum events, late night openings, outreach and educational programmes. The Islamic Arts Museum in Malaysia has a range of programmes that cater to people from pre-school to university level as part of their objective to encourage new audiences at the museum. The Kyoto National Museum differentiates its lectures and events according to the degree of intensity, from the children's club to Saturday lecture series for working adults and international symposiums for museum experts.

The museum's collection is also more transparent for other curators and collections managers around the world. Data is available in both on-line and off-line status. Curators can choose to stage successful exhibitions selected from a diversified array of paintings, sculptures or installations, and also work towards possible cross-cultural collaborations and inter-visiting exhibitions. These could be exhibitions that are popular with visitors or sponsors, or exhibitions which coincide with the city's trend at a particular point in time.

The National Museum of Contemporary Art, Korea, has pages dedicated to the 'Travelling Art Museum'. Short descriptions of the exposition themes are placed in clear order which allows curators to select their choice. An annual schedule, indicating the next exhibition location and duration, further allows curators (other museums) to plan exhibition schedules ahead of time. To further attract visitors, cultural events are accompanied with the exhibitions to the next locations.

From the survey data, Asia museums utilize e-marketing more in the aspects of education and information resource.

Recommendations

Marketing versus e-marketing

An important strategic consideration lies in ensuring e-marketing components complement and do not become independent of overall, more traditional marketing strategies in community outreach, branding and corporate communications. An international tourist's museum experience anywhere in this world remains, more likely than not, tangible, sensory and deeply personal.

For example, the Singapore Art Museum's media familiarity tours, exhibition press conferences, press kit distributions and other media efforts work towards listings and editorials for its exhibitions on international news agencies with high on-line presence (e.g., Bloomberg, International Herald Tribune, MSNBC-Newsweek). This reaches informed business travellers particularly well—likely visitors of both art museums and Business Travel, Meetings, Incentives, Conventions and Exhibitions (BTMICE), centric Singapore. The editorials and write ups by these international news agencies are then picked up by other websites, for example absolutearts.com, virtualtourist.com, artnet.com and artfacts.net, reaching a larger pool of travelling art lovers.

Customer relationship marketing is an imperative strategic function which has evolved from direct customer contact to direct e-mail contact. The method of contact should be differentiated between different visitor groups. Relationship marketing as part of the overall marketing strategy creates a solid base of supporters and visitors for the museum (Runyard and French, 1999, p. 105).

'Gartner Group predicts that the "e" will soon be dropped, making electronic business just part of the way things are done' (Strauss et al., 2006, p. 9). As Aronica and Fingar predict, 'E-business has become just business. E-commerce has become just commerce. The new economy has become just the economy'. The global marketplace has set the scene for websites and e-mail marketing as essential components in any cultural organization. The natural process of evolution brings about another level of marketing with global advancements.

Communications and information

The marriage between technology and the arts often results in two common problems, among other things, faced in all marital relationships: over-reliance and miscommunication. In today's paperless economy, over-dependency on any information-receiving appliances may result in undesirable consequences for the management as well as the international tourist. Websites have to be constantly well maintained, updated and forecast a few months in advance. The international tourist's on-line experience solely relies on the information, design and navigation properties of the website.

Information technology now redefines itself with its own lingo and special programming of HTML pages for upload onto the Internet to accommodate the ease of navigation for user search properties. A whole new communications channel is being developed. Researchers are currently investigating the 'e-language' that is used on websites, blogs, SMS and MSN to understand how this has influenced communications between the younger generations. Websites with unattractive usage of words may deter young visitors from visiting the website and going to the museum.

The knowledge economy brings with it a vast multitude of new media content and channels. One strategic consideration lies in ensuring the marketing message reaches the greatest number target audience without drowning in this sea of information. While the international tourist has greater control over their museum experience, they also need to exercise caution because not all information may be bona fide.

Summary

Digitization is the most influential contributing factor to globalization. With increasing appliance convergence and improved Internet strategy integration, e-marketing can reach a broader audience base more effectively at lower costs. The audience group expands to include a younger generation who are fervent users of the computer and Internet as well as overseas visitors, both of whom adopt technology for an enhanced museum experience.

E-marketing and communications should complement and not become independent of overall, more traditional marketing strategies. E-marketing tools are used more in terms of access, outreach, education and research. Growing trends depict usage of e-marketing to boost funding, sponsorship and other forms of museum support.

Due to the number of uncontrollable variables with specific exhibitions, it is beyond the scope of this chapter to isolate the statistical significance of specific e-marketing strategies on international tourist numbers across exhibitions. Since the implementation of strategies like the examples above, however, there have been significant increases in the numbers (reach) and countries of origin (expansion) of Museum visitors.

References

Aronica, R. and Fingar, P. (2001). Ten myths of the new economy. *The Business Integrator Journal*, Fall, 14–22.

Desmarteau, M. (2003). Art museum web sites: from information medium to learning medium. *Museums and the Web Conference 2003*, North Carolina. <http://www.archimuse.com/mw2003/abstracts/prg_195000640.html> (accessed 9 December 2006).

Kotler, N. and Kotler, P. (1998). *Museum Strategy and Marketing*. Jossey-Bass. Wiley Print, San Francisco, United States of America.

Mclean, F. (1997). *Marketing the Museum*. Routledge, London.

Report in Office of Arts and Libraries (1991). *Volunteers in Museums and Heritage Organization: Policy, Planning and Management*. HMSO, London.

Runyard, S. and French, Y. (1999). *Marketing and Public Relations Handbook for Museums, Galleries and Heritage Attractions*. Alta Mira Press, United States of America.

Strauss, J., El-Ansary, A. and Frost, R. (2006). *E-Marketing* (Fourth edition). Pearson Education. Pearson Prentice Hall, United States of America.

2

Major case study: Vietnam Museum of Ethnology

Huong Le

Vietnam Museum of Ethnology in a broader context

The contemporary economy is based on the digital revolution and the management of information (Kotler, 2003). This means markets that offer customers a variety of choices become more competitive. The consuming culture in Vietnam has also experienced this global trend.

Since the implementation of the 'open door' policy, the Vietnamese economy, and the living standard of its people, has improved significantly. Cultural and artistic activities have progressively developed in Vietnam since the mid-1990s as a result of economic reforms. Compared with pre-1990s, the Vietnamese entertainment industry has become diverse; numerous Western movies, Internet, bars and many other types of entertainment are now present. Part of the reason for this is the vital influences of the global economic integration and cultural globalization, which has encouraged and motivated Vietnam to develop its own national identity, and exchange culturally with other parts of the world. This case study focuses on the Vietnam Museum of Ethnology (VME) within this context. It will explore initial efforts of this museum in visitor development and focus on a shift from traditional functions of the museum to activities for stronger connections with visitors. It will conclude with implications and recommendations for marketing strategies for museums in Vietnam.

Museums and efforts to attract audiences in the contemporary marketplace

The entertainment industry has become much more competitive and diverse than was previously the case. Kotler's (2003) analysis shows that due to the digital revolution, consumers today have:

- a substantial increase in buying power;
- a greater variety of available goods and services;
- a great amount of information about anything;
- greater ease interacting with suppliers, placing and receiving orders, and an increased ability to compare notes on products and services.

Not surprisingly, the museum has persistently and significantly changed its academic and intellectual frameworks in response to economic pressures (Kotler and Kotler, 2000; McPherson, 2006). Museums compete in an expanding leisure market and face common challenges in varying degrees (Kotler, 2001). Museums have made a clear shift from being static storehouses for artefacts into active learning environment for people (Hooper-Greenhill, 1994). They also redirect their traditional and singular focus on collection and exhibitions to two trends: attending to sociable, recreational and participatory experiences; and becoming parts of a cultural mosaic (Kotler, 2001). Hooper-Greenhill (1994) emphasized 'it is now no longer enough to collect as an end in itself; collecting has become the means to an end, that of making connections with people, and making links with their experience' (p. 1).

Notably, arts organizations cannot afford to ignore marketing tools or the general principles of management in securing their finances, audience and ultimately their survival. Marketing is no longer defined as the provision of required goods or services at a profit but has switched to the satisfaction of consumer wants and, more generally, to sensitively serving the needs of a particular society (Sargeant, 1999). Although concern that the above-mentioned shift undermines the quality of the museum experience for all visitors has been noted (Bradburne, 2001), many museums choose 'blockbuster' exhibitions to reach a broader public (Kotler and Kotler, 2000; Bradburne, 2001; Kotler, 2001). Strategies to build audiences, including improving the museum-going experience, community service and market re-positioning towards entertainment, are analysed thoroughly in Kotler and Kotler's article (2000). The authors indicate that to improve the museum-going experience for visitors, museums need to provide richer exhibits and programmes, better services and design elements, more accessible and comfortable facilities. Indeed, consumers often seek benefits and values in creational activities in their museum visitations, such as being with people and social interaction; enjoying the challenge of a new or unusual experience; having a learning opportunity; doing something worthwhile; and participating actively. The audience research apparently contributes to these findings.

Compared with other art-type museums in Vietnam confront even more serious difficulties in promoting themselves to the market. 'Going to the museum' is perhaps either uncool for the majority of young people or unattractive to the mature generation. Vietnamese audiences are also seduced by Americanization, Western popular culture and stylist entertainment. Also, government-reduced subsidies available to the cultural sector (Hoang, 1993) pose new challenges for the cultural sector in Vietnam. Lidstone and Doling (2000), in *Arts Management in Vietnam*, pointed out that 'from 1988 onwards the government reluctantly decided that hitherto generous state financing for arts and culture organizations should be reduced, and in some cases abolished altogether in favour of self-financing' (p. 7). In this context, marketing is sought as a new survival strategy for Vietnamese museums, given that marketing activities are newly utilized in this sector. Initial efforts of the VME in building audiences, including improving the museum-going experience and increasing community focus, will be discussed in the following sections.

Organizational profile

The impetus to establish the VME was to preserve the values and cultures of 44 ethnic groups in Vietnam. The proposal to establish the VME in Hanoi was approved by the government in 1987 but officially opened to the public in November 1997 after a long construction period. The VME is located in an open area in the Cau Giay District (which is about 8 kilometres from the centre of Hanoi, capital city of Vietnam). The museum has been managed by the National Centre for Social Sciences and Humanities and directed by Professor Nguyen, Van Huy.

The museum is both a research centre and a public museum, exhibiting the traditional cultures of Vietnam's 54 ethnic groups. The mission of the museum is to undertake scientific research, collection, documentation, conservation, exhibition and to preserve the cultural and historic patrimony of the nation's different ethnic groups. The museum also serves to guide research, conservation and technology specific to the work of an ethnographic museum.

It is noted that good architecture is an important factor to attract visitors (Bradburne, 2001; McPherson, 2006), and this is the case with the VME. The museum has very special architecture, presenting specific features of ethnic groups of Vietnam and their daily life activities. The collection includes 15,000 artefacts, 2190 slides, 42,000 photographs, 237 audiotapes, 373 videotapes and 25 CD-ROMS (Vietnam Museum of Ethnology, 2006). It is divided into two parts: an indoor and an outdoor exhibition. The indoor section includes the exhibition building, offices, the research centre and library, while the outdoor section displays different types of houses of minority groups in Vietnam, such as Ede long house, Tay stilt house, Yao house half on stilts and half on the ground, and the Giarai tomb.

The museum's existence and development has been secured by government funding and also from admission fees, sponsorships, donations and other trading services. A strengths–weaknesses–opportunities–threats (SWOT) analysis will be presented in the next section.

SWOT analysis

Strengths

- Owns and exhibits a collection of invaluable products from all of Vietnam's ethnic groups.
- Well-organized and displayed products according to their functions, to artefacts of each ethnic group or to different customs with clear explanations in three languages, good use of light and accessibility.
- Sets out clear organizational missions.
- Has strong staff (who are experts on the different ethnic groups).
- Has been given priority of government in preserving ethnic identity of Vietnamese culture.
- Receives sponsorships from many organizations such as the Embassy of France, Embassy of the Federal Republic of Germany, the Ford Foundation, the Rockefeller Foundation and many other corporations in Vietnam.
- Starts to utilize marketing strategies to attract visitors.
- Emphasizes the role of education programmes to develop young educated visitors through reduced prices for university, college and school students, free admissions fee for children under 6 years old and for Vietnam's ethnic minority members.
- Plans to present the cultures and civilizations of other countries in Southeast Asia.
- Has its website, comments and other services in three languages: Vietnamese, English and French to facilitate overseas visitors.

Weaknesses

- Lack of funding.
- Depends much on sponsorships of both the government and organizations.
- Does not have long-term museum marketing experience or large marketing department (e.g., there are only 2 staff in the Marketing Section while Department of Education has 11 people, Department of Conservation and Restoration of Collections (5 people) and Administration (23 people).
- No research on visitors or attendees or any other types of market research.

- Less accessible location compared with other museums (about 8 kilometres from the centre which is rather far for a small city, such as Hanoi).

Opportunities
- Attracts tourists, interests and collaborations of overseas museums due to its collections of artefacts of Vietnam's ethnic groups.
- A growth of tourism in Vietnam opens great opportunities for the VME to expose to foreigners who are keen on learning uniqueness of the Vietnamese culture.

Threats
- Many small, medium and large museums and galleries located in crowded cities such as Hanoi and Ho Chi Minh City. For example, some large national museums in Hanoi are the Vietnam Military Museum, Vietnam Historical Museum, Museum of Ho Chi Minh, Vietnam Fine Arts Museum (Ministry of Culture and Information of Vietnam, 2005). These other museums may attract more visitors due to advantages of location and accessibility, and specific exhibitions about Vietnamese wars, arts and history.
- Coping with a real difficulty in attracting visitors.
- New government policy which allows individuals or organizations to open private museums or galleries (Ministry of Culture and Information of Vietnam, 2006). The prevalence of private galleries is growing.

The above strengths and opportunities have helped the VME attract many more visitors in recent years, including tourists. Director of the VME Mr Nguyen indicated that the museum has increasingly attracted visitors since its opening: 37,000 visitors in 1998; 91,000 in 2003; 128,000 in 2004 and 163,000 in 2005. He added that approximately 45 per cent of visitors are foreigners, including many Westerners and recently more visitors from Japan and Korea.

Understanding the competition of the current entertainment market, much of the VME's initial efforts focused on improving the museum-going experience. The museum improved its activities and exhibitions, such as by creatively exploiting its current collections and displays; organizing regular temporary exhibitions; and improving lightings, accessibility, services, gift shop, communications and website. A new exhibition section about other Asian cultures will be opened to diversify its collections and particularly to reach international markets.

Beyond the traditional focus on objects, collections and education, where visitors are merely spectators, the museum's marketing strategies now include involving visitors in direct participation in activities (Kotler and Kotler, 2000; Kotler, 2001). The VME conducts interactive programmes which are a combination of entertainment and education to increase audiences. For example, as water puppetry has drawn great interest from foreigners, monthly performances have been organized since early 2006. The highlight point of the programme is a time for visitors to talk to the puppetry artisans, and make and practice controlling puppets. In addition, traditional food programmes were organized during this time so that visitors can try Vietnamese cuisines.

The VME also had special programmes to teach children to make traditional toys in which ethnic crafters were invited to exhibit their works and show children how to make them. Craft classes such as textiles class to make bags, purses or dolls with appealing messages are advertised on the VME's website to attract audiences. Indeed, these activities have brought in a large number of visitors and encouraged repeat visits. Also, as Kotler and Kotler (2000) suggested, such programmes help young people appreciate traditional arts, craftsmen and artists. The VME also attends to sociable, recreational and participatory experiences as is the current trend in museums (Kotler, 2001).

Many museums have, as Davies (1994) noted, encouraged visitation of target audiences by increased community focus and offering temporary exhibitions to suit apparent needs of these communities. According to its website and the director, the VME organized a successful exhibition which reflected the life and contemporary issues of Hanoi's people. Many people were invited to participate in the production process of this exhibition. The audiences did not simply see products and listen to comments but they also discovered themselves and their lives through the exhibition. The director indicated:

> to draw more attention of audience, we've expanded community services, we've built up 'friends of museum' includes a network of ethnic groups living in Hanoi; we've organized seminars, workshops, events to preserve heritages and develop a sense of community. We've tried to make the museum become a forum for community.
>
> (VME Director, Correspondence, September 2006)

Nowadays, museums are also increasingly using new media and Internet to expand visitors (Kotler and Kotler, 2000). Internet is effectively used to introduce, promote and market the VME's activities. Despite the fact that most museums in Vietnam have no website, the VME's activities, virtual visitation and services are published in detail online. Its activities are advertised in the media in three languages. The VME may be a pioneer in Vietnam to have a bulletin in which the coming 3 months of activities and exhibitions are published in advance, although this sounds common to many museums around the world. In the age of globalization when reliance on Internet is widespread, using good marketing communications helps the VME reach a broader audience. This also attracts sponsorships and collaborations with overseas museums. Indeed, in March 2003, the VME held a special exhibition in collaboration with the American Museum of Natural History (AMNH) entitled 'Journeys of Body, Mind & Spirit' in the USA (Cotter, 2003). This collaboration provided an ideal opportunity to reveal the richness of Vietnamese culture to

American audiences. The VME and staff also benefited from the experience and expertise of the AMNH and its curators.

However, in comparison with numbers of tourists visiting Vietnam annually (about 1 million), the number of visitors to the VME is modest (maximum 90,000 visitors). Conducting market research into audiences, why they go to performances and/or make a purchase, their level of satisfaction, the psychological and demographic aspects, significantly helps arts organizations evaluate ways to meet audiences' needs, as well as design marketing plans (Dickman, 1997; Australia Council, 1998; Close and Donovan, 1998; Rentschler, 1999; Dickman, 2000; Byrnes, 2003; Colbert, 2003; Wiggins, 2004). Such research and evaluation seems unfamiliar to marketers of the VME. The director noted that the VME has done neither market or visitor research nor has staff skilled in this area. Indeed, the museum has only one marketing officer who mainly focuses on public relations. The director noted that 'although we occasionally visited travel agencies to collect comments of visitors on our exhibitions and activities, it was just simple data' (VME Director, Correspondence, September 2006). As indicated in the SWOT analysis, marketing is a small department and that may not actively function as it should. The museum would be advised to conduct marketing research so that it can plan marketing strategies to maximize cultural tourism in Vietnam and compete with the entertainment market, particularly as public funding has declined (Ministry of Culture and Information of Vietnam, 2005).

Conclusion

The core organizational mission of the VME, to preserve the identity of Viet-namese culture, provides impetus for development of the museum. Together with government funding, the museum also generates incomes from corporate sponsorships, ticket sales and other trading. The VME has initially used marketing strategies such as improving the museum-going experience, emphasizing community aspects, and using Internet and media to build audiences. However, to reach a broader market and in turn ensure financial viability, marketing research into visitors is highly recommended, given that such research is an important tool to assist managers make better programming and marketing decisions, and identify and serve better the needs and wants of the audience (Hill et al., 1995; Kotler and Kotler, 2000).

Some research and development activities could be as follows:

● Conducting marketing research should be implemented annually at the VME. For example, research on consumers (existing, potential, lapsed consumer and consumers' behaviour, attitudes and satisfaction), research on products and services (existing and potential product and services, competitor's products, packaging), and other research on competitors and on four 'P's (Hill et al., 1995; Dickman, 1997; Kotler and Kotler, 2000).

- Training skilled staff who can conduct effective market research and apply findings for marketing plans and museum activities. Furthermore, the marketing department needs to be expanded.
- Identifying market segments and having relevant goals and strategies to meet different segments and target groups.
- Redisplaying and diversifying the VME's collections to help further interaction with and link to the community and in turn attract more local visitors.
- Entertainment should be greatly developed and exploited so that the museum can maintain target markets and also develop new markets.
- Setting out more customer-oriented goals, clear and realistic marketing and financial goal strategies rather than focusing on traditional functions of the museum, as indicated in current organizational missions.
- Making use of other promotional strategies, marketing mix to improve product positioning to domestic market.
- Given that Vietnam has not had a long-term experience in museum marketing, learning from and collaborating with overseas museums is a great opportunity for long-term development of the VME in a competitive age of globalization.

Acknowledgement

The author would like to thank the Director of the VME Mr Nguyen, Van Huy and other administrators of the VME for corresponding and assisting in completion of this case study.

References

Australia Council (1998). *The World Is Your Audience: Case Studies in Audience Development and Cultural Diversity*. Australia Council, Melbourne.

Bradburne, J. M. (2001). A new strategic approach to the museum and its relationship to society. *Museum Management and Curatorship*, 19(1), 75–84.

Byrnes, W. J. (2003). *Management and the Arts* (Third edition). Boston: Focal Press.

Close, H. and Donovan, R. (1998). *Who's My Market? A Guide to Researching Audiences and Visitors in the Arts*. Sydney: Australia Council.

Colbert, F. (2003). Entrepreneurship and leadership in marketing the arts. *International Journal of Arts Management*, 6(1), 30–9.

Cotter, H. (2003). Vietnam's subtle culture, prolific in its nuances. *New York Times*, 14 March, E.2:35.

Davies, S. (1994). Attendance records. *Leisure Management*, 15(2), 41–4.

Dickman, S. (1997). *Arts Marketing: The Pocket Guide*. Melbourne: Australia Council and Centre for Professional Development.

Dickman, S. (2000). *What's My Plan? A Guide to Developing Arts Marketing Plans.* Sydney: Australia Council.

Hill, E., O'Sullivan, T. and O'Sullivan, C. (1995). *Creative Arts Marketing.* Oxford: Butterworth-Heinemann.

Hoang, T. Q. V. (1993). Dau Tu Ngan Sach Nha Nuoc cho Van Hoa trong Dieu Kien Chuyen Sang Nen Kinh Te Thi Truong [The Government Budget for Culture in a Transition of Market Economy in Vietnam]. Unpublished PhD, The National Economics University.

Hooper-Greenhill, E. (1994). *Museums and Their Visitors.* London: Routledge.

Kotler, N. (2001). New ways of experiencing culture: the role of museums and marketing implications. *Museum Management and Curatorship*, 19(4), 417–25.

Kotler, N. and Kotler, P. (2000). Can museums be all things to all people? Missions, goals, and marketing's role. *Museum Management and Curatorship*, 18(3), 271–87.

Kotler, P. (2003). *Marketing Management* (Eleventh edition). London: Pearson Education International.

Lidstone, G. and Doling, T. (2000). *Arts Management in Vietnam: Towards a Market Economy—Research Report.* Hanoi: Visiting Arts.

McPherson, G. (2006). Public memories and private tastes: the shifting definitions of museums and their visitors in the UK. *Museum Management and Curatorship*, 21(1), 44–57.

Ministry of Culture and Information of Vietnam (2005). Ministerial Decree on Restructuring of the Vietnamese Museum System until 2020 (156/2005/Q-TTg). <http://www.cinet.gov.vn/detail.aspx?source=4&catid=44&newsid=1352> (accessed 23 June 2006).

Ministry of Culture and Information of Vietnam (2006). Vietnamese private museums and challenges of government regulations. <http://www.cinet.gov.vn/detail.aspx?source=1&catid=21&newsid=9020> (accessed 25 June 2006).

Rentschler, R. (ed.) (1999). *Innovative Arts Marketing.* Sydney: Allen & Unwin.

Sargeant, A. (1999). *Marketing Management for Non-profit Organizations.* Oxford: Oxford University Press.

Vietnam Museum of Ethnology (2006). Website of Vietnam Museum of Ethnology. <http://www.vme.org.vn/index.asp> (accessed 20 June 2006).

Wiggins, J. (2004). Motivation, ability and opportunity to participate: a reconceptualisation of the RAND model of audience development. *International Journal of Arts Management*, 7(1), 22–33.

Part B
The audience experience in a leisure context

3

Major case study: Shape shifters—the role and function of modern museums

Leonie Lockstone

The museums of today are dramatically different from their earlier counterparts. Trends both internal and external to the museum sector have combined to necessitate these institutions adapt at an extraordinary pace in order to survive. This case study examines these trends, in particular the shift in function and purpose from museums having an educational role to one that entertains. Factors contributing to this trend and associated changes will also be examined. Where relevant, insights are provided in relation to two prominent Australian institutions that exemplify the changing nature of museums: the National Museum of Australia and the Melbourne Museum. The case study concludes with a brief summary of these trends and their implications for museum marketing.

The case study commences by providing some background on the National Museum of Australia and the Melbourne Museum to set the scene.

Case in point

The day-to-day functions of the National Museum of Australia and the Melbourne Museum are highly comparable; however, the core mission of each does differ. The former was established in Canberra, at a cost of $155 million in March 2001, as Australia's first dedicated social history museum. The latter, founded in central Melbourne during the late nineteenth century and relocated to its present site (4 kilometres outside of the CBD) in 2000, may be considered a more traditional type of museum in terms of content, showcasing Victoria's natural science, science, technology and social history collections. Reflective of its size as the largest museum complex in the Southern Hemisphere (Museum Victoria, 2001), the establishment cost of the re-engineered Melbourne Museum was $290 million, almost double that of the National Museum of Australia. Both museums are government run and funded, and have comparable policy frameworks.

Museums: what they were and what they are now

The first public museums took the form of what would today be considered natural history museums. These institutions displayed curiosities of animal, plant and human or natural origin (Whitehead, cited in Valdecasas et al., 2006, p. 32). Other forms of museum have emerged over time; for example, social history museums where the focus is not so much on the exhibition of objects but rather on the telling of stories about peoples' lives. Regardless of form, all museums have had to adapt to a shift in emphasis in roles undertaken. As Trotter (1998, p. 47) contends, 'the older notion of the museum as a treasure house has given way to a stronger educative role and, more recently, an information centre and also a site of leisure, entertainment and identity-formation'. Relationships with external stakeholders (visitors, communities and governments) have also altered significantly. Serving the visitor has become the overriding focus of museums. The reasons for this fundamental shift and its ramifications for museum operations, in particular the focus on edutainment, will now be discussed.

Edutainment

Before examining the trends that have influenced the re-engineering of museums in the modern age, it is worthwhile to provide a definition of a central concept of this case study, 'edutainment'. Kotler and Kotler (2000, p. 283) suggest that edutainment represents presentation styles and designs that fulfil the dual goals of entertaining and educating the visitor. Museums have adopted this concept to varying degrees. In the extreme, McPherson (2006, p. 53) notes that 'indeed, many of today's entertainment-oriented museums, such as Disney's

Epcot [in Florida], are primarily based on experience and popular ideas of what is fun, rather than on specific objects'. If not to this extent, to build visitor audiences, modern museums have incorporated more sensory experiences that involve sight, sound and motion, and allow visitors to participate rather than act as spectators to the museum experience (Kotler and Kotler, 2000).

Critical questions to ask in light of the shift from education to entertainment are why this trend has occurred in museums and what factors have influenced it? A starting point is two trends that have been identified as having a major influence on museums during the latter part of the twentieth century. These include the growing expectation that museums should generate revenue, all the more important considering that there have been significant reductions in public funding over time, and the increasing use of new technologies in museums (Rottenberg, cited in McPherson, 2006, p. 52). Adding to the problem of fewer resources, museums are increasingly being asked to do more with their resources in order to improve community access and public accountability (Kotler and Kotler, 2000). Together, these trends indicate that museums are operating in a difficult environment where the visitor is vitally important to these institutions achieving their revenue and access goals. The flow-on effect has been that museums must satisfy visitor needs in order to survive. The related trends of edutainment and the repositioning of museums as cultural tourism resources appear to be products of this environment. Some of the factors influencing these particular trends include technology, blockbuster exhibitions, architecture and design and retailing. Each of these will be discussed in turn after a fuller discussion of museums from the entertainment and tourism perspective.

Edutainment and museums as a cultural tourism resource

Market repositioning towards an entertainment experience has been suggested as a deliberate strategy museums can use to build audiences and improve the museum-going experience (Kotler and Kotler, 2000). The point is made, however, that in their pure form, museums will continue to differ from other forms of entertainment through 'collections of authentic objects and materials, assembled and conserved in accordance with the core purposes of preservation, enlightenment, edification and education' (Kotler and Kotler, 2000, p. 283). The compromise is hybrid museums offering a mix of the old (collections) and the new (technology driven). Criticisms have been raised in relation to this strategy with it being suggested that museums may be in danger of losing focus on their core mission, while at the same time exposing themselves to competing interests in the entertainment industry that are far better resourced, particularly if privately funded (Kotler and Kotler, 2000).

Case in point

This criticism has been levelled at both the National Museum of Australia and the Melbourne Museum in relation to the increasing use of interactive technologies in their displays. At the time, Director of the South Australian Museum, Tim Flannery, suggested that this came at the cost of museum research activities (Musa, 2001).

Regardless of whether such repositioning is pursued as a proactive strategy, most institutions have had to adapt to some extent as museums have become more commonly regarded as cultural tourism resources that can be used to generate visitation and subsequently revenue to the host destinations. The compatibility of museum and tourism activities has been recognized. Bruner (cited in Harrison, 1997, p. 23) suggests that the common ground between the two includes 'the production and exhibition of culture, a dependence on an audience, their construction and invention of what they display, and that they are both the result of travel'. Tourism offers museums the opportunity to extend their reach and access visitors from outside the local market.

Case in point

Visitor statistics support this potential in relation to the Melbourne Museum. Figures for the year ending June 2005 indicate that 40 per cent of the 1.3 million international visitors to Victoria attended a museum or gallery during their stay (Tourism Victoria, n.d.).

Factors influencing the shift to edutainment

Several factors have enabled museums to adapt to a greater focus on edutainment in order to build audiences. Probably the most profound of these, as previously mentioned, is the introduction of new technologies. In the edutainment context, technologies such as videos and computers have been used to enhance museum exhibits by making them more interactive and attractive to visitors. The other main area where museums have employed technology is towards the creation of 'virtual museums'. Photographic technologies and the Internet now enable greater access to information and objects, in a visual sense, than ever before. As a result, museums can now access audiences beyond the number of on-site visitors (Trotter, 1998, p. 54).

Case in point

Prior to the opening of the National Museum of Australia in 2001, it was suggested that 'new technologies will play an important role in the ways this new museum is reinventing or reshaping how the museum interacts with its users—be they domestic or tourist audiences, sponsors, corporate bodies, politicians, real or virtual visitors' (Trotter, 1998, p. 58).

As a cautionary note, it has been suggested that virtual visitation may have a negative effect on actual visitation to museums (Tufts and Milne, 1999, p. 623). It is probably too soon to adequately assess this impact, given the relatively new and evolving nature of the technologies involved.

Due to their scale and intensity, blockbuster exhibitions have been used by museums as an increasingly common way to attract first-time and repeat visitation (Kotler and Kotler, 2000, p. 277). The origin of this type of exhibition, which showcases theme-based works from across the globe, has been traced back to the 1960s (Bradburne, 2001, p. 75). Blockbusters can be expensive and time consuming to organize; however, this is generally offset by travel to several museums over an extended period of time. For individual museums, a temporary increase in visitation may be sufficient reason to organize and host these exhibitions.

Case in point

The Melbourne Museum's recent blockbuster 'Mummies: Ancient Egypt and the Afterlife', held between June and October 2005, exceeded projected visitation figures. It has been followed by one of the museum's largest exhibitions to date, displaying items from the Melbourne 2006 Commonwealth Games' opening ceremony (Usher, 2006).

Despite the positive of increased visitation, it has been recognized that blockbusters do not necessarily result in an enhanced museum experience. Bradburne (2001, p. 75) notes that 'increased attendance at blockbusters tends to reduce the actual amount of time visitors spend in the exhibition, and, given the crush of visitors, drastically reduces the possibility to enjoy the masterpieces on display'. Furthermore, to what extent such short-term surges in visitation accelerate museum wear and tear has yet to be fully assessed.

Architecture is another means museums are using to enhance visitation. In relation to new museums such as the Guggenheim in Bilbao (Spain), Bradburne (2001, p. 76) notes that 'due to their striking architecture, the new buildings themselves also draw huge numbers of visitors—often hundreds of thousands per year—visitors whose main interest is in the building's architecture, not necessarily the museum's collections'. With the creation of the National Museum of Australia and the re-engineering of the Melbourne Museum, this strategy was also pursued.

Case in point

Both museums offer innovative building designs that have received several architectural awards. For example, the National Museum of Australia was awarded Best New Public Building Award 2001 at the Blueprint International Architecture Awards in London, and the Melbourne Museum was awarded the 2001 Sir Zelman Cowan

Award for Best Public Building Australia by the Royal Institute of Architects. Furthermore, whether it is the Garden of Australian Dreams outdoor courtyard at the former institution, or the Rubik's Cube shaped Children's Galley at the latter, both museums incorporate design elements that directly influence the visitor experience. Despite formal recognition, the designs of both museums have been criticized. Controversy at the National Museum of Australia ranges from the 'borrowing' of certain features from the Jewish Museum in Berlin (Duffy, 2001) to more practical matters such as the orientation of its exhibitions, which may be a typical problem for first-time museum visitors (Kotler and Kotler, 2000, p. 278). Comparing the design approaches of the National Museum of Australia and the Melbourne Museum, Morgan (2002) suggests that the latter museum is more traditional, incorporating separate gallery spaces leading into common thoroughfares. While the Melbourne Museum has not escaped criticism, with comment made in reference to empty exhibition spaces (Bolt, 2003), it has been noted generally that museums now 'tend to be more open and organic in their layouts' (McPherson, 2006, p. 47). By doing so, a welcoming and inviting image can be presented that is often in stark contrast to older style museums.

Finally, it has been recognized that retailing (restaurants, gift shops) is becoming increasingly important to visitors as part of the museum experience. McPherson (2006, p. 53) suggests that 'museums have not just attempted to improve their exhibits, but have also engaged services previously regarded as ancillary, such as retailing, and turned them into a core part of the "recreation experience", as they are in visitor attractions'.

Conclusion

The case study outlines several trends and factors that have either brought about the related movement of museums towards edutainment and cultural tourism or enabled it to occur. While a vast oversimplification of the material covered, for review purposes these are listed as being either drivers or enablers.

The drivers include:

- A greater push to generate revenue.
- Reduced government funding for museums.
- A greater push to enhance community access and build visitor audiences.

The enablers include:

- Technology.
- Blockbusters.
- Architecture.
- Retailing.

For museum managers, what marketing implications arise from these drivers and enablers? It would be stating the obvious to say that a key focus of the marketing function in museums is directed towards attracting physical and virtual visitors, of the first-time and repeat variety. As a result, methods to assist museums in this task are being applied on an increasing basis. Among the most relevant of these are market research, market segmentation and relationship marketing. These are being used to better identify visitor needs and expectations, segment the market appropriately and develop strategies to build customer loyalty (for a fuller discussion of museum marketing, see Kotler and Kotler, 2000). As the case study demonstrates, with particular reference to the National Museum of Australia and the Melbourne Museum, museums are operating in a changed environment. They face competition from those not just within their own sector, but the wider entertainment and tourism industry. In light of reduced public subsidies, it is safe to predict that the visitor, as a much needed generator of revenue, will continue to play a key role in shaping the destiny of museums.

References

Bolt, A. (2003). Too soft on our museum. *Herald Sun*, 20 February, p. 19.

Bradburne, J. M. (2001). A new strategic approach to the museum and its relationship to society. *Museum Management and Curatorship*, 19(1), 75–84.

Duffy, M. (2001). Museum impressive work in progress. *Courier Mail*, 31 May, p. 15.

Harrison, J. (1997). Museums and touristic expectations. *Annals of Tourism Research*, 24(1), 23–40.

Kotler, N. and Kotler, P. (2000). Can museums be all things to all people? Missions, goals, and marketing's role. *Museum Management and Curatorship*, 18(3), 271–87.

McPherson, G. (2006). Public memories and private tastes: the shifting definitions of museums and their visitors in the UK. *Museum Management and Curatorship*, 21, 44–57.

Morgan, G. (2002). Has the National Museum got it all wrong? *Quadrant*, April, 23–9.

Musa, H. (2001). Director rejects museum criticism. *Canberra Times*, 14 August, p. 3.

Museum Victoria (2001). Museums Board of Victoria Annual Report 2000/2001. Museum Victoria.

Tourism Victoria (n.d.). Tourism Victoria, Victoria market profile, year ending June 2005. <http://www.tourismvictoria.com.au/images/assets/All_PDFs/research/victoria-tourism-profile-year-ending-june-05.pdf> (accessed 29 June 2006).

Trotter, R. (1998). The changing face and function of museums. *Media International Australia Incorporating Culture and Policy*, 89, November, 47–61.

Tufts, S. and Milne, S. (1999). Museums: a supply-side perspective. *Annals of Tourism Research*, 26(3), 613–31.

Usher, R. (2006). Numbers game for museum head. *The Age*, 27 January, p. 17.

Valdecasas, A. G., Correia, V. and Correas, A. M. (2006). Museums at the cross-road: contributing to dialogue, curiosity and wonder in natural history museums. *Museum Management and Curatorship*, 21, 32–43.

The Boag's Centre for Beer Lovers: building brand with a corporate museum

Kim Lehman and John Byrom

In the twenty-first century we are surrounded by brands. Born out of the Industrial Revolution, when factories needed to 'brand' their barrels, branding as a marketing phenomenon has risen in prominence over the last 50 years. Modern branding is linked to the rise of the television and the consequent need to drive consumption to a mass market. Marketers then had to find ways of differentiating their products. Today, few areas of modern life have escaped the influence of branding; from the shoes on our feet to the food that we eat and the cars that we drive. There are even self-help books showing how individuals can brand themselves for a more successful career!

Briefly, brand refers to a combination of factors relating to a good or a service, such as its name, logo and symbols, its design and packaging, as well as its performance. Branding encompasses the associations that come to mind when consumers think about a brand, as well as all instances of contact that customers may have with a brand. Brand identity involves those facets of the brand that represent the brand visually and verbally. Importantly, these facets are constructions of the firm concerned. Brand image is, then, concerned with the perceptions of the brand in the minds of the consumer.

Many products are advertised and promoted to build brand. Fast moving consumer goods in particular, what marketers call FMCGs, make extensive use of marketing communication tools such as direct mail, the Internet and sales promotion. Another tool, given little attention in either the academic or general press, is the corporate museum.

Launceston, Tasmania, is home to one striking example of a corporate museum, the Boag's Centre for Beer Lovers, operated by J. Boag and Son. Though it is a tourist attraction in its own right, the Boag's Centre for Beer Lovers also illustrates how the establishment of a corporate museum can be used to communicate with a firm's key customer base and assist in building a brand image in the consumer's mind.

The Boag's Centre for Beer Lovers is located in William Street, just across the street from Boag's Launceston brewery. The carefully renovated three-storeyed Georgian building—a former pub, the Tamar Hotel, one of the oldest buildings in Launceston—in which the centre is housed, serves to highlight the value of locating a corporate museum in a building that encourages people 'through the door', allowing them to interact with the corporate brand on a one-to-one basis. In this way a corporate museum can act in the same manner as the shop window of a retail outlet.

Corporate museums like the Boag's Centre for Beer Lovers occupy a difficult position, straddling both the cultural and traditional world of the public museum, and the profit-motivated and ever-changing business world. Nonetheless, they have become an increasingly prevalent feature of the organizational landscape. Firms across the world have sought to preserve and exhibit elements of their history by opening corporate museums. Well-known examples include the BMW Museum in Munich, the Wells Fargo Museum in San Francisco and the Guinness Storehouse® in Dublin.

The presence of a managed collection of objects sets the corporate museum apart from its more common bedfellow, the company visitor centre. Corporate museums typically include not only company records and artefacts, thus aiding in the preservation of 'corporate memory', but also information on the broader industry within which the firm operates. At the same time, corporate museums have the potential to be an explicit representation of the brand if they are supported by appropriate managerial strategies. They can be a device by which a firm will seek to communicate a certain image to their customer. If the message is received by the consumer as intended then the corporate museum will have played a part in establishing a positive brand image for the firm.

Founded in 1883 in Launceston, Tasmania, J. Boag and Son is a brewer of premium beers for the Tasmanian state market and the national Australian market. The company forecasts that within 5 years, 85 per cent of its production will be for the national market. At present, Boag has only a 2.5 per cent share of the latter market, but it has won a number of national and international awards and has strong national brand recognition. Though it is now owned by the Philippines-based brewing giant San Miguel, its marketing communications consistently highlight the brand's local heritage, its history and a tradition of brewing excellence. The J. Boag and Son's corporate museum is an integral part of the Boag's Centre for Beer Lovers. Its promotional material notes that the centre includes 'a museum of the Brewery's memorabilia giving an insight into the Boag family and the development of the Boag's brands throughout the last century' (Boag, 2006).

Inside the centre, the top two floors contain various displays and artefacts relating to both the brewing industry and the history of J. Boag and Son. On the first floor one area contains the original brewery manager's office of James Boag II, complete with company records on the bookshelves. In use from approximately 1905 to 1920, the office provides a glimpse to visitors of the brewery business of the era. On the same floor is a detailed display illustrating the long tradition of coopering, the art of hand making wooden barrels—an example of a corporate museum promoting the history of the industry of which it is a part.

On the second floor a number of rooms are devoted to product packaging and advertising merchandise. In the past it has been considered unnecessary to keep such material, but recent times have seen a shift, not least because it can successfully be used to inform both new products and advertising campaigns. In addition, visitors are genuinely interested in historical bottles and cans. Also on the second floor is the James Boag's Premium Gallery, an exhibition of the photographs of the late Helmut Newton, the internationally known photographer who was responsible for many of the iconic images J. Boag and Son have used to promote the Boag's Premium brand.

Clearly, with branding now a marketing priority for many firms, brewers included, it is not surprising that corporate museums have been used as devices for building the brand. Indeed, this focus on promotion of the brand, mixing corporate and industry memory as the Boag's Centre for Beer Lovers does, is common to many corporate museums. The Guinness Storehouse® museum, for instance, states that visitors can embark on 'an incredible journey throughout 250 years of brewing history, discover the pride and passion which goes into making this world-famous beer' (Guinness & Co., 2006). There is a clear link in the advertising copy between brand statements, referencing the firm's heritage as displayed in the corporate museum, and the intended brand image.

Similarly, J. Boag and Son is clear about the place of the Boag's Centre for Beer Lovers within its corporate strategy. Managing Director Pat Riley was the prime instigator of the renovation of the heritage building in which the centre is housed and has been a strong supporter of preserving the company's historical documents and artefacts. Nonetheless, there is no doubt that the primary aim of the centre is to assist the company in developing what it calls 'brand ambassadors'. Talking with staff from all levels of J. Boag and Son, it is apparent that the focus is on providing visitors to the centre with a level of brand experience that exceeds their expectations of what a traditional museum should deliver. Although Boag's brewery tour commences and concludes at the centre, where Boag's merchandise is also on sale, the museum collection serves a very strategic purpose. J. Boag and Son feels that having a museum increases credibility with consumers. That is, it supports the message of tradition and heritage consistently communicated through its advertising. The company understands that simply claiming a tradition for brewing premium beers since 1883 is not sufficient to impress today's highly informed consumers. It uses the museum at the Boag's Centre for Beer Lovers to prove it.

The Boag's Centre for Beer Lovers might not fit the definition of a museum as commonly perceived by the general public. For example, it does not have professional curatorial staff, and the collection is centred around one company's products and history. As well, it is housed in a building with multiple company functions, all principally aimed at promoting J. Boag and Son's product brands. That said, the museum *is* considered by all at the company as a 'real' museum and that view is not negated by the museum's primary purpose as a tool for building its brand. Certainly, many modern museums would benefit by having such a clearly defined role.

Acknowledgement

The authors would like to thank the staff of J. Boags and Son for their kind assistance in the preparation of this case study.

References

J. Boag and Son (2006). Boag's Centre for Beer Lovers. <http://www.boags.com. au/Files/00268-Boags-Centre-for-Beer-Lovers.asp> (accessed 10 December 2006).

Guinness & Co. (2006). Guinness Storehouse. <http://www.guinness-storehouse.com/> (accessed 14 February 2006).

Knowing how to look at art

Dirk Vom Lehn

Introduction

Marketing research and sociology suggest that participation with and understanding of artworks depend on knowledge about art and a 'cultural code' (Bourdieu, 1993, p. 215) acquired in and through socialization and education. Art-specific knowledge and the cultural code are marks of 'distinction' that reflect people's social position in society (Bourdieu, 1989). In the light of these debates, museum visiting has long been considered as an activity undertaken by people who have acquired knowledge about art and culture while those lacking the cultural code are seen to stay away from museums (Bourdieu, 1990; DiMaggio, 1998).

In recent years, the argument that cultural participation reflects the social structure has been challenged by studies that see people's lifestyles and habits as critical for their position in society. They consider the relationship between cultural consumption and social position as more fluid and dynamic (Schulze, 1992). They show that people have become 'cultural omnivores' (Peterson, 1992) who participate in both, 'high-' and 'low-brow' activities; museum visiting does not mark anymore a distinction between people of diverging cultural understanding and participation, but has become one among a range of social activities in which people engage. This change in cultural participation, coupled with a renewal of museum exhibitions, has stimulated an increase in visitor numbers (MORI, 2001; DiMaggio and Mukhtar, 2004).

Despite museum managers' delight with the growing popularity of museums, there is a growing concern that visitors' understanding of exhibits rarely coincides with the intentions of the museum managers and curators (Baker, 1998). They employ visitor researchers to explore people's behavioural and cognitive response to exhibits and exhibitions. Visitor research produces findings that inform the development of exhibits and exhibitions that are attractive and facilitate learning about art, science and culture (Falk and Dierking, 2000). Yet, due to the focus on learning, visitor research largely fails to address other aspects of the museum visit, in particular it does not explore the practices through which people examine and make sense of exhibits.

This chapter argues that social interaction is critical to the ways in which people view and inspect artwork. It explores how people coordinate their navigation of exhibitions with companions and other visitors, how they examine exhibits and how they interleave looking at artworks with the use of novel touch-screen information systems.

The analysis is based on a substantial corpus of video-recordings and field observations of conduct and interaction in museums and galleries. The corpus includes material from art and decorative art museums such as the Victoria and Albert Museum, the Tate Britain and Modern, the Musee des Beaux Arts Rouen, the National Gallery in London and the Science Museum London, as well as science centres such as Green's Mill (Nottingham) and Explore@ Bristol. Through the detailed analysis of single instances, and comparing and contrasting characteristic actions and activities between various fragments, we begin to identify the patterns and organization of conduct and interaction. In common with more traditional ethnography, the instances discussed in this chapter have been chosen as they provide interesting or particularly clear instances to reflect the more common themes that we explore (Heath, 2004; vom Lehn and Heath, 2006). The analysis of the video-data is based on ethnomethodology (Garfinkel, 1967) and conversation analysis (Sacks, 1992; Have, 1998). Various publications discuss the detailed, sequential analysis of video-data (Heath, 2004; vom Lehn and Heath, 2006).

Background

Museums have recently undergone a fundamental transformation. The dusty, object-centred institution has been turned into a modern, visitor-focused leisure and education centre. Marketing research has played an important part in this development. By exploring the relationship between museums and their audiences, marketing research has provided information critical to understanding, and segmenting the audience and revealing why some people visit museums while others stay away (Kirchberg, 1996; McLean, 1997; Kotler and Kotler, 1998). Yet, relatively little marketing research has been undertaken on the exhibition floor where, so to speak, the eye hits the canvas—'the point of experience' (vom Lehn, 2006).

The gap in museum marketing research is partly filled by visitor studies. This largely applied field of research explores how museums can be turned into effective learning environments. While being primarily concerned with people's behavioural and cognitive response to exhibits (Screven, 1969; Serrell, 1998; Shettel, 2001) visitor studies have recently become interested in the ways in which social interaction and talk influence the museum experience (Falk and Dierking, 2000; Leinhardt et al., 2002). Their principal focus, however, has remained with the learning outcome of people's visits to museums. They prioritize questions for people's understanding of exhibits over those concerned with how people practically explore and examine exhibits and exhibitions.

This chapter draws on three bodies of research: marketing and consumer research, audience research and sociology.

Marketing and consumer research offer methods and techniques to broaden the scope of visitor studies, and shed light on people's behaviour and experience of shopping and retail outlets as well as of cultural events (Penaloza, 1998; 2001; Goulding, 2001; Rentschler, 2001; Sherry et al., 2001; Gilmore and Rentschler, 2002; Kozinets et al., 2002; Rentschler and Gilmore, 2002). They increasingly undertake studies of people's behaviour at the 'point of sale' (Phillips and Bradshaw, 1993), where buying decisions are actually being made. These studies reveal how the design and layout of shops, as well as the presence of other people, may affect shopping behaviour (Arnould and Wallendorf, 1994; Underhill, 1999; Harris and Baron, 2004; Nancarrow and Tinson, 2005).

Audience research sheds light on the ways in which people watch television, listen to music and use new media. It reveals that media perception is a social activity, embedded within people's everyday lives and undertaken in social interaction with others. People watch TV with their families, visit cinemas in groups, and listen to music and play computer games with friends (Lull, 1990; Silverstone and Hirsch, 1992; Ang, 1995; Srinivas, 2002).

In *sociology* there is a long-standing interest in behaviour in public places. Research shows how people socially organize their action and interaction in public places. Studies using audio- and video-recordings of people's conduct and interaction show how people coordinate their actions with each other when navigating streets, crossing pedestrian pathways and sitting on park benches (cf. Goffman, 1963; 1971; Ryave and Schenkein, 1974; Lofland, 1985; 1998; Kendon, 1990).

These different bodies of research highlight the importance of the circumstances in which consumption actually takes place. They reveal that people's behaviour and experience of shopping and cultural environments are not prefigured by their knowledge about and disposition towards the particular institution or event; rather, how people explore, make sense of and 'consume' these environments arises in the situation at hand.

Configuring view spaces

People often explore exhibitions together with companions. They walk together to the galleries, walk past some exhibits and stop at others to view them in more detail. As they navigate the gallery, they meet other people who also examine the artefacts. Let us consider a first fragment to explore how companions and other people coordinate their exploration of galleries. The fragment has been recorded in the Courtauld Galleries in London.

We join the action when Max and Flora examine a drawing at the other end of the gallery. Both visitors stand at the exhibit and read the associated label. The position and posture of their feet indicate the potential trajectory of their exploration of the exhibition; both of Max's feet as well as Flora's right foot point to this end of the gallery and Max stands sideways to the exhibit, viewing it with a slightly twisted posture and head (Image 1.1). After about a minute, Max and Flora have moved on and reached the middle of the gallery. They view a drawing and then read the label nearby. To their right, a woman reads a poem and in the gallery corner a small group of visitors examines another exhibit (Image 1.2).

Image 1.1

Image 1.2

When Max and Flora look up, the woman still reads the poem which attracts Flora's attention. Flora points towards the poem and then, together with her companion, leaves this area of the exhibition (Image 1.3). They go to the centre of the gallery where they view drawings displayed on a table. While standing at the table, they remain sensitive to the events around the poem. As soon as the woman and the small group of visitors move elsewhere, Max and Flora complete their current activity and go to read the poem.

Image 1.3

They approach the exhibit and configure a view space where they inspect the piece. They stand side by side and read the poem. By virtue of their bodily positions and their head movement, they display the focus of their actions. For example, when they arrive by the exhibit they both look at the poem. After a few moments, they shift their orientation to the label and then consider the exhibit in the light of information provided by the museum (Images 1.4 and 1.5).

We begin to see how visitors coordinate their action and interaction with their companions and others when navigating an exhibition and inspecting exhibits. As Max and Flora approach the poem, they configure a view space

Image 1.4

Image 1.5

where they look at the object and read the label. They form a side-by-side arrangement at the exhibit that shields their view space from others. They align their bodily positions at the exhibit with each other to view the object together, thereby neatly coordinating their reading of the poem and the label. Their activities at the exhibit are visible and intelligible for others who keep a distance from the view space. Like Max and Flora earlier in the fragment, they may become third-party participants and look at the piece from a distance, or engage in activities close-by where they unobtrusively monitor the inter-action at the exhibit until it becomes available (vom Lehn et al., 2001; cf. vom Lehn, 2006).

In coordinating their navigation and exploration of museums with compan-ions and others, people employ practical knowledge about human conduct. It allows them to anticipate the trajectory of other people's actions by virtue of their posture, feet position, their gaze and head movement (Goffman, 1971). Thus, people can coordinate their actions with others to foster an environment where, relatively undisturbed and uninterrupted, they can view and appreci-ate artworks. In and through the design of their actions, people produce the museum visit as a seamless movement along the exhibits, neatly coordinated between all those in the locale.

Discovering art

Theories of the ways in which people look at art often presume that the per-ception of artwork is shaped by the structure of the piece and the knowledge people have of art and culture (Acton, 1997). They largely ignore that people view artworks together and influence how each other is seeing the pieces. When examining artworks, people employ a range of methods to invite others to look and see for themselves. We will now consider one or two fragments to shed light on some of these methods. The following Fragment 2 shows the arrival of Jimmy and his father Paul, at a painting in the National Portrait

Gallery in London. When the two participants arrive near the piece the boy notices something unusual in the material used for the piece.

The transcript uses conventions from conversation analysis (Jefferson, 1984). Pauses between utterances are indicated by (3.6), meaning a pause of three seconds or two-thirds of a second; underlining is used to show where an utterance or parts of an utterance are stressed; a question mark (?) shows the lowering of the voice; square brackets ([) indicate overlapping talk; a colon shows an elongation in a syllable; and (......) stands for an utterance that could not be heard on the tape. The purpose of the transcript is to illustrate the sequential organization of talk. It shows not only what has been said, but also how an utterance has been produced and where in a conversation it has occurred.

Transcript Fragment 2: NPG—Jimmy and Paul

```
J:  do you know what that's made of?
    (.6)
P:  It's oil paint (.) eh very thick oil paint you put it
    on put it on
         [
J:       what's at the back it must be a board or
    something what is behind it
P:  I'm not sure yah probably on a board yah
    (3.6)
    So thick took ages to dry he
                                 [
J:                               he
```

As he arrives at the artwork, Jimmy points at it. He holds his gesture just long enough for his father to notice and turn to it. Just when Paul stands next to his son to view the portrait, Jimmy poses a question, 'Do you know what that's made of?'. Paul attends to his son's question by providing him with a description of the materiality of the piece, 'it's an oil painting (.) a very thick oil painting' (Image 2.1). He describes the painting in a way that allows him to continue with a comment on the technique used to create such artworks, 'you put it on put it on'. As he begins to explain the artist's technique, Paul steps closer to the piece and moves his right hand in front of it as if using a brush to spread paint onto a canvas (Image 2.2). Yet, Jimmy is not interested in the technique of spreading paint onto the canvas but in the material of the canvas itself that keeps the paint in place. He moves a step closer to the painting and asks, 'what's at the back it must be a board or something what is behind it' (Image 2.3). The fragment continues for a little while before father and son leave the exhibit.

Image 2.1

J: do you know what that's made of?

Image 2.2

P: it's oil paint

Image 2.3

P: you put it on you. . .

We can begin to see how knowledge about art and the practical work of artists become relevant for people's looking at and understanding of artwork. Jimmy notices that the painting has been produced in a curious way. He voices his interest in the piece by drawing his father's attention to the material aspects of the artwork, 'Do you know what that's made of?'. His question encourages, if not demands, a particular response from his father; it evokes Paul's know-ledge about art and materiality. Paul briefly looks at the piece and notices its texture. He draws on his knowledge and characterizes the piece as 'a very thick oil painting', and provides Jimmy with information that occasions him to produce a follow-up question concerned with the technique of the artist. The father displays he is 'not sure' about the material of the canvas or board the paint has been applied to. Instead, he revisits the thickness of the paint and brings the examination of the piece to an end by making a little joke, 'so thick took ages to dry he'.

Fragment 2 illuminates how people develop an understanding of an art-work by voicing and using knowledge about art and materiality that shapes the way in which they view and make sense of the object. While numerous other ways of seeing the portrait are conceivable, in this specific situation the participants come to focus on the material aspects of the painting rather than on its content. The focus of their interaction arises as a result of the initial utterance Jimmy produces on the arrival of his father. His question requests, if not demands, his father produce an answer that attends to the way in which the son orients to the piece. Questions coupled with bodily and visual con-duct specifying what a visitor looks at are one method that people employ to draw others to an exhibit and display how they wish to examine the object in this particular moment. In other cases, people approach an exhibit and notice aspects of its content and composition. They employ methods to engage a companion in a particular way with the same piece. Consider the following fragment recorded at 'Mississippi', a photograph by Henri Cartier-Bresson (1961) shown in a photography exhibition at London's Victoria and Albert Museum. We join the action after Douglas has inspected the photograph for a few moments.

Transcript Fragment 3: V&A Douglas and Jane

```
D:  I tell you what Jane (.) this is interesting
    (.)
    this is Mississippi in nineteensixtyone
    (1.9)
    You have a Cola sign depicted in
    nineteensixtyone
J:  hhmmmh
```

Douglas examines the photograph and discovers a Cola sign. He is surprised to find such an advertisement in a photograph from 1961. He summons Jane, one of his companions, to have a look, 'I tell you what Jane (.) this is interest-ing'. On the onset of her companion's utterance, Jane turns her head and then her body around to join Douglas by the photograph. He notices her shift in orientation and moves his upper body and gaze back to the exhibit, anticipat-ing that she will join him by the exhibit (Image 3.1).

Image 3.1

D: I tell you what Jane (.)

Image 3.2

D: this is interesting

Jane moves towards him as he produces a general description of the exhibit, 'this is Mississippi in nineteensixtyone' (Image 3.2). The utterance gains its importance later in the sequence, when Douglas points with his small finger across the bottom of the photograph. This reference stimulates Jane's interest in the details of the image, and occasions her to bend down and move her face close to the image. His gesture is designed to encourage Jane to adopt a viewpoint where she can see details of the photograph, but still withholds the phenomenon Douglas actually wants to show her (Image 3.3). A moment

Image 3.3

D: This is Mississippi in nineteensixtyone

later, Douglas moves his little finger up to the Cola sign, 'a Cola sign depicted in nineteensixtyone' (Image 3.4).

Image 3.4

```
D: a Cola sign depicted in nineteen-sixty-one
J: hhmmmh
```

Douglas tries to kindle the same kind of surprised response towards the Cola sign in Jane that he has experienced when he discovered this particular exhibit feature for the first time. He invites her to join him by the piece and by gesturing with his little finger he progressively occasions Jane to lean forward and inspect a particular part of the object. The progressive organization of the reference kindles interest and curiosity in Jane. She gradually moves to the viewpoint configured by Douglas's actions. He then thrusts his finger up to the Cola sign to generate surprise in the light of his prior statement that the photograph has been taken in 1961. Jane looks up and briefly says 'hhmmmh', confirming that she has seen the Cola sign without displaying surprise and excitement at this discovery.

We can see how people use knowledge about an artwork acquired by inspecting it, in their interaction with others. The analysis illuminates how knowledge about particular features of a piece arises in and through people's action and interaction at the object. They view and examine the artwork and learn about some of its features. They employ this knowledge when they draw their companions in to look at the piece and to discover it like they have a few moments earlier. In creating an experience for another, they draw on their knowledge about people's conduct and experience; for example, knowing about ways in which to stimulate another to closely inspect an object, they design their talk and gesture to come close to the piece and examine it from close distance; and knowing how to kindle surprise in another, they produce their actions at an exhibit to occasion a surprised response.

The companion's experience of the artwork is, in turn, fundamentally different from that of the original discoverer of the object's features. The companion approaches the object anticipating that the discoverer is about to show some-thing to them. As they arrive at the exhibit, they align their orientation to the artwork with that of the discoverer. They display their alignment by virtue of their bodily movement and position, as well as brief utterances like 'yes', 'yah', 'mhm' or even an outburst of laughter, revealing that they have seen an object in the same way as the discoverer.

Ways of seeing artwork often arise in interaction between people. How people see and understand a piece is contingent upon the specifics of the situation in which they encounter and view it (Heath and vom Lehn, 2004). The knowl-edge that they bring to bear at an artwork is not (primarily) an art-specific knowledge acquired through education and upbringing, but the mundane and commonplace practical knowledge about human conduct, the 'ethnometh-ods' as Garfinkel (1967) has called them. This knowledge allows people to orient towards and view artworks in social situations, and to render their ways of seeing the piece visible and intelligible for others. It provides them with resources to create shared perspectives and inter-subjective ways of see-ing artworks.

Seeing art through technology

Museum managers and curators are increasingly held accountable for the effectiveness of their exhibitions in attracting visitors and communicating knowledge and understanding about art and culture. Therefore, they are immensely concerned about the contingency of people's actions in and experi-ence of exhibitions. They increasingly address their concerns by deploying new, digital technologies in their exhibitions to enhance the interpretation of the exhibits and to engage people in new ways. These digital devices, such as stationary touch-screen information kiosks and portable personal digital assistants (PDAs), provide visitors with information about the museum, specific galleries and particular exhibits. Digital devices deliver information through text, images and/or short audio- or video-clips con-cerned with the exhibition or particular exhibits. The information is presented to be read, viewed or listened to. Relatively little is known of how people look at and see artworks when they use these devices (see vom Lehn and Heath, 2005).

Let us consider an example that has been recorded at a touch-screen infor-mation kiosk deployed near a nineteenth century washstand by William Burges in the British Galleries at the Victoria and Albert Museum in London. The monitor is placed on a low stand to the right of the washstand. It shows a short film, lasting about 3 minutes. The film illustrates the design and oper-ation of the washstand. It consists of a series of interconnected but continu-ous parts of information that focus on particular aspects of the piece. Each of these parts includes one or two subtitles summarizing a particular feature of the piece. The film begins by touching the screen and continues without inter-ruption until the end.

The fragment begins when Paul and Anna stand at the system and view the film. After about 1 minute, the film shows fish on the bottom of the bowl that becomes visible when water is filled in. This event occasions Paul to lean forward and Anna to say that there are 'fishes in the bowl' (Images 4.1a and 4.1b).

Transcript Fragment 4: V&A—Paul and Anna

```
A: fishes in the bow:: 1 (.) (but you can't see from
   here)
   (5.6)
   silver carp (2.6) mh:::m
   (1.3)
P: that bit
   (32)
   You just so wanna try it
A: mhm
```

Image 4.1a   Image 4.1b

```
A: fishes in the bow::1
```

When Anna completes her utterance, Paul approaches the washstand to inspect the bowl. As he arrives at the object, he leans forward and looks into the bowl where the fish can be seen (Images 4.2a and 4.2b). A moment later he returns from the exhibit. He stands next to Anna who voices parts of the subtitle off the monitor, 'silver carp'. A moment later the film moves on and shows the image of one of the fish in the bowl, occasioning Paul to produce a short utterance, 'that bit', and then to move close to the exhibit. He looks into the bowl and returns to view the film. While the film continues, the two participants glance to the washstand when a new exhibit feature is shown on the monitor.

Image 4.2a

Burges based the carp on a Japanese print

Image 4.2b

A: silver carp

After the conclusion of the film, they both approach the exhibit and inspect some of its features in detail; yet, without having access to the information provided by the system. Paul points out some of the details in the bowl that he has seen a few moments earlier and his wife examines them before they both move on (Images 4.3 and 4.4).

Image 4.3

Image 4.4

P: You just so wanna try it

The system is very well designed and very successful with visitors. Yet, we can see that people have some difficulties in interweaving the information they receive from the system with their viewing of the washstand and their interaction with each other. The difficulties arise from the stationary position of the system and the structure of the content delivered by the device. Where people stand they cannot see parts of the washstand highlighted by the system. But when they leave the monitor to view the exhibit, they inevitably miss parts of the information. The two visitors come to an interesting solution to this problem. Paul coordinates his inspection of the piece with the content delivery by the device. While he inspects the washstand, his wife continues to view the film. On his return, she provides her husband with additional information about the fish that he may have missed while examining the original object; for example, when returning from the inspection of the fish in the bowl Anna informs him that the fish are 'silver carp'. They repeat this organization of viewing the film and inspecting the washstand a few times. When the film ends they both move to the exhibit and Paul, who has seen the bowl in more detail, points out some of the features he has noticed to Anna.

The analysis reveals how the two participants apply knowledge to create a shared experience of the object. The two participants acquire different knowledge about the piece through the ways in which they examine it; Paul views parts of the film and inspects the piece, while Anna primarily views the film and occasionally looks up at the piece. As Anna views the film she remains aware of Paul's actions at the washstand, knowing what parts of the exhibit he inspects. By voicing segments of the subtitles to the film, Anna provides her husband with information of what she has seen and what it is he is looking at. On completion of the film, they both move to the washstand and Paul points out some of the features in the bowl, thus showing Anna what they both have seen in different ways a few moments earlier. Thus, the two participants manage to constitute the viewing of the washstand as a shared experience although they have seen the object in very different ways.

We can see how people use information delivered by a digital system to align each other's perspective to an exhibit. Touch-screen systems like the one at Burges' washstand provide visitors with art-specific knowledge about particular exhibits. The information displayed by the systems often surpasses what can be seen in the original object. It may highlight features of the exhibit and also offer contextual and historical information or show the working object. Participants who view the film therefore may have a very different understanding of the exhibit than those examining only the original object. They align each other's understanding of the exhibit by using their know-ledge about the object as well as their knowledge of the other's activity; for example, by monitoring Paul's actions, Anna knows that he has inspected the bowl and reveals to him that the fish he has been looking at are 'silver carp'; and Paul, who knows that Anna has been watching the film, uses his knowledge of the bowl to show its features to her when they both approach the washstand. How people see the original object therefore is not defined by the information delivered by the system but by their shared understanding of the piece in interaction with and around the exhibit and the information system.

Discussion

In the light of recent changes in museum funding and a political agenda that promotes social inclusion and diversity, museums increasingly use new techniques and technologies to provide visitors with art-specific knowledge in exhibitions; for example, by deploying novel digital technologies like information kiosks and PDAs. Thus, museums hope to attract larger parts of the population to participate with and develop an understanding of art and culture in museums.

This chapter has shown that knowledge is critical for people's visit to and experience of museums. Yet, art-specific knowledge is only one kind of knowledge people may bring to bear when exploring exhibitions. The analysis has begun to reveal the importance of practical knowledge that people bring to bear when examining and making sense of artworks. They particularly rely on knowledge of human conduct and experience to foster environments where they can view the pieces and share their experience of the art with each other. This knowledge allows them to coordinate their actions in museums with companions and others who happen to be in the gallery at the same time. It facilitates the seamless flow of visitors through museums and makes it possible for people to view exhibits relatively undisturbed from events around them. Visitors use this practical knowledge to align each other's perspectives to exhibits; for example, by kindling a surprised response to an artwork. Hereby, they may interweave art-specific knowledge and knowledge they have just acquired about an artwork, with knowledge about human conduct and experience to influence how others look at, see and respond to a piece.

The experience and understanding of artworks in museums is subject to the complex and contingent situation in which people approach and examine the exhibits. Which exhibits people look at, for how long and how they see them may be affected by the conduct of companions and other people with whom they are not familiar. The deployment of novel, digital devices is an attempt to address the uncertainty concerning people's understanding of exhibitions. Touch-screen systems like those at the Victoria and Albert Museum or PDAs currently deployed in various art museums, contextualize the pieces and often show the objects in a way they would otherwise not be seen in the gallery. The information delivered by the systems can often stand by itself and is sometimes made available through CD-ROMS, DVDs or on the Web. (For example, the video-clip on Burges' washstand that can be seen on the system in the V&A can be downloaded from <http://www.vam.ac.uk/collections/british_galls/video/washstand/index.html>.) It is up to the visitors to link the information about the artwork to the original object.

This chapter hopes to make a small contribution to current museum marketing research concerned with people's conduct in and experience of museums. The discussion sheds light on the different facets of the museum experience as it arises in and through people's conduct and interaction at the exhibit-face. Such detailed understanding of the relationship between social interaction and the museum experience is of critical importance for the design of new exhibitions and information technologies to enhance people's experience of museums. When social interaction is considered critical for people's experience of artworks, then museums may consider developing and deploying exhibitions that facilitate and support the collaborative viewing of exhibits. Thus, marketing research on the exhibition floor can complement visitor studies that focus on people's learning from exhibits by highlighting the practical and social aspects of knowledge that people bring to bear when looking at artworks.

Acknowledgement

Dirk vom Lehn is a Research Fellow in the Work, Interaction and Technology Research Group based in the Department of Management at King's College London (UK). The research reported in this contribution has been funded by the AHRC grant 'Enhancing Interpretation: new techniques and technologies in museums of fine and decorative art' (AR17441). The author wishes to thank his colleagues at WIT for their help with the analysis of the data, the museums' management and staff for helping with the research and the visitors who kindly agreed to participate in the study.

References

Acton, M. (1997). *Learning to Look at Paintings*. Routledge.
Ang, I. (ed.) (1995). *Living Room Wars: Rethinking Media Audiences for a Postmodern World*. Routledge.
Arnould, E. J. and Wallendorf, M. (1994). Market-oriented ethnography: interpretation building and marketing strategy formulation. *Journal of Marketing Research*, 31, 484–504.
Baker, M. (1998). Museums, collections and their histories. In *A Grand Design* (M. Baker and B. Richardson, eds.), pp. 18–19. Harry N. Abrams.
Bourdieu, P. (1989). Social space and symbolic power. *Sociological Theory*, 7(1), 14–25.
Bourdieu, P. (1990). *Distinction: A Social Critique of the Judgement of Taste*. Routledge.
Bourdieu, P. (1993). *The Field of Cultural Production*. Polity.
DiMaggio, P. (1998). Sociological perspectives on museums. In *The Encyclopedia of Aesthetics* (M. Kelly, ed.). Oxford University Press.
DiMaggio, P. and Mukhtar, T. (2004). Arts participation as cultural capital in the United States, 1982–2002: signs of decline? *Poetics*, 32(2), 169–94.
Falk, J. and Dierking, L. (2000). *Learning from Museums. Visitor Experiences and the Making of Meaning*. Alta Mira Press.
Garfinkel, H. (1967). *Studies in Ethnomethodology*. Blackwell.
Gilmore, A. and Rentschler, R. (2002). Changes in museum management: a custodial or marketing emphasis? *The Journal of Management Development*, 21(10), 745–60. New York: The Free Press.
Goffman, E. (1963). *Behavior in Public Places. Notes on the Social Organization of Gatherings*. New York: The Free Press.
Goffman, E. (1971). *Relations in Public. Microstudies of the Social Order*. Basic Books.
Goulding, C. (2001). Romancing the past: heritage visiting and the nostalgic consumer. *Psychology and Marketing*, 18(6), 565–92.
Harris, K. and Baron, S. (2004). Consumer-to-consumer conversations on service settings. *Journal of Service Research*, 6(3), 287–303.
Have, P. (1998). *Doing Conversation Analysis: A Practical Guide*. Sage.

Heath, C. (2004). Analysing face-to-face interaction: video, the visual and material. In *Qualitative Research: Theory, Method and Practice* (D. Silverman, ed.), pp. 266–82. Sage.

Heath, C. and vom Lehn, D. (2004). Configuring reception: (dis-)regarding the 'spectator' in museums and galleries. *Theory, Culture and Society*, 21(6), 43–65.

Jefferson, G. (1984). Transcript notation. *Structures of Social Action: Studies in Conversation Analysis* (J. M. Atkinson and J. Heritage, eds.), pp. ix–xvi. Cambridge University Press (Cambridge, London, New York, New Rochelle, Melbourne and Sydney).

Kendon, A. (1990). *Conducting Interaction. Patterns of Behavior in Focused Encounters.* Cambridge.

Kerrigan, F., Fraser, P. and Özbilgin, M. (eds.) (2004). *Arts Marketing.* Elsevier.

Kirchberg, V. (1996). Museum visitors and non-visitors in Germany: a representative survey. *Poetics*, 24(2–4), 239–58.

Kotler, N. and Kotler, P. (1998). *Museum Strategy and Marketing.* Jossey-Bass.

Kozinets, R. V., Sherry, J. F., Deberry-Spence, B., Duhachek, A., Nuttavuthisit, K. and Storm, D. (2002). Themed flagship brand stores in the new millennium: theory, practice, prospects. *Journal of Retailing*, 78(1), 17–29.

Leinhardt, G., Crowley, K. and Knutson, K. (eds.) (2002). *Learning Conversations in Museums.* LEA.

Lofland, L. H. (1985). *A World of Strangers. Order and Action in Urban Public Space.* Basic Books.

Lofland, L. H. (1998). *The Public Realm. Exploring the City's Quintessential Social Territory.* De Gruyter.

Lull, J. (1990). *Inside Family Viewing: Ethnographic Research on Television's Audiences.* Routledge.

McLean, F. (1997). *Marketing the Museum.* Routledge.

MORI (2001). *Visitors to Museums and Galleries in the UK.* re:source.

Nancarrow, C. and Tinson, J. (2005). The influence of children on purchases: the development of measures for gender role orientation and shopping savvy. *International Journal of Market Research*, 47(1), 5–28.

Penaloza, L. (1998). Just doing it: a visual ethnographic study of spectacular consumption behavior at Nike Town. *Consumption, Markets and Culture*, 2(4), 337–400.

Penaloza, L. (2001). Consuming the American West: animating cultural meaning and memory at a stock show and rodeo. *Journal of Consumer Research*, 28(3), 369–98.

Peterson, R. (1992). Understanding audience segmentation: from elite and mass to omnivore and univore. *Poetics*, 21(4), 243–58.

Phillips, H. and Bradshaw, R. (1993). How customers actually shop: customer interaction with the point-of-sale. *Journal of the Market Research Society*, 35(1), 51–62.

Rentschler, R. (2001). Entrepreneurship: From Denial to Discovery in Nonprofit Art Museums. Working Paper. Brisbane.

Rentschler, R. and Gilmore, A. (2002). Museums: discovering services marketing. *International Journal of Arts Management*, 5(1), 62–72.

Ryave, A. L. and Schenkein, J. N. (1974). Notes on the art of walking. In *Ethnomethodology: Selected Readings* (R. Turner, ed.), pp. 265–74. Penguin.

Sacks, H. (1992). *Lectures on Conversation*. Blackwell.

Schulze, G. (1992). *Die Erlebnisgesellschaft. Kultursoziologie der Gegenwart*. Campus, Frankfurt/New York.

Screven, C. G. (1969). The museum as a responsive learning environment. *Museum News*, 47(10), 7–10.

Serrell, B. (1998). *Paying Attention: Visitors and Museum Exhibitions*. American Association of Museums.

Sherry, J. F., Kozinets, R. V., Storm, D., Duhacheck, A., Nuttavuthisit, K. and DeBerry-Spence, B. (2001). Being in the Zone. Staging retail theatre at ESPN Zone Chicago. *Journal of Contemporary Ethnography*, 30(4), 465–510.

Shettel, H. (2001). Do we know how to define exhibit effectiveness? *Curator*, 44(4), 327–34.

Silverstone, R. and Hirsch, E. (eds.) (1992). *Consuming Technologies. Media and Information in Domestic Spaces*. Routledge, London and New York.

Srinivas, L. (2002). The active audience: spectatorship, social relations and the experience of cinema in India. *Media, Culture and Society*, 24(2), 155–73.

Underhill, P. (1999). *Why We Shop: The Science of Shopping*. Simon & Schuster.

vom Lehn, D. (2006). Embodying experience: a video-based examination of visitors' conduct and interaction in museums. *European Journal of Marketing*, 40, 1340–59.

vom Lehn, D. and Heath, C. (2005). Accounting for new technology in museums. *International Journal of Arts Management*, 7, 11–21.

vom Lehn, D. and Heath, C. (2006). Interaction at the exhibit-face: video-based studies in museums and galleries. In *Video-Analysis Methodology and Methods* (H. Knoblauch and B. Schnettler, eds.), pp. 101–13. Peter Lang.

vom Lehn, D., Heath, C. and Hindmarsh, J. (2001). Exhibiting interaction: conduct and collaboration in museums and galleries. *Symbolic Interaction*, 24(2), 189–216.

'Constructive chillers': a new market for museums

Alix Slater

Introduction

The modern museum has become unrecognizable in comparison to its predecessors. This is the result of new technologies used in exhibition development, better interpretation, international blockbuster and touring exhibitions, websites and other on-line resources, and professionally managed visitor facilities including cafés, restaurants and retailing outlets. Museums continue to retain their dual focus, juggling learning and entertainment while at the same time generating income to support their activities. Despite the changes inside the museum, and many publicly funded museums attempting to diversify their audience base, the visitor profile at museums and within the sector as a whole has altered very little. However, in the future there are a number of trends that potentially threaten their market. This chapter explores these trends and discusses a new market for museums, 'constructive chillers' who are looking for leisure experiences that enable them to recuperate and have a worthwhile experience. British case studies illustrate this chapter, however many of these trends are applicable elsewhere.

The British Museum context

There are approximately 2000 museums in the UK (Museums Association, 2006). Like most countries, British Museums are diverse, in terms of scale, operation and governance, and include national, regional, city, local authority and independent museums. Museums have undergone significant changes over the last 25 years. This is partly due to the pressure that the Conservative Government put on them in the 1980s and early 1990s to become more market-orientated and accountable for their public funding. Secondly, the introduction of The National Lottery in the UK in the mid-1990s, initially with funds dedicated to culture and the new millennium, fuelled a welcome and long overdue investment in museum buildings. A number of flagship venues were built to celebrate the year 2000 such as Tate Modern in London and The Lowry in Salford. Other museums and galleries have applied for funds from the lottery since, to support extensions and refurbishments. This has resulted in numerous museums and galleries having new galleries, exhibits and temporary exhibition spaces with the latest technology as well as large public areas such as the Great Court at the British Museum. Museums have also recognized the importance of retail and catering outlets in the visitor experience and their value financially. This opportunity has allowed museums not only to develop facilities to support their core activities, but has also put them on a platform where they can compete in the broader visitor attractions' market of which they make up a third of the venues (Leisure Intelligence, 2006a).

Museum attendance

Each year, between 80 and 110 million visits are made to British Museums and Galleries (Davies, 2005; Museums Association, 2006). Visitor research suggests that somewhere between a quarter and a third of the adult population visit at least once a year (Skelton et al., 2002; MORI, 2004; Davies, 2005; Leisure Intelligence, 2006a) of which nearly half visit three or more times each year (Skelton et al., 2002). The current New Labour Government has introduced free admission at those national museums and galleries that formerly charged, for example the Victoria and Albert Museum (V&A), the Natural History Museum and the Science Museum. This was part of government policy to make museums more accessible, but, despite an increase of more than 5 million visits since charging was first withdrawn in 2000 (DCMS, 2006), participation across all social groups has not grown at an equal rate (Leisure Intelligence, 2006a, b). The largest growth in attendance has been from traditional visitors who are attending more frequently but for shorter periods of time.

Sturgis and Jackson's (2003) broader study of leisure participation identified five groups among the population of which three (22 per cent in total) visit museums and galleries: family day trippers (9 per cent), high culture vultures (5 per cent) and heritage seekers (8 per cent). What is agreed is that the market appears to be relatively stagnant and that there is a group of frequent visitors, accounting for a disproportionate share of visits. Attendance varies across regions (partly due to opportunities to visit as cities tend to have more museums) and by gender, age, life-stage, class, household income and education. Men are more likely to visit than women, 35 to 44 year olds, couples without children, dual income households and older parents (compared to the retired, singles and young parents). Also more likely to visit are groups described under the ACORN (A Classification of Residential Neighbourhoods) classification system as 'wealthy achievers', 'urban prosperity' and 'comfortables', car owners, households with incomes of more than £50,000 per annum, and those in employment, particularly those in professional occupations.

Sociologists have attempted to explain why some people visit museums while others do not for the last half century. The most famous of these, Bourdieu (1984), argues that family and social environments provide people with cultural capital that enables them to participate. Personal and social

factors have been found to be important as these offer opportunities economically and because individuals see visiting museums as a choice. However,
this is only part of the picture (Merriman, 1991). Academics writing more
broadly about leisure, for example Iso-Ahola (1980), argue that people are
escaping from their everyday life and also seeking psychological (intrinsic)
rewards when they make choices as to how to spend their leisure time.

Motivational factors

In a recent study of the museum sector in the UK (MORI, 2004), 49 per cent
of respondents said that they normally visited a museum 'to see a particular
exhibition or event of interest'. Among families the figure was even higher.
While this indicates that exhibitions prompt visits, it does not explain the
underlying motivations of visitors. Hood's (1983) seminal study at the Toledo
Art Museum and the surrounding area explored attributes of leisure participation among a small group of frequent visitors and larger groups of occasional and frequent visitors. Frequent visitors valued all of Hood's criteria, in
particular learning, the challenge of new experiences and doing something
worthwhile. In comparison, occasional and non-visitors had similar characteristics to each other and valued the same three criteria: being with people,
participating actively and feeling at ease in their surroundings. The occasional
visitors went to museums when there were special exhibitions, events or if
they had friends or relatives visiting, and Hood suggested that they related
'leisure' with 'relaxation' compared to the frequent visitors who were motivated by learning. Miles (1986) also identified a small group who saw their visit
as educational and were highly committed to learn.

Longhurst et al. (2004) examined the use of museums by middle-class arts
audiences in their everyday life; how people saw, used and valued them. The
middle classes saw museums as part of their local area, visited them on holiday (or felt that they should) and thought visiting was part of what defined a
good parent. These findings support a number of theories that argue that people
take part in leisure activities they value and which they know will fulfil their
psychological needs (Fishbein and Azjen, 1975; Hood, 1983; Rojek, 1999).

Other academic studies of visitor motivations have revealed similar findings
that people visit in a variety of social groups for education, fun, social interaction (Falk and Dierking, 1992) and to escape from the daily routine (Graburn,
1977; Falk and Dierking, 1992; Jansen-Verbeke and Van Redom, 1996; Slater,
2007). Increasingly, it is being recognized that visitor perceptions of learning are broad and may include seeing something knew, learning something
or sharing an interest with another person(s). Mousourri's doctoral research
in the UK and USA (1997 in Falk and Dierking, 2000) and Falk et al. (1998 in
Falk and Dierking, 2000) follow up study found that visitors did not perceive
education and entertainment as mutually exclusive but as complementary
aspects of a single, complex leisure experience and are looking for 'a learning-
orientated entertainment experience' (p. 73). Bourgeon-Renault (2000) argued

that visitors have multiple motivations including socializing, consumption, relaxation and escapism as individuals have complex identities influenced by their different roles, for example as a parent and colleague. Richards (1999, 2001, 2002) found that younger, highly educated tourists see modern art galleries as a leisure experience and are seeking relaxation and entertainment. Motivations are therefore complicated, and it would appear from recent research that people may have multiple motiv-ations, and that education is not necessarily the 'core' factor (Slater, 2007).

A changing society

While museums have been improving facilities and gaining a strong position in the wider leisure sector, a number of social and cultural trends have been occurring that are likely to influence the core market for museums. In the UK, the demographic structure of the population is shifting. A declining birth rate will lead to fewer children and young people in the population and, over time, a greater proportion of older people.[1] Household structures are changing as there are fewer married couples, more singletons, lone parents, and an increase in people cohabiting and living in multi-person households.[2] Natural growth and migration will result in an ethnically and culturally diverse population.[3] More young people are participating in further and higher education, and an increasing proportion of older people are involved in learning. Employment levels are rising as more adults work; in particular, women and retirement ages are rising.[4] For some, working hours are increasing and leisure time is declining.[5] Others are caring for family and friends. The middle classes are expanding as a result of a more educated, affluent and mobile

[1] In 2004, there were only 11.6 million children 16 years or under, a decline of 2.6 million from 1971 while 9.6 million persons are now over 65 years, an increase of 2.2 million in the same period (ONS, 2006). By 2010, there will be nearly 2 million fewer 25 to 34 year olds and nearly 3 million more 45–64 year olds in the UK (The Henley Centre, 2000).

[2] By 2011, 28 per cent of the population will be living as a couple with children, 23 per cent as a couple with no children, 34 per cent in one-person households, 9 per cent in other multi-person households and 6 per cent as lone parents (ONS in The Henley Centre, 2000).

[3] The non-white population in the UK grew by 53 per cent between 1991 and 2001. Just over 7 per cent (7.1 per cent) of the UK population are now from non-white ethnic groups, the largest of which are Asian, Black/Black British and Mixed Race (ONS, 2006).

[4] Almost three-quarters (73 per cent) of the adult population in the UK are economically active or actively seeking work, a rise of 7 per cent since 1984. This has largely been due to more females working, particularly with young children (Hibbett and Meager, 2003; Leisure Intelligence, 2006b).

[5] Working hours are now declining in the UK, although 22 per cent still work for more than 45 hours per week, particularly fathers aged 30 to 49 years in the private sector (CIPD, 2006).

society illustrated by rising levels of car ownership and expenditure on leisure[6], and all social groups have better access to technologies such as computer ownership, the Internet, broadband and mobile telephones.

Some of these trends, for example a more educated society, bode well for museums but there is also a key barrier that crosses groups—time—that is likely to result in a blurring of work and leisure. The Henley Centre (2000) analysed peoples' working and leisure time by dividing individual's activities into four categories: 'work', 'time robbers' (chores), 'constructive time' (worthwhile leisure activities such as visiting museums) and 'chilling' (less demanding activities such as home-based entertainment, e.g., watching TV and listening to music to recuperate from work). They found that the number of people who feel pressurized by a lack of time had increased and the number of respondents who agreed with the statement 'I never seem to have enough time to get things done' rose from 52 to 63 per cent between 1991 and 1998, rising to 75 per cent among those who work.

In the UK many dual-income middle-class families are affluent but work some of the longest hours, while the group with the least amount of leisure time is full-time working mothers with children and other high-income groups. These groups are responding by buying their way out of time robbing activities, for example shopping on-line. When they come to spend their leisure time they are looking for 'perfect moments and low-risk activities'. The study also found that despite the development and growth of home entertainment, people still want to escape from daily routine and their homes, thus the continued popularity of cinema.

Leisure time in museums

So how do museums react to these trends? It is not entirely clear at this stage whether any of these demographic and employment related trends will be reversed. Despite government initiatives to increase the share of the population from specific social groups visiting museums, participation rates among working-class people remain relatively low. And while the middle class is expanding economically and educationally, many people in this group would classify themselves as working class and have probably, according to Bourdieu, not been socialized into museum visiting by their parents. Museums also face competition for the traditional museum visitor as this group tends to participate in a range of leisure activities. New leisure complexes offer experiences that combine activity, retailing and food, and budget airlines mean it is often cheaper to go to a European city for the weekend than to visit a British city. In the family market there are new entrants, such as Gambado which sells itself as 'stimulation, education and enjoyment' in an 'innovative, safe and above all extraordinary environment' (Gambado, 2006). Museums need to

---

[6] The share of household income spent on leisure doubled from 10 to 18 per cent between 1976 and 2001 in the UK (ONS, 2006).

understand visitor motivations, lifestyles, aspirations and perceptions to enable them to consider different approaches to segmentation and identify appropriate marketing communication strategies to attract visitors.

Traditionally museums have thought about their markets in geo-demographic terms. However, by adopting the Henley Centre's method of segmenting individual's time into different activities, museums can understand when, how, where and with whom potential visitors spend their time. The modern museum is ideally positioned to meet a combination of needs—fun, learning, social interaction and escapism—in a safe environment and should be marketing itself to people who want to do something worthwhile and at the same time recuperate.

This group have been termed 'constructive chillers'. They could be tourists on a weekend break to Edinburgh or Paris, a dual-income family looking to spend some quality time with their children on a Sunday afternoon, or a singleton meeting a friend after work. They are likely to be existing or lapsed visitors but the mindset of the museum needs to change when thinking about what visitors are seeking, when and how much time they have, and in response re-position itself so that it is perceived and used in new ways. It is likely to be cost effective as local residents visit most frequently, bring friends and relatives to local places of interest and are most likely to be friends and supporters. They also visit other cultural venues on holiday.

Constructive chilling is a spectrum that offers experiences that allow visitors to do something worthwhile and relax at the same time (see Figure 3.1). On the left-hand side of the spectrum, the focus is on recuperation and on the right-hand side on doing something worthwhile—learning in the broadest sense. For example, visitors might meet a friend in the museum for lunch and then browse in the shop. As they move across the spectrum they might attend an art workshop with their child on a Sunday afternoon and have a coffee afterwards. At the extreme right of the spectrum they volunteer or attend a short course. The list of activities on the spectrum is illustrative rather than exhaustive and reflects those activities the visitor might do in the museum or at home in a virtual museum environment.

The left-hand side of the spectrum is characterized by relatively passive experiences where the visitor is more likely to be a spectator than participant. The activities require less planning, time and the depth of engagement, prior knowledge and personal commitment is less than on the right-hand side of the spectrum. Visitors are also less likely to have specific desired outcomes from their visit. As discussed previously, individuals have multiple motivations and roles and are often pressurized for time. Figure 3.1 illustrates the variety of experiences that a museum can offer this group, combining worthwhile experiences and relaxation rather than limiting itself as a place to see a temporary exhibition.

The 'Ace Café with quite a nice museum attached' slogan for the V&A in the late 1980s was controversial and since museums have perhaps been reluctant to promote their location and facilities too explicitly. However, the National Gallery's restaurant has a prime position overlooking Trafalgar Square. The

• Meeting a friend • Visiting the café/restaurant • Having a drink in the Members' bar • Browsing or making a purchase in the museum shop • Taking a stroll through the garden of a museum • Shopping on the museum website • Selecting an e–card from the museum website	• Visiting the core collection • Attending a temporary exhibition • Meeting a friend at a private view • Hiring an audio-guide • Going on a guided tour • Participating in a family workshop • Attending a lunchtime talk • Viewing an on-line exhibition • Surfing a museum website • Participating in on-line forums • Using on-line resources, e.g., children • Zones within museum websites • Searching for an artefact on a museum database	• Attending a short course or study day • Volunteering

'Constructive chilling'

Figure 3.1 A spectrum of 'constructive chilling'

Members' Room at Tate Modern has spectacular views over the River Thames and its bar has gained a reputation as a 'hip' place to hang out on Friday and Saturday evenings. The cafés of both the Horniman Museum and the Dulwich Picture Gallery in South London are used by locals as places to meet friends; they are set in lovely gardens and in the former are very family friendly. Many museums have excellent shops offering a different leisure experience, shopping. On-line museum shops can also provide mementos of a virtual experience.

These examples illustrate the potential resources museums have and how museum cafés and shops offer an alternative venue to relax. They also have the advantage that to the 'constructive chiller' they seem more worthwhile than having coffee in a high street coffee chain, as the income is support- ing a good cause and they have the option of popping into the museum to have a quick look at an exhibit or a temporary exhibition. Museums such as the Tate have realized the potential of their members and the exclusivity of Tate Modern in particular that appeals to young 'arty' audiences.

The people who might 'chill' in museums are likely to visit them in other contexts, as it would be unusual for somebody who wasn't comfortable with the venue to use it in this way. However, this should not be dismissed; it is just one experience a museum can bring and contributes much needed revenue. Of course there are other events that museums could host to attract specific audiences that sit towards the left-hand side of the spectrum, for example 'speed dating'!

Vignette 1: The Horniman Museum and Gardens, Forest Hill, London

The Horniman Museum and Gardens (2006) has an impressive collection, and loyal audience of adults and families who see it as a place to spend their leisure time. Nearly 5000 visitors chill at the annual World Music Festival, local residents pop in to use the cafe, and adults and families take part in their regular programme of events. During the school summer holidays performances are held in the gardens for children, themed events in the museum's 'Hands On Base', and under fives can take part in story telling. As well as a loyal local audience, visitors come from across London and the Southeast, and it attracts some international visitors. It has a high level of repeat visitation as residents bring their friends and relatives and spend different types of leisure time in the museum due to the range of experiences it provides.

The middle section of the spectrum represents activities that require more commitment on the part of the visitor. Many are typical of how museums are perceived, as places to visit a temporary or permanent exhibition. Some require more commitment on the part of the visitor, for example hiring an audio-guide or taking part in a workshop. To 'constructive chillers' they are perceived as worthwhile although not necessarily in the way museums intended. Museums tend to focus on 'learning' which to this type of visitor is an implicit assumption. The visitor might be a working mother who is seeking half and hour of escapism from the daily routine of family and work, or a family who value the opportunity it has given them to spend time doing something worthwhile with their children. This is supported by the research that suggests frequent museum visitors do not cite the educational or cultural value of a visit as a motivation because it is an implicit assumption. For example, in an evaluation of art workshops in a major London gallery, one participant described the workshop as 'a chance to learn together in an informal way' and another 'we have come for a year. It is always fun with great activities'. In contrast, infrequent visitors do cite education as an explicit reason for visiting, as was seen in Hood's (1983) research.

The spectrum is a continuum. The positioning of activities is indicative rather than set in stone and inevitably some blurring or discussion as to whether some activities should be positioned more towards the left-or right-hand side will occur. For example, a visitor might walk through an exhibition not taking much notice of what is on the walls because they are having an hour away from the office, while in another case they might attend to all the labels with the intention of learning something about an artist. Interpretative tools that will affect the museum experience should probably be positioned further towards the right-hand section of the spectrum as they reflect a greater level of investment and engagement, and doing something worthwhile is likely to be more important to the visitor. Friends' organizations could also host events that would sit in this section as would concerts and musical events in the museum or its grounds.

There is also a group of web-based activities that are important as they show how globalization and technological change enable museums to have a global audience. Vignette 2 focuses on the Tate Galleries and illustrates the range of experiences that a museum might offer. This is not an isolated example and quick searches on our personal computers enable us to visit museums such as Museum of Modern Art (MOMA) in New York, the collection in the National Palace Museum in Taipei (and to make a purchase inspired by the collection) explore and read labels in the Louvre in Paris or take an on-line guided tour.

Vignette 2 The Tate Galleries

The National Gallery of British Art opened on the bank of the River Thames in 1897 to house the works of art Henry Tate had gifted to the British nation. Just over a hundred years later there are four galleries in the Tate 'family', Tate Britain and Tate Modern in London, Tate St Ives in Cornwall and Tate Liverpool. An estimated 6 million visits will have been made to the four sites in 2005–2006 (Tate, 2005). Tate also has a significant web presence in the form of Tate Online that has an estimated 7 million visits each year (Tate Online, 2006).

The capacity and reputation of Tate clearly puts it in a strong position. Each of the galleries has its own visitor profile. Due to technological advances the audience is global and Tate has more 'hits' on its website than pairs of feet walking through its doors. The range of experiences it offers, both at the galleries and through the web is staggering. The two main galleries in London have temporary exhibitions and a programme including films, music and performances, courses and workshops, family activities, lectures, gallery tours, symposia and seminars. Audiences can visit the galleries on-line through multimedia tours, download tours to their MP3 players, talk to artists through interactive videos, be taken on a journey through a themed 'archive journey' or test their knowledge in on-line quizzes. In recent months, Raw Canvas Artlookers Podcast created a sound tour of Tate Modern's New Collection Displays. Independent learners can take on-line courses, with materials provided in English, Simple and Traditional Chinese. Tate Tales encourages children to be 'art detectives' and explore pictures, create stories in response to images and submit them on-line. In Imaginary City they create their own paintings.

Visitors can even have a Tate image delivered to their front door. Create Art on Demand allows shoppers to customize images by choosing from a variety of sizes and frames, and viewing their potential purchase against the colour of their living room wall.

The website is translated into 12 languages and British Sign Language and i-maps are provided for the visually impaired. Visitors who are unable to physically visit can become members and keep in touch through *TATE ETC.* the Gallery's magazine.

The far end of the spectrum shows those activities where the visitor is most likely to be looking to do something worthwhile; however, the chilling aspect should not be disregarded as motivations are often complex and the social aspects and location of museums are also important. Of course hundreds of thousands of children and young people visit museums as part of their curriculum with the specific intention of learning. However, the spectrum has been designed to show those activities that could potentially appeal to one market, 'constructive chillers'.

Conclusions

Globalization is extending the reach of museums and their potential audience is limitless (subject to technology being available) but at a local level the audience base might be limited due to a changing society, demographically, culturally and socially. Museums need to be aware of these changes; for example, a smaller share of the population being children, a more culturally diverse population, different family structures, time pressures and their impact on leisure time. Although it may not be 'politically correct' to say so, higher economic social groups ('the middle class') are likely to be the core audience for museums in the future and an important stakeholder group as potential supporters, yet they are most likely to be short of time. The harder they work, the more time they will want to spend chilling and the fewer risks they will be prepared to take.

Thinking about potential visitors' time and how they might want to spend their leisure time produces a new approach to segmentation. Segmentation shows that museums have the potential to appeal to existing and new audiences as they offer a range of experiences. Museums do not need to become 'populist' or 'dumb down' as some museums have been accused of, rather they need to communicate their offering to visitors to demonstrate that they offer edutainment, places to have fun, escape and spend time together; for example, a 'place to get away from it all', 'to see a little bit of . . .' and 'to have fun with family and friends'. For many people, learning is an implicit assumption.

The challenge will be to communicate this, to appeal to the individualism of some subgroups and to develop this audience by broadening and deepening their engagement with the museum. Families are likely to be a core market segment. The 'constructive' end of the spectrum will attract visitors with greater levels of time and the motivation to engage at a deeper level and this group may well be friends or members of the museum.

In conclusion, museums need to capitalize on and change the way they market themselves by communicating their diversity, flexibility, facilities and the experiences they can offer in contrast to their competitors in the wider leisure market. They need to consider people's 'leisure maps'; what they are seeking, when, why and how.

References

Bourdieu, P. (1984). *Distinction: A Social Critique of the Judgement of Taste.* Harvard University Press, Cambridge, Mass.

Bourgeon-Renault, D. (2000). Evaluating consumer behaviour in the field of arts and culture marketing. *International Journal of Arts Management,* 3(1), 4–18.

CIPD (2006). Working hours in the UK. <www.cipd.co.uk> (accessed 29 June 2006).

Davies, S. (2005). Still popular: museums and their visitors 1994–2004. *Cultural Trends,* 14(1), 53, 67–105.

DCMS (2006). Four years after scrapping entry charges: free admission is still a growing success. Press release 032/06, 20 March. <http://www.culture.gov.uk/museums_and_galleries/> (accessed 27 June 2006).

Falk, J. and Dierking, L. (1992). *The Museum Experience.* Whalesback, Washington D.C.

Falk, J.H., T. Moussouri and Coulson, D. (1998). The effect of visitor's agendas on museum learning, Curator, 41(2), pp. 106–20.

Fishbein, M. and Ajzen, I. (1975). *Belief, Attitude, Intention and Behaviour: An Introduction to Theory and Research.* Addison–Welsey, Reading, MA.

Gambado (2006). <http://www.gambado.com/home.html> (accessed 1 July 2006).

Graburn, N. H. H. (1977). The museum and the visitor experience. In *The Visitor and the Museum,* pp. 5–32, prepared for the *72nd Annual Conference of the American Association of Museums.* Seattle, Washington.

Hibbett, A. and Meager, N. (2003). *Labour Market Trends,* October, 503–11.

Hood, M. G. (1983). Staying away: why people choose not to visit museums. *Museum News,* April, 50–7.

Horniman Museum and Gardens Online (2006). <www.horniman.ac.uk> (accessed 30 June 2006).

Iso-Ahola, S. E. (1980). *The Social Psychology of Leisure and Recreation.* W.C. Brown. Dubuque, Iowa.

Jansen-Verbeke, M. and Van Redom, J. (1996). Scanning museum visitors: urban tourism marketing. *Annals of Tourism Research,* 23(2), 364–75.

Leisure Intelligence (2006a). Days Out: UK Pursuits. Leisure Intelligence Standard: Leisure Intelligence.

Leisure Intelligence (2006b). Leisure Time: UK Pursuits. Leisure Intelligence Standard: Leisure Intelligence.

Longhurst, B., Bagnall, G. and Savage, M. (2004). Audiences, museums and the English middle class. *Museum & Society*, 2(2), 104–24.

Merriman, N. (1991). *Beyond the Glass Case, the Past, the Heritage and the Public in Britain*. 1e. Leicester University Press, Leicester.

Miles, R. (1986). Museum audiences. *The International Journal of Museum Management and Curatorship*, 5, 73–80.

MORI (2004). *Visitors to Museums and Galleries, Research Study Conducted for the Museums, Libraries and Archives Council*. Museums, Libraries and Archives Council, London.

Mousourri, T. (1997). Family agendas and family learning in hands-on museums. Doctoral Dissertation, University of Leicester. In *Learning from Museums* (J. Falk and L. Dierking). Alta Mira Press. Walnut Creek, CA.

Museums Association (2006). <www.museumsassociation.org/faq> (accessed 27 June 2006).

Office of National Statistics (ONS) (2006). <www.statistics.gov.uk> (accessed 13 June 2006).

Richards, G. (1999). Heritage visitor attractions in Europe: a visitor profile. *Interpretation*, 4(3), 9–13. Wallingford.

Richards, G. (ed.) (2001). *Cultural Attractions and European Tourism*. CAB International, Wallingford.

Richards, G. (2002). Tourism attraction systems exploring cultural behaviour. *Annals of Tourism Research*, 29(4), 1048–64.

Rojek, C. (1999). *Leisure and Culture*. Palgrave Macmillan, Basingstoke.

Skelton, A., Bridgwood, A., Duckworth, K., Hutton, L., Fenn, C., Creaser, C. and Babbidge, A. (2002). *Arts in England, Attendance, Participation and Attitudes, 2001. Research Report 27*. The Arts Council of England, Resource. London.

Slater, A. (2007/in press). Escaping to the gallery: understanding the motivations of visitors to galleries. *International Journal of Non-profit and Voluntary Sector Marketing*, 12(2), 149–162.

Sturgis, P. and Jackson, J. (2003). Examining participation in sporting and cultural activities: analysis of the UK 2000 Time Use Survey Phase 2. Department of Culture Media and Sport.

Tate (2005). Tate Funding Agreement 2005/06–2007/08. <www.tate.org.uk/about/governancefunding/funding/fundingagreement060001.pdf> (accessed 13 June 2006).

Tate Online (2006). Tate Online: British and international modern and contemporary art. <http://www.tate.org.uk/> (accessed 23 November 2006).

The Henley Centre (2000). Towards 2010 new times new challenges for the arts. Arts Council of England.

Further reading

Burton, C. and Scott, C. (2003). Museums: challenges for the 21st century. *International Journal of Arts Management*, 5(2), 56–68.

Foley, M. and McPherson, G. (2000). Museums as leisure. *International Journal of Heritage Studies*, 6(2), 161–74.

Goulding, C. (1999). Contemporary museum culture and consumer behaviour. *Journal of Marketing Management*, 15, 647–71.

Huber, J. and Skidmore, P. (2003). *The New Old: Why the Baby Boomers Won't be Pensioned Off*. Demos, London.

McPherson, G. (2006). Public memories and private tastes: the shifting definitions of museums and their visitors in the UK. *Museum Management & Curatorship*, 21, 44–57.

Stephen, I. (2001). The contemporary museum and leisure: recreation as a museum function. *Museum Management & Curatorship*, 19(3), 297–308.

Sport museums: marketing to engage consumers in sport heritage

Pamm Kellett

Sport has long been of enormous cultural significance around the globe. In ancient Greece, games and contests were grounded in mythology and religious beliefs. Folk games and tournaments in medieval times reflected and reproduced gender and social class differences in European cultures. More recently, Australia directly inherited British sports and games, which have played an important role in the development of Australian values and influenced Australian's views of nationalism, social cohesion (in the form of mateship), tenacity and development of a culture of volunteering (Bloomfield, 2003).

The earliest reported competitive sport played in Australia was cricket. British military and administrators, having maintained their strong links with England, challenged ex-convicts (who saw themselves as Australians) in various sports, the first being cricket. For the colony to compete against the 'English' in cricket (the Brit's own game), and more importantly to win against the 'mother country' was considered to be a signal of the penal colony society's determination, mateship, social development and maturity (Shilbury et al., 2006). These values and social meanings continue to influence modern-day rivalry (particularly in the sport of cricket) between Australia and England. As this example suggests, sports are inextricably linked to a nation's culture.

Sporting heritage, such as significant sport stadia, objects, artefacts, rituals and retro apparel, is increasingly recognized, by governments and sport organizations alike, as representations of important legacies for individuals, regions and nations. As a result, there is a burgeoning sport museum industry. This chapter aims to summarize current research that examines motives for individuals to visit sport heritage sites (such as sport museums) and to understand the implications for marketing museums.

The proliferation of sport museums and halls of fame

The importance of sporting heritage to societies is demonstrated in the proliferation of sporting museums, halls of fame and sites of special sporting significance around the globe. The Picasso Museum in Barcelona is the second most-visited museum in the city—behind Futbol Club Barcelona's Football

Museum, while the Baseball Hall of Fame and Museum in Cooperstown, USA, has attracted over 12 million visitors since 1939 (Gammon and Ramshaw, 2005).

Sport museums have been established to celebrate individual athletes; such as the US$70 million Muhammad Ali Centre in Louisville, Kentucky (Kindred, 2006) or the Sir Donald Bradman Museum in Bowral, rural Australia (Bradman Museum, 2000). Sport 'halls of fame' have been established in cities and towns to celebrate the region's athletes (such as the Wagga Wagga Sporting Hall of Fame in Wagga Wagga, a rural city in southern New South Wales, Australia; or the Australian Capital Territory (ACT) Hall of Fame). Sport clubs and associations have also developed places to celebrate their own sport heritage (such as the Melbourne Cricket Club Museum; the Surfworld Museum and Hall of Fame and the Master Scuba Diver Hall of Fame). Further, specific groups of athletes have developed sites to celebrate their sporting heritage (such as the African American Sporting Hall of Fame and Museum; the 'Super [sports] Women' display at the Boston Children's Museum and the National Collegiate Athletics Association Hall of Champions).

The Olympic Movement has its own Olympic Museum in Lausanne, Switzerland—the home of the International Olympic Committee. It reported unusually high numbers of daily visitors in the week 18–26 August 2006, with more than 600 visitors during the weekdays and nearly 1500 on the Sunday. The record number of visitors to the museum was 2546 in July 1998. Interestingly, the Summer Olympic Games did not occur during either of these years, therefore excitement for the Games cannot explain the high visitation rates.

In the USA, demand for preservation of historic sports facilities is increasing as franchise owners build facilities with new modern revenue-generating structures and amenities. Franchise owners are incorporating historical elements into the design of new facilities to capitalize on the growing demand for sport heritage (Mason et al., 2005), particularly following the success of the first acknowledged 'retro' ball park (Oriole Park at Camden Yards) built in 1992 (Friedman et al., 2004).

Despite the number of sport museums, halls of fame and stadia tours that have been created, most are not-for-profit organizations, funded by contributions from a variety of interested individuals and corporations, with revenue from admission and/or memberships providing minimal income. Very few, however, are financially viable (Frost, 2005). The costs of housing, insuring and appropriately displaying memorabilia (that may require expensive restoration and subsequent temperature and humidity controlled environments) can be exorbitant. However, when connected to larger marketing strategies for teams, destinations or sport stadia it is suggested that sport museums and heritage displays can generate additional revenue (Wood, 2005) and help to offset the seasonal nature of sport competitions (Higham, 2005).

Sport heritage: part of a tourism portfolio

Perhaps the most important indicator of the importance of sporting heritage is the way many nations now include sports museums as part of their tourism marketing strategies. For example, Futbol Club Barcelona's football museum is the most-visited museum in the city, and in London the cricket museum at Lords and the tennis museum at Wimbledon have become important components of the city's tourism strategy (Fairley and Gammon, 2005). Other cities have followed their lead. For example, the Sporting Scotland Gallery at the Museum of Scotland in Edinburgh was opened during 2006 (anonymous, 2006), while construction was scheduled to start in 2006 for the for-profit National Sports Museum in New York City that houses a theatre, a hall of fame for female athletes and more than 25,000 square feet of display area (Sandomir, 2006). The Federal Government of Australia recently invested A\$15 million to assist the development of the National Sports Museum at the Melbourne Cricket Ground (the MCG) in Melbourne. The National Sports Museum will be the permanent home of the Sport Australia Hall of Fame, the Australian Gallery of Sport and Olympic Museum, the Australian Cricket Hall of Fame and the Melbourne Cricket Club Museum.

Sport-related heritage, of which sport museums are a part, is becoming recognized as a powerful catalyst for sport tourism (Fairley, 2003; Adair, 2004; Hinch and Higham, 2004; Frost, 2005; Mason et al., 2005). It is only recently that the area of sport tourism has received academic attention. Gibson (1998a) identified three broad categories of sport tourism: active sport tourism which involves travel to participate in sports (e.g., Hall, 1992a); event sport tourism which involves travel to watch a sport event (Hall, 1992b) and celebratory or nostalgia sport tourism which involves travel to attractions associated with the history of sport, such as museums, halls of fame and sites of historical importance such as stadia (Gibson, 1998b; Fairley, 2003). In the non-sport literature, scholars have examined the way in which sites of historical importance including museums, heritage sites and attractions evoke nostalgia (Peleggi, 1996; Goulding, 2001). The phrase 'nostalgia sport tourism' has been developed by sport scholars who have been informed by the non-sport literature that links nostalgia and tourism.

While the focus of this chapter is to explore what has been referred to as 'nostalgia sport tourism', of which sport museums, halls of fame and significant historical sport sites such as stadia are a part, it must be noted that all types of sport tourism identified by Gibson (1998a) (active sport tourism, event sport tourism and nostalgia sport tourism) are potentially complementary insomuch as they can foster or facilitate each other (Chalip, 2001; Fairley, 2003). In other words, after viewing an event or participating in an event, a sport spectator might be more likely to attend a sport-related museum or sport heritage site.

Nostalgia sport tourism: understanding motivations to visit sport heritage sites

Nostalgia, in the context of sport tourism, has been defined as 'a preference (general liking, positive attitude or favourable affect) towards objects (people, places experiences or things) from when one was younger or from times about which one has learned vicariously, perhaps through socialization or the media' (Fairley, 2003, p. 288). Sport has been identified as a potent instigator of nostalgia as it represents personal and collective life-markers that can, over time, be edited and generously enhanced by individuals. People can recollect sporting moments (as spectators and/or participants) that reinforce their self-concept, or that represent the way a sport or game was originally meant to be played (such as without performance enhancing drugs, training regimes or scientifically developed equipment) (Fairley and Gammon, 2005). Historical sport artefacts, objects and sites of significance can therefore evoke nostalgic reactions. Not surprisingly, nostalgia has been central to the (limited) empirically based exploration of motives for travel to sport museums, sport halls of fame (Redmond, 1991; Snyder, 1991), and stadia and arenas with historical significance (Wilson and Gibson, 2005).

As a result of ongoing research in sport tourism, nostalgia sport tourism has been categorized into two broad and independent areas (Fairley and Gammon, 2005). First, nostalgia sport tourism where nostalgia is triggered by place or artefact (object-based) elements (such as objects, music, scents, products and possessions). Second, nostalgia sport tourism where nostalgia is triggered by social experience (group-based) events (such as friends, family members, reunions, picnics and social gatherings).

Object-based nostalgia sport tourism includes stimuli from sport heritage such as that contained in sport museums, halls of fame, stadia and other monuments linked to sport history. Nostalgia has been found to be an important motive for individuals to visit the Baseball Hall of Fame and Museum (Snyder, 1991) and Wrigley Field—a historically significant sport site which has been the home of the Chicago Cubs baseball team since 1914 (Wilson and Gibson, 2005).

In her study of fan groups who repeat-travel to events, Fairley (2003) found that travel to take part in a sport event and travel to spectate at a sport event 'may engender memories that motivate subsequent sport tourism, and that those memories become meaningful and motivating because of the social experiences through which they are engendered' (p. 285). Nostalgia was evoked, not from any tangible event facility or object, but rather from the social interaction between the fan group members travelling to an event site. Similarly, in their exploration of nostalgia in junior hockey in Canada, Mason et al. (2005) found that nostalgia experienced reflected a feeling for the social experience (the act of attending a game) rather than for a hockey arena or significant hockey site.

Interestingly, in their study of fans who travel to see live National Hockey League (NHL) games because their home team (the Hartford Whalers) relocated to a different city, Kulczycki and Hyatt (2005) found that nostalgia sport tourism does not exist without artefacts or objects. They suggest that Whaler fans can have a nostalgic experience when watching ex-Whaler players, or when seeing or wearing ex-Whaler jerseys, and when discussing the team in the stands when attending NHL games. A combination of the objects and social interaction creates the positive nostalgic experience for Whalers when they travel to other cities and recreate past experiences of being Whaler fans.

Implicit in the resulting proliferation of sport heritage sites, and the examples of empirical study described above, nostalgia is an important and meaningful element in the consumer experience at sport heritage sites; however, so too is social interaction. It is possible that museums and sites of sport heritage may be able to deepen nostalgic experiences by allowing for opportunities to combine both nostalgia for objects with nostalgia for social interaction. Research work thus far has not encouraged consideration of the two broad categories working together; however, implicit in some research (Fairley, 2003; Kulczycki and Hyatt, 2005; Mason et al., 2005) is that this should be an important element to consider in developing sites of sport heritage.

The way in which sites are presented (either at the site or through promotional and marketing material) has a role in constructing nostalgic perceptions. For example, museums instigate nostalgia because they display any miscellaneous heritage connected to the sport, regardless of how trivial it is, as well as honour the elite, while halls of fame celebrate the gifted and exceptional (Fairley and Gammon, 2005). It is possible that design, marketing, programmatical and promotional elements need to further develop concepts that allow for nostalgic experiences through social interaction in addition to nostalgia through objects and artefacts. Although the work on understanding motives to travel to sites of significant sport history has been greatly informed by the studies that use nostalgia to understand consumer behaviour, there has been a call from scholars to broaden the studies of nostalgia sport tourists beyond mere nostalgia.

Heritage sport tourism

Academic literature that attempts to understand travel to venerate sport-related sites is in its infancy. It has been dominated by a perspective that understands nostalgia to be a core motivation for those who visit sport heritage sites. More recently, a body of knowledge is emerging that suggests that the term 'nostalgia' sport tourism should be replaced by 'heritage' sport tourism (Ramshaw and Gammon, 2005). It has been argued that nostalgia sport tourism is more usefully categorized as one part of a larger category called sport heritage tourism (Ramshaw and Gammon, 2005). They suggest that 'nostalgia is associated more with motivation than destination, while heritage must have a location for the tourist to *visit*' (p. 239). Their argument is two-fold. First, they suggest that nostalgia can only be evoked if there is a site for an individual or group to visit that has heritage characteristics related to sport. Second, they suggest that nostalgia is only one motivation for people to visit sport heritage sites.

Drawing from the broader field of tourism, Ramshaw and Gammon (2005) argue that some tourists will choose to visit locations and attractions at destinations that are associated with a distinct sporting past and sporting culture for motives that might be linked, not necessarily or solely with nostalgia, but with other motives such as pilgrimage or education (Hinch and Higham, 2004). In practice, museums already incorporate many elements that promote learning. The Olympic Museum includes a large reference library, as does the Tennis Museum at Wimbledon. Theoretically, to Ramshaw and Gammon (2005), positioning this type of sport tourism as 'heritage' rather than 'nostalgia', 'places the emphasis on the heritage characteristics of the attraction rather than the perception or motivation of the tourist' (p. 237), therefore allowing multiple motives to be considered.

In line with this view, Wood (2005) suggests that London must develop local sport heritage projects and initiatives considering the opportunities that 2012 London Olympics represent for the city and the country. He proposes a plan that incorporates a variety of programmes, sites and celebrations to tap into multiple motivations beyond nostalgia. It is in an examination of categories and characteristics of heritage elements and empirical research, that is grounded in the study of heritage attractions rather than reasons people attend them, that we may be able to build on the extant knowledge to gain substantial practical implications for heritage sites such as museums, halls of fame and sport stadia.

Categorizations of sport heritage

Sport-related heritage has characteristics that identify particular artefacts, location, experiences, rituals and the like that are expressions of this heritage. Drawing from characterizations of heritage, Ramshaw and Gammon (2005) identify four categories: tangible immovable (such as buildings); tangible moveable (such as artefacts and objects); intangible (such as memories and rituals) and goods and services (such as retro apparel products and purpose-built amenities to provide a heritage feel for customers). Ramshaw and Gammon (2005) suggest that sport-related heritage may fall into multiple categories. In the next section, research that has explored the tangible categorizations of heritage characteristics as central to understanding sport tourism will be discussed.

Sport stadiums as heritage sites

The sport stadium is an example of a heritage building within the tangible immoveable category. Sport stadiums have evolved from being functional buildings to places that hold instant recognition for sport fans and non-sport fans (Gammon and Fear, 2005). In their need to position themselves in the global marketplace, cities have often used sport stadia and the inclusion of heritage elements in their design, as part of a broader strategic positioning strategy to attract visitors from out of town (nostalgic sport tourists) (Mason et al., 2005). Fairley and Gammon (2005) refer to stadiums as 'huge emotional receptacles' (p. 189). Gammon and Fear (2005) explored the reasons for growth and popularity in stadium tours. They found that not only did stadium tours appeal because of their symbolism of local, national and international heritage, but also because they can give an experience that goes beyond the superficial features of the structure and beyond what can be experienced during an event. In their study of tours of the Millennium Stadium in Cardiff (a multi-use stadium that is the home of the Welsh Rugby Team), Gammon and Fear found that the appeal of a stadium tour was in the ability of people to glimpse the places that are usually hidden or protected from view, and for many, it was the ultimate backstage experience. Interestingly, volunteers report this experience—to witness behind the scenes of an event through a volunteer assignment at an event—is a factor in repeat volunteering (Farrell et al., 1998).

Mason et al. (2005) note that facilities built for major junior hockey in Canada (as opposed to professional NHL franchises) have built their facilities based purely on functionality rather than to incorporate any nostalgic or heritage features to attract attendees. Junior hockey facilities have not been built with tourism in mind; however, this is not to say that attendees do not experience nostalgia. Nostalgia sport tourism exists, but is associated with the social experience of the game attendance and not the actual venue itself. Mason et al. (2005) suggest that there is scope for professional franchises and their host cities to link with junior hockey franchises to assist in creating a market where many motivations can be catered for through resource sharing and making associations between local notions of hockey, community and identity with facilities. This is perhaps an important lesson in creating new markets and further penetrating existing markets through the characteristics of heritage sites.

Sport museums and halls of fame

Sport museums and halls of fame are examples of collections of tangible moveable heritage. Often, sport museums and halls of fame are incorporated into stadia as part of heritage displays. In this way, museums and halls of fame can exist in multiple categories—the moveable and immoveable heritage categories. Certainly, placing museums and halls of fame within venues can add to their appeal, but can also allow marketing and ticket sales strategies to 'piggyback' on each other. The proliferation of sport halls of fame and museums raises questions about their sustainability. Should organizations attempt to run them as for-profit enterprises or should the sport organizations and related events subsidize the heritage attractions? In his analysis of the Australian Football League (AFL) Hall of Fame, Frost (2005) provides some definitive answers.

Frost (2005) reports that the AFL Hall of Fame gathered A$2 million in debt in less than 3 months of operation in 2004. The AFL Hall of Fame and Sensation had two components: the heritage-based hall of fame and a football-themed interactive parlour. It was located in a shopping complex in the central business district of Melbourne. Frost (2005) outlined three major problems for the AFL Hall of fame: concept, location and price. First, he suggests that the concept of a hall of fame, while successful in other sports, was flawed in AFL football, because the heritage of the sport lies in individual clubs rather than the league in general. Some clubs had already established their own heritage attractions, some including a hall of fame. Further, the concept confused heritage with a fun parlour—advertising featured a current player with children and did not mention any heritage components. Second, Frost (2005) suggested that the location (in the central business district) was flawed and the

AFL Hall of Fame should have been located at a stadium (such as the MCG). Third, admission prices for the AFL Hall of Fame were too expensive when compared with other substitute attractions. Clearly, sport heritage attractions are not guaranteed of success.

Wilson and Gibson (2005) studied visitors to the Baseball Hall of Fame and Museum at Wrigley Field stadium. With regard to the heritage characteristics on display, they found differences between the way in which male and female attendees experienced and interpreted them. Although they did not offer any solutions for those who manage and create museums and halls of fame, it might be important to incorporate different elements that may appeal differently to both sexes for sports.

The culture of sport: the intangible elements of heritage

Sport has had a distinctive influence on the culture of society. Moreover, each sport also has its own unique culture and sets of stories, rituals, ceremonies and myths. Smith and Shilbury (2004) suggest that sports, until recently, have not been as effective in leveraging their own culture in reaching for organizational objectives (in human resource management, marketing, promotional strategies and the like). A recognition of sporting heritage and displaying and celebrating cultural elements is perhaps testament to the changing role that culture plays in sport. Indeed, one of the appeals of the Olympic Games is not just the athletes themselves, but also the intangible elements that include the ideologies of the Olympic Movement. The Olympic Museum in Lausanne, Switzerland, is built so that people can learn from the vast Olympic Library about the history of the Olympic Movement and its ideals, the meaning of the ceremonies, as well as its athletes and host cities. In this way, the museum attempts to continue interest about the Olympics during the 4-year hiatus between events (although the Summer and Winter Games really make this hiatus only 2 years) (Adair, 2004).

It is well recognized (by practitioners at least) that museums and halls of fame can provide learning environments. This is particularly instructive when considering the work of Fairley et al. (in press) who have found that an important factor in Olympic volunteer travel and repeat event volunteering (at the Olympic Games) is the opportunity to learn about the Olympic Movement, as well as to learn about the history of the Olympic Games. Museums and halls of fame may provide important educational and experiential facilitation of volunteers in sport.

Conclusion

Sport heritage tourism is an exciting and rapidly expanding industry. The academic literature that explores sport heritage and related heritage sport tourism and nostalgia sport tourism is in its infancy. The sport heritage industry is burgeoning, with museum and heritage facility planners, designers, architects and managers providing high-class facilities that allow nations, sport organizations and fans to celebrate the rich history and culture that sport offers. Scholars have yet to 'catch up' with practitioners in detailed studies of the consumers and consumption of sport heritage sites and experiences; however, with continued dialogue between scholars and practitioners, our knowledge of sport heritage and all that it offers society will move forward, and important lessons will continue to be learned about the management and marketing of sport heritage.

References

Adair, D. (2004). Where the Games never cease: The Olympic Museum in Lausanne, Switzerland. In B. Ritchie & D. Adair (eds.), *Sport Tourism Interrelationships, Impacts and Issues*. Clevedon: Channel View Publications.

anonymous (2006). Sporting heritage goes on show. *The Herald*, 22 June, p. 9.

Bloomfield, J. (2003). *Australia's Sporting Success: The Inside Story*. Sydney: University of NSW Press.

Bradman Museum (2000). Bradman Museum. <http://www.bradman.org.au/html/s01_home/home.asp?dsb=2> (accessed 7 July 2006).

Chalip, L. (2001). Sport and tourism: capitalising on the linkage. In D. Kluka & G. Schilling (eds.), *The Business of Sport* (D. Kluka and G. Schilling, eds.), pp. 77–89. Oxford, UK: Meyer and Meyer.

Fairley, S. (2003). In search of relieved social experience: group-based nostalgia sport tourism. *Journal of Sport Management*, 17, 284–304.

Fairley, S. and Gammon, S. (2005). Something lived, something learned: Nostalgia's expanding role in sport tourism. *Sport in Society*, 8(2), 182–97.

Fairley, S., Kellett, P. and Green, B. C. (2007). Volunteering abroad: motives for travel to volunteer at the Athens Olympic Games. *Journal of Sport Management*, 21(1), 41–57.

Farrell, J. M., Johnston, M. E. and Twynam, G. D. (1998). Volunteer motivation, satisfaction, and management at an elite sporting competition. *Journal of Sport Management*, 12, 288–300.

Friedman, M., Andrews, D. L. and Silk, M. (2004). Sport and the facade of redevelopment in the post-industrial city. *Sociology of Sport Journal*, 21, 119–39.

Frost, W. (2005). The sustainability of sports heritage attractions: lessons from the Australian Football League Hall of Fame. *Journal of Sport Tourism*, 10(4), 295–305.

Gammon, S. and Fear, V. (2005). Stadia tours and the power of backstage. *Journal of Sport Tourism*, 10(4), 243–52.

Gammon, S. and Ramshaw, G. (2005). Editorial: placing heritage in sport tourism. *Journal of Sport Tourism*, 10(4), 225–7.

Gibson, H. (1998a). Active sport tourism: who participates? *Leisure Studies*, 17, 155–70.

Gibson, H. (1998b). The wide world of sport tourism. *Parks and Recreation*, 33(9), 108–15.

Goulding, C. (2001). Romancing the past: heritage visiting and the nostalgic consumer. *Psychology and Marketing*, 18, 565–92.

Hall, C. (1992a). Adventure, sport and health tourism. In B. Weiler & C. M. Hall (eds.), *Special Interest Tourism*, pp. 141–58. London: Bellhaven Press.

Hall, C. (1992b). *Hallmark Tourist Events*. London: Belhaven Press.

Higham, J. (2005). Sport tourism as an attraction for managing seasonality. *Sport in Society*, 8(2), 238–62.

Hinch, T. and Higham, J. (2004). *Sport Tourism Development*. Clevedon: Channel View Publications.

Kindred, D. (2006). Still the greatest – and getting better. *Sporting News*, 5 May, 230, 18, 56.

Kulczycki, C. and Hyatt, C. (2005). Expanding the conceptualization of nostalgia sport tourism: lessons learned from the fans left behind after sport franchise relocation. *Journal of Sport Tourism*, 10(4), 273–93.

Mason, D., Duquette, G. H. and Scherer, J. (2005). Heritage, sport tourism and Canadian junior hockey: Nostalgia for social experience or sport place? *Journal of Sport Tourism*, 10(4), 253–71.

Peleggi, M. (1996). National heritage and global tourism in Thailand. *Annals of Tourism Research*, 23, 432–48.

Ramshaw, G. and Gammon, S. (2005). More than just nostalgia? Exploring the heritage/sport tourism nexus. *Journal of Sport Tourism*, 10(4), 229–41.

Redmond, G. (1991). Changing styles of sports tourism: industry/consumer interactions in Canada, the USA and Europe. In M. T. Sinclair & M. J. Stabler (eds.), *The Tourism Industry: An International Analysis* pp. 107–20. Wallinford, UK: CAB International.

Sandomir, R. (2006). Museum to display sports, and hopes to earn a profit. *New York Times*, 2 July, 155, pp. 1–7.

Shilbury, D., Deane, J. and Kellett, P. (2006). *Sport Management in Australia: An Organisational Overview*. Bentleigh, VIC: Strategic Sport Management.

Smith, A. C. T. and Shilbury, D. (2004). Mapping cultural dimensions in Australian sporting organisations. *Sport Management Review*, 7(2), 133–66.

Snyder, E. E. (1991). Sociology of nostalgia: sport halls of fame and museums in America. *Sociology of Sport Journal*, 8, 228–38.

Wilson, A. and Gibson, H. (2005). Something old, something new: motivations of nostalgia sport tourists at Wrigley Field. Paper presented at the *20th Annual Conference of the North American Society for Sport Management*.

Wood, J. (2005). Olympic opportunity: realizing the value of sports heritage for tourism in the UK. *Journal of Sport Tourism*, 10(4), 307–21.

By the community, for the community: exhibiting New Model Army's 25 years of rock visual heritage

Daragh O'Reilly

Introduction

When one thinks of rock music heritage, one thinks perhaps of rock celebrities, for example Bono or the Sex Pistols, being inducted into the Rock and Roll Hall of Fame, or perhaps of media stories about Beatles or Rolling Stones memorabilia being auctioned for large sums of money. It is less usual for a rock band to work quietly with local museum services in order to organize a touring display of its visual heritage.

In 2004, New Model Army (NMA), the English rock band, set up a free-of-charge exhibition of its art and artefacts in collaboration with the local museum service in West Yorkshire. The event was entitled 'One Family, One Tribe'. Initially, the Old Courthouse in the small town of Otley, a community arts centre which is generally the preserve of arts events appealing to a different kind of audience, was invaded by an excited group of rock music fans. The exhibition later moved to the larger Cartwright Gallery in Bradford, West Yorkshire, where it received approximately 10,000 visits. It has since been shown in Hamm, Germany, under a municipal twinning arrangement between Hamm and Bradford, and Salford, near Manchester, England.

In a cultural policy climate which favours the broadening of access to museums and heritage services, this was a powerful example of a successful project. For arts and heritage marketers, or audience developers, the challenge of broadening access is considerable. Theoretical notions of re-segmenting the market can easily founded on the practical problems of persuading people to give up their leisure time to visit venues which are not necessarily salient for them. Simply targeting new audiences with the same offering is also unlikely to work. Consequently, there needs to be a rethinking of the offering as well as of the audience. The NMA project was effective not only in the way it provided a new offering to existing and new audiences, but also in the way in which it involved the band and its fans in developing the exhibition, and in the way in which the art and artefacts themselves can be seen as community-building resources.

Music and heritage

The heritage of a rock band, in the widest sense, includes all of the meanings which it has ever negotiated with its fans—musical, visual and experiential. In order to conceptualize this heritage, it is necessary to turn to the culturalist approach to understanding music (Middleton, 1990, 2003). The conceptual framework in Figure 3.2 is offered as a means of facilitating thinking about important meaning aspects of popular music from a culturalist point of view. In this framework, I adapt the circuit of culture model (Du Gay et al., 1997; Hall, 1997; Du Gay et al., 2000) and make use of the notion of phenomena as texts (Lewis, 1992, pp. 52–5; Longhurst, 2007, pp. 195–202; Titon, 2003; Frith, 1996, p. 158ff; Gelder and Thornton, 1997, pp. 254–60; Shuker, 1998, p. 301ff; Horner and Swiss, 1999; Middleton, 2000, p. 1ff; Johnson, 2002, pp. 704–12), as well as earlier work in this area (O'Reilly, 2004).

According to this framework, music is produced within a band's culture of production, in which the salient aspects are the *people* who produce the music,

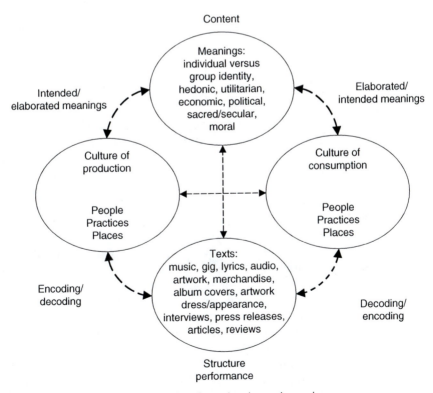

Figure 3.2 The production and consumption of meanings in popular music

the *places* in which it is produced (sites of production) and *practices* (creative, musical, managerial and communicative) by means of which the production happens. Band members, crew and cultural intermediaries such as music producers play the key parts in the production of live or recorded music. On the consumption side are individual and grouped consumers, fans and audiences, who engage in consumption practices which include attending, listening, watching, reading, talking, dancing and singing. Both producers and consumers encode and decode meanings in their interaction with each other. The production and consumption of music are articulated (linked) by cultural texts of different kinds. These texts are produced, performed and consumed by bands, their fans and by third parties. They include musical sounds, lyrics, artwork, merchandise, publicity photographs, live performances, DVDs, and so on. The meanings of these texts are negotiated between bands and fans, and include the hedonic, sacred, secular, utilitarian, economic, political and social resonances of the band's work. While the fans are free to make their own response to the texts, their interpretation is shaped or constrained by the way in which these texts are encoded by the band. In this way, producer culture shapes consumer culture. At the same time, the fan-base of any particular band constitutes an interpretive community, an audience, whose sense-making, imagination, emotional reaction and creativity may to some extent, in its turn, shape and constrain the band's production. The places or sites in which music is produced may be either distant from the places of consumption—for example, when a fan listens to a recorded track on an iPod—or both band and fans may gather in the same place at a live performance.

New Model Army

NMA has survived for since the early 1980s, in a difficult business, for most of that time without mass media attention and without a major label recording contract. This chapter emerges from an ongoing empirical study of the band and its fans using a variety of data collection methods, including on-line and live performance observation, videography, interviews with band-side figures and fans, and analysis of visual texts. This approach is broadly suited to a tribal study (Cova and Cova, 2002), and indeed notions of tribe have featured heavily in NMA's past (see O'Reilly and Doherty, 2006), including in the title of the exhibition which is the focus of this chapter 'One Family, One Tribe'. The band played its first live performance in Bradford, England, in 1980. Since then, 17 albums have been released to date, including compilations, and the band currently operates its own label and recording studio. Earlier in its existence, it had 12 chart singles. The band still records and tours regularly in North America and Europe, and has a strong following in the UK, the Netherlands and Germany, in particular. It is important to understand that many of this band's fans have been listening to its music and attending its live performances for many years. Not a few of the fans have occupied, or currently occupy, music-related jobs, either as musicians, music journalists or venue promoters. Although NMA is close to their hearts, it is by no means the only band whose music they listen to. Many of the fans have a very wide repertoire of musical and band taste, though NMA fans often speak of their particular affection, or love, for NMA above all others. The experience of being an NMA fan is fed of course by listening to their music on CD, but the particular sense of community which the band and fans create is fostered by attendance at live performances, by regular participation in the website discussions (<www.newmodelarmy.org>), and by the notions of 'emotional politics' and family, offered in the band's songs and interviews.

Visual culture

In this section, I outline the kinds of visual culture which the band seeks to create, and go on to discuss how particular visual texts find their place in the band–fan cultural circuit. The fan culture of any particular band is shaped by the texts which the band encodes, by the structures of these texts and by the ways in which the fans respond to, use and discursively elaborate their responses and uses of these texts. The NMA exhibition collected the key elements of the band's visual heritage together for the first time. Such an exhibition is unusual in the music business—although an exhibition entitled 'Punk: Sex, Seditionaries and the Sex Pistols' took place at the Urbis Centre in Manchester, England, from 26 May to 11 September, 2005. For the first time, it was possible for NMA fans and other visitors to have a historical retrospective of the entire history of the band as related through visual objects. It is interesting to note the kinds of art and artefacts which the curators selected for the collection. The visual texts exhibited included those generated by the band, by fans and by third parties. The band-originated material included text panels containing a document entitled 'What is the "NMA Family"—some thoughts by Joolz Denby' (posted 15 February 2004 – see Talk pages). The piece is in part a fierce polemic, partly a retrospective essay and partly a manifesto communicating band values (see O'Reilly and Doherty, 2006, for a fuller account). The 'Family' is a place of emotional sanctuary and a place to experience solidarity and protection, in contrast to the cynical consumerism of mainstream music. In the following paragraph, I examine the role of the family in relation to the exhibition.

The 'Family' and social inclusiveness

NMA comes with a pre-existing inclusive community of fans (the family) who love the band's music. If the museum service had simply put on a rock artefacts exhibit it would no doubt have had some success, but the collaboration with NMA brought the idea to a whole new level. The idea for the exhibition came from Joolz Denby, who has been responsible for almost all of the album cover artwork for the band, since the early 1980s. A family member who worked closely with Joolz in developing the event was the audience development manager for the Museums, Libraries and Archives Council. Together, they planned for a small opening event (Otley Courthouse) and secured the funding. Artefacts and artwork which had been lying under beds and in cupboards were given professional curatorial treatment and put on display. This event was visited by a museum service team and, on the basis of this appraisal, the event was permitted to move to the Cartwright Hall in Bradford, where exhibition space is usually reserved for major artists—Anish Kapoor had been a recent exhibitor. It is interesting to note that Joolz Denby actively solicited the support of the fans in the exhibition grant bid. Using the website and e-mail, Joolz Denby appealed for fans to 'e-mail why you think such an exhibition is important, what it would mean to you and how NMA has inspired you over the years'. Stories of what NMA means to fans came flooding in. This produced a strong file of evidence which helped to persuade the Otley and Bradford venues it would be worthwhile to programme their spaces with the NMA exhibition. In this way, the new audience, the family, was already involved in advocating the exhibition. In addition, the physical work of setting up the initial Otley and subsequent Bradford exhibitions involved different members of the local family volunteering time and effort, doing favours and lending resources.

The exhibits: visual culture and community

A wide range of items were displayed at the exhibition. Objects generated by the band included lyrics notes and books, paintings, portraits, photographs, a photo-collage, the original painted leather jacket from the Ghost of Cain album cover, posters, CDs and album cover artwork. Two displays occupied the particular attention of fans, namely a reproduction merchandise booth and an altar. Other items included stage costumes and banners, as well as a selection of electric guitars and keyboards. The fans were also represented, as some of the e-mails which helped to advocate the grant were displayed in a scrapbook near the entrance. In addition, in an interesting response to the band's music, a fan had drawn a comic strip in three panels interpreting a particular NMA song. A band DVD was playing on a large wall screen. There were also objects which originated from outside the immediate band–fan community, including laminated backstage passes, press cuttings, clogs and a hat worn by Justin Sullivan on 1980s videos. There were, finally, quite a few objects pointing to death (skulls, skeletons) and spirituality (a serpent on a cross, Tarot cards, a framed painting and statuette of the Blessed Virgin Mary). In the following paragraphs, I examine particular texts which were on display in the exhibition and how they help to build community. Lack of space prevents a detailed analysis of all of the texts, but the following are selected in order to give a flavour of how the visual texts are used as resources for the construction of a sense of community.

The NMA logo

On entering the Bradford exhibition, the first thing the visitor saw was a kind of altar structure. On a dais about 12 centimetres off the ground, stood two very tall candlesticks wrapped in a white fabric and holding thick red candles. Midway between them, against a white-emulsioned back panel, was a framed copy of 'Celtic knot' original artwork for the 'Thunder and Consolation' album (1989). The sign underneath the artwork read 'Band logo'. This is an appropriate designation for the image which has become perhaps *the* key signifier of NMA. Its location in the exhibition in the centre of the altar is a clear sign of its importance. In a Catholic church, for example, it is the tabernacle which is in the centre of the altar; the object of worship is central. In this exhibition, the centre of the altar was the recognized symbol for the community—a visual cue that the most important thing is the bond with one's emotional family. Joolz Denby drew on George Bain's 'Celtic Art: The Methods of Construction' (1996) in developing this image. The following passage from an interview with Joolz explains her approach to the emblem:

> People very often want to know about Celtic work, and what drew me to it. That's easy—it's beautiful and it is the expression of spiritual dedication and prayer. It expresses a link between mathematics (which are my own, personal mystery) and art (which I do understand). The piece that symbolises 'Thunder and Consolation' came from a Pictish stone carving—now people have it on a record cover, it serves its purpose again through another medium.

The Celtic symbol points to a kind of spirituality and culture which is pre-Christian, and to the idea of a time and place when society was organized tribally. In this way, it contributes to a certain notion of community of the band and the fans.

Tattoos

Some NMA fans have had the Celtic knot tattooed onto their skin. In this way, they put this key community symbol into circulation in their everyday lives. In interview, Joolz made the following comment about tattoos:

> Music fans—especially rock or alternative music fans—very often seek to publicly declare their allegiance to their chosen band by being tattooed with the band's logos, record /CD covers, lines from songs that have particular meaning to the tattooee, or names of band members, portraits, etc. This is done to demonstrate solidarity not so much with the band itself but with the other fans who are part of the tattooee's 'family' or clique. Fans of rock/alternative bands also have a perception of themselves as 'individuals', 'outlaws', rather more discerning and daring than 'the average person'. Tattooing, which in the West has ambiguous status within the dominant culture and associations with punitive or stigmatized sub-cultures, and thus a 'daring' image presents a relatively safe way of expressing 'otherness'.

In some contexts, of course, it may not be possible or advisable to reveal the tattoo, for example, working in some health care, educational or corporate environments. Otherwise, the tattoo can function as a discussion point, a prompt for narratives of community affiliation and musical experiences. In the case of NMA, the Celtic knotwork tattoo functions as a signifier of allegiance to a community which includes the band and the fans.

Album covers

The band artwork acts to encode certain qualities or values of the band. As one fan commented on his copy of a band album:

> The Thunder and Consolation album, I've got—it's a gatefold, vinyl record. It is a beautiful piece of just something to have. It's done in a sort of a parchmenty thing, it's got the drawings on it, it's all hand written lyrics and the thing is itself is a work of art [. . .] It feels quality but not in a sort of quality money gone into it, but the thought gone into it and there's pride gone into it and that shows through.

The notion that money can buy quality would be contested by NMA fans. The community ethos favours the idea that what goes into an object's making is important, the love and pride with which an object is made, and how this is evidenced in the appearance and attributes of the object itself.

As a material signifier, band artwork can function as a trigger for emotion. For example, here is a fan talking about an NMA record sleeve:

> If I see the Poison Street EP, and I look at the cover, I really love it you know, like, there's a boy and a girl standing on a hilltop kissing and you see the valley and all the lights—I really love that drawing and why? Because it reminds me of me kissing with a girl once [. . .] it was really romantic, and that's my connection with that cover.

This connects the fan with a moment in his own personal life, and serves to bind this moment to his memory of the band.

T-shirts

As well as being used as a tattoo pattern, the NMA Celtic knot has been used by the band on T-shirts, along with other images, song lyrics and sayings. T-shirt markings help to point out NMA fans to each other at pre-gig pub meets or music festivals, in the street or on television. The wearing of the T-shirt is a visual signifier of affiliation with the fan group and an act of symbolic consumption which helps to link the community.

Images of spirituality and death

There is a sense in which any museum collection is a shrine, a preservation of cultural resources which are sacred to a particular society. In this sense, the art and artefacts exhibition might be regarded as a touring shrine to NMA. There are also particular reasons for using the word 'shrine' in this instance, however. This has to do with the ways in which the sacred is represented or perhaps even invoked there. One key display which connects the sacred and the mundane is the altar to community already mentioned. The reproduction merchandise booth is also an important exhibit with spiritual 'content'. The booth consists of a cloth-covered table spread with objects, including Tarot cards, a candlestick with thick red candle, a framed icon and a statuette of the Virgin Mary—her heart radiating love and her right hand raised in a gesture of blessing. It might be considered unusual to find this kind of object on a merchandise booth, which is after all a place for doing commerce, for selling CDs and T-shirts. However, the booth is also a place where fans can talk with band associates—engage in social commerce. And, arguably, there is a third kind of commerce going on, namely, the commerce between the living and the 'dead', the transcendent world beyond.

Images of death are present in the shape of a skeleton which hangs from a string on the back wall of the booth, over some band T-shirts, and an almost-human sized skull which sits on a tiny skeleton frame on the booth table. A skull with an angry expression and staring green eyes is also found in a separate glass showcase which contains a guitar and a collection of artiste backstage passes. This skull is topped off with a kind of topknot and hair, which makes it look like a tiny Japanese samurai. According to Joolz, skulls are a symbol for truth: 'When you are talking to a person you can never know what hides behind this person's skin. A skull is clear and true'. These images, like vanitas themes in seventeenth-century paintings, invoke a sense of the proximity of death and of the beyond. It is noteworthy, too, that the exhibition was dedicated to the memory of a family member, Darryl Charles Kempster (1967–2004), who was tragically killed earlier in the year of the first NMA exhibition, 2004. The community also lost, in the same year, Robert Heaton, who had been the drummer and a key member of the band from 1982 to 1998. It is in the interest of the band and the fans that NMA's creative and musical project be sustained, but these deaths were reminders that the community and its members are mortal.

Each of these texts in circulation in the band–fan economy has its own structural and performative aspects, of course, and suggests its own meanings. Together they function to bind the fans to the band and to each other, and are a key element in building a sense of community or tribe.

Visitors

The promotional material positioned the exhibition as:

> an unrivalled opportunity for music fans to see a unique archive of paintings, photographs, concert footage and objects. The collection is a 'must-see' for contemporary music fans, highlighting the roles of art and music, bringing together different backgrounds, ages and cultures.

In fact, the exhibition had a variety of audiences. First of all were the NMA fans who travelled from far away to see it. It was possible to schedule some band gigs in venues which were quite close to Bradford (Manchester), so that some fans were able to combine gigs with a visit to the exhibition. Then there were other music fans, not necessarily fans of NMA, who were also interested. The existing audience of the museums came to see something different. Large numbers of school children also made the trip. Ten thousand people travelled to the Bradford Cartwright Hall venue, including people who flew from the USA to see the exhibition.

A museums officer explained that the exhibition had been among Cartwright Hall's most popular shows in recent months:

> I've been here 9 months and it's one of the busiest [exhibitions] . . .
> it's a whole new audience that might never normally go to a museum.

Touring bands, touring exhibitions

In addition to the art and artefacts considered above, a band may build a strong sense of community with its fans in three principal ways: through live performances, through its website and through touring. Live performances offer an intensity of experience that can go far beyond that of listening to a recorded track. The band website functions in a unifying, socially inclusive way across vast geographical distances. But in the context of this exhibition, it is worth pointing to the idea of the band tour. Touring is an experience shared by musicians, actors, travellers, circus people and others. In order to build and retain audiences, bands need to go on tour; touring is a key stage of a band's cycle of activity. To take a small number of examples: a favourite song of many NMA fans is 'Vagabonds', with its connotation of wandering travellers, which contains the lines 'We follow the tail-lights out of the city/Moving in a river of red/As the colours fade away from the dusky sunset/We roll for the darkness ahead' (Sullivan, 1987). Bruce Springsteen's fans have been referred to as 'tramps' (Cavicchi, 1998). Fans of Killing Joke are sometimes referred to as 'Gatherers'. 'Tales of the Road' is the name of a song written by Sullivan in 1996, of a live CD issued in 2004 from the Justin Sullivan and Friends tour, and of a fan website. Diaspora is a centrifugal force carrying members of a tribe or people out of and away from a homeland, driven by famine, war or persecution. The touring activity of a band also involves a going out but it has a kind of centripetal force too. A band on tour gathers people in to share musical experiences. For those far away from the band's home base, and/or who may not have seen the band live for a long time, the gig experience is a repatriation to the inner core—the heart, the family and the healing power of creative and musical imagination.

The exhibition itself has, of course, also gone on tour, offering another moving 'assembly point' for the fans. In fact, the band's 2006 German tour began in Hamm, where the exhibition toured after leaving Bradford (both cities are linked under a twinning arrangement). The exhibition, too, is therefore playing its part in offering an opportunity to partake in a deeper sense of community.

Conclusion

The generation of new audiences in line with an inclusive cultural policy is a difficult task. It is not enough to find new audiences, segments or markets; they may well need to be offered something new which it may not be within the power of the museum service to offer immediately. In any case, conventional marketing wisdom suggests that to offer new products to new audiences can be a highly risky strategy. We have seen how in this case, many factors came together to produce a successful outcome. These included the determination of the band's artist, Joolz Denby, the fortunate presence of a fan who was familiar with how the museums service worked and with funding sources, the prior existence of a community with a strong ethic of commitment and loyalty, and of course the band itself with its rich musical and visual heritage. These particular circumstances may not be so easily replicable, but they may at least help to inform thinking about museum service development—by a community and for the community.

Acknowledgement

The author works at the Sheffield University School of Management. He wishes to thank Joolz Denby, Nina Baptiste and Danijela Bogdanovic for their kind help with preparing this material.

References

Bain, G. (1996). *Celtic Art: The Methods of Construction*. London: Constable and Robinson.

Cavicchi, D. (1998). *Tramps Like Us: Music and Meaning Among Springsteen Fans*. New York: Oxford University Press.

Cova, B. and Cova, V. (2002). Tribal Marketing: The Tribalisation of Society and its Impact on the Conduct of Marketing. *European Journal of Marketing*, 36, 5/6, 595–620.

Du Gay, P., Hall, S., Janes, L., Mackay, H. and Negus, K. (1997). *Doing Cultural Studies: The Story of the Sony Walkman*. London: Sage.

Du Gay, P., Evans, J. and Redman, P. (eds.) (2000). *Identity: A Reader*. London: Sage.

Frith, S. (1996). *Performing Rites: On the Value of Popular Music*. Cambridge, Massachussetts: Harvard University Press.

Gelder, K. and Thornton, S. (eds.) (1997). *The Subcultures Reader*. London: Routledge.

Hall, S. (ed.) (1997). *Representation: Cultural Representations and Signifying Practices*. London: Sage.

Horner, B. and Swiss, T. (ed.) (1999). *Key Terms in Popular Music and Culture*. Oxford: Blackwell Publishers.

Johnson, B. (2002). Unsound Insights, in Looking Back, Looking Ahead: Popular Music Studies 20 Years Later. In *Proceedings of the Eleventh Biannual IASPM Conference July 6–10, 2001* (K. Karki, R. Leydon, and H. Terho, eds.) pp. 704–12, IASPM-Norden.

Lewis, L. (ed.) (1992). *Adoring Audiences: Fan Culture and Popular Media*. London: Routledge.

Longhurst, B. (2007). *Popular Music and Society*. Cambridge: Polity Press.

Middleton, R. (1990). *Studying Popular Music*. Buckingham: Open University Press.

Middleton, R. (2000). *Reading Pop: Approaches to Textual Analysis in Popular Music*. Oxford: Clarendon Press.

Middleton, R. (2003). *The Cultural Study of Music: A Critical Introduction*. London: Routledge.

O'Reilly, D. (2004). The marketing of popular music. In *Arts Marketing* (F. Kerrigan, P. Fraser, and M. Özbilgin, ed.). Oxford: Elsevier.

O'Reilly, D. and Doherty, K. (2006). *Music B(r)ands Online and Constructing Community*. New York: Peter Lang.

Shuker, R. (1998). *Key Concepts in Popular Music*. London: Routledge.

Sullivan J. (1987). *Vagabonds*. New Model Army Web-Site. [online]. Available from: http://www.newmodelarmy.org [Accessed 30th April 2007].

Titon, J. T. (2003). Text. In *Eight Words for the Study of Expressive Culture* (B. Feintuch, ed.). Champaign: University of Illinois Press.

4

Major case study: Tennis Australia—what to do with a heritage collection of great significance

Pamm Kellett

In its Strategic Plan 2004–2008, Tennis Australia has signalled its desire to take care of the heritage of the sport and their Grand Slam event (The Australian Open Tennis Championships). Tennis Australia has listed 16 strategic priorities, of which one is 'Strengthening, protecting and promoting the wonderful heritage of Australian tennis as a Grand Slam nation and arguably Australia's largest participation sport' (Tennis Australia, 2004, p. 9). Tennis Australia aims to protect and promote the heritage of Australian tennis, and the role that the sport has played in the social history of Australia.

Tennis Australia's commitment to this aim was consolidated in 2004 when it purchased a collection of tennis memorabilia. An entrepreneur from the USA owned the collection and had initially invited the US Tennis Association to purchase it. However, that organization declined. The president of Tennis Australia, a sport history enthusiast, showed an interest in the collection, and having once view the collection, very quickly arranged for its purchase and shipment to Australia. In 2005, Tennis Australia celebrated 100 years of its Grand Slam event, The Australian Open, and has demonstrated a commitment to preserving the sport's history by producing a number of products (such as the DVD '1905–2005 Australian Open: 100 Years in the Making') that celebrates tennis history.

The collection is yet to be catalogued or valued. Of the full shipping-container load of memorabilia, only two boxes have been opened and placed on display. Only the president of Tennis Australia has knowledge of the extent of the collection. Regardless, the limited collection on display is breathtaking. The collection is international in scope with memorabilia from European clubs dating back hundreds of years. As one might imagine, the collection includes a variety of specific items directly related to the sport, such as historic wooden tennis racquets used in indoor 'Royal Tennis' (the first version of the game), white tennis balls, tennis ball storage boxes and tins, tennis string and storage tins, as well as clothing, shoes and boots.

The collection also includes a fascinating array of artefacts related to the game of tennis, but not specifically to the sport. For example, the collection includes: a grandfather clock from a French tennis club dating back to the early 1800s that has a French tennis club scene painted on porcelain set in the clock cabinet; silver gongs once used to signal breaks for 'tea', where the ball is the gong which is struck with a silver replica racquet; china sandwich plates and tea sets with tennis racquets and related scenes painted on them; silver tennis toast racks; statues of elegant tennis players in dresses and suits; children's building blocks with scenes of a tennis country club on them; jewellery, such as cameo necklaces and brooches with tennis players elegantly poised; as well as a collection of tennis artwork. Tennis Australia would like to build a facility to display the memorabilia; however, the organization is at a crossroad as to what to build, where to build it and what elements to include.

Wood (2005) suggests that in order to capitalize on the increasing demand for sports heritage tourism, organizations will need to 'identify imaginative projects and initiatives to mark and celebrate the tradition of sports clubs and places, while at the same time meeting key government objectives for regeneration, education and healthy living' (p. 309). Tennis Australia is faced with the desire to display its collection, but with the dilemma of how to do so.

Internationally, the sport of tennis has experienced some success with its sport museums, and this may also have factored in the president's decision to buy the rare collection. For example, the Lawn Tennis Museum at Wimbledon opened in 1977, however, in 2006 it moved to a new purpose-built facility in the grounds of the All England Club (where the Wimbledon Championships are staged each year). The museum provides visitors with a tour through the men's dressing room of the 1980s, with a digital projection of John McEnroe opening lockers; a cinema that screens a movie of the science of tennis and of great Wimbledon matches of the previous three decades; and static displays and interactive exhibits. A visitor to the museum can also combine it with a guided tour to some of the inner sanctums of the All England Club (however, this is limited during the time of the championship event); a visit to an extensive library for scholars of the game and a viewing of the championship trophies. More than 3000 school children have visited the museum in the year 2005–2006

(Mercer, 2006). For most of the year, the museum reports less than 500 visitors per day; however, during the fortnight of the Wimbledon Championship tournament, the museum reports more than 2000 visitors per day (Sanderson, 2006).

At Roland Garros, the home of the French Open Tennis Championships, the Tenniseum was opened in 2003. It has similar attractions and characteristics to the Lawn Tennis Museum at Wimbledon but includes an exhibition from a French photographer (Jaques-Henri Lartique who died in 1896), including his work on the art of 'fleeting' where some of his photographs are of tennis players in action. It also includes extracts from his writings and drawings. Another exhibition in the Tenniseum contains works from the artist who designed the 2006 Roland Garros poster. The Tenniseum has included artefacts that are certainly important in the history of tennis; however, perhaps less directly linked to the sport than one might normally expect to see in a sport museum.

These two examples, along with lessons from empirically based research as outlined in the chapter entitled 'Sport museums: marketing to engage consumers in sport heritage', might be instructive for Tennis Australia to consider its own collection and potential for a sport museum. Unlike many other sports, tennis is international. The Lawn Tennis Museum at Wimbledon and the Tenniseum have both located their facilities in the grounds of their respective championship tournament facilities. Lessons from other sport heritage sites such as the (successful) Baseball Museum at Wrigley Field and the (unsuccessful) location of the Australian Football League Hall of Fame at a shopping mall suggest that locality within or adjacent to major sporting venues is crucial to success. It is possible that the location adds to the felt experience of nostalgia, or the added excitement of being at a large public stadium, that may be symbolic of a destination in its own right. It is possible that the location places the sport and artefacts in a larger cultural context, therefore assisting the meanings that people take from and socially construct about the heritage sites and objects.

Further, both sports have used their respective championship tournaments as the central theme through which internationally relevant artefacts, rituals and objects are incorporated. In this way, halls of fame have been deliberately created within the museum (and stadia) facility. It is possible that an addition of nostalgic elements has been made by incorporating each of the different heritage characteristics, and an appeal to multiple motives such as learning and pilgrimage by layering heritage elements. Catering for multiple motivations in this way can, without doubt, expand the potential consumer base. Further, both museums incorporate libraries, and tours of the tournament stadia which further caters for multiple motivations of consumers beyond mere nostalgic experiences. This is supported by the advocates of sport-heritage tourism (Gammon and Ramshaw, 2005; Ramshaw and Gammon, 2005).

Opportunities for the future

Tennis Australia has some exciting opportunities when considering location. Its championship tournament is played at Melbourne Park, Melbourne's sporting precinct. Melbourne has had a specific sport-event tourism strategy for some time, and the Australian Open has been a very successful part of the strategy to date. The facility already has some tournament-specific heritage elements such as monuments of past players, and intangible stories, rituals and ceremonies that are attached to the event. Further, also located in the precinct (in the Melbourne Cricket Ground stadium) is the new National Sport Museum. In keeping with lessons from the Australian Football League Hall of Fame (Frost, 2005), Tennis Australia would need to be mindful of ensuring pricing strategies are congruent with those of the National Sport Museum and other substitute services or products in the vicinity. It would seem that opportunities might also exist for linkages and cross promotions between the museums, to engage the heritage or nostalgia sport tourist.

Further cross-promotional opportunities might be considered by Tennis Australia. Volunteers play an important role in the sport of tennis. Museums may be able to assist in volunteer recruitment and retention strategies. It has already been noted that learning about events (behind the scenes experiences) (Farrell et al., 1998) and learning about the culture and ideology of sport organizations (such as the Olympics) (Fairley et al., in press) can assist in repeat volunteering. Tennis Australia must be mindful of incorporating opportunities to visit any heritage sites (including the tournament stadium) that they may develop, into a marketing strategy for volunteer recruitment and retention. Volunteer training or reward programmes might include museum visitation opportunities in the non-event periods.

Cross-promotional opportunities for developing participation might also be considered. The work of Mason et al. (2005) is instructive in asking managers to consider why we build facilities for professional sports as tourist attractions, but do not build large facilities (for junior sport) with tourism strategies in mind. Sport participation pathways (for people to move through the levels of sport participation) must be smooth (Shilbury et al., 2006), and it is interesting to consider the gap in strategic thinking that Mason et al. (2005) allude to. Junior sport is the future of the sport and there is no reason to suggest that this might be beyond the realm of heritage or nostalgia tourism. It is interesting to consider the links between active consumption at a museum and pathways to active consumption of the sport as a participant. This has yet to be explored.

The Tenniseum example of including works and exhibits of French artists (who have a minimal link to the sport itself) may be instructive for the future of sport museums. Sport has had, and continues to have, an impact on the broader culture and vice versa. Sport heritage that recognizes and celebrates the inextricable link between sport and society will serve educational purposes, as well as potentially broaden the appeal for sport heritage sites.

Similar to sport competitions, museum visitation has been reported to be seasonal (IOC, 2006; Sanderson, 2006). Although it has been found that museum visitation might be useful as part of a broader strategy for offsetting the seasonal nature of sports (Higham, 2005), it is obvious that sport competitions are useful for increasing traffic in museums, although on a seasonal basis. This is a delicate balance of facility design and construction. What capacity crowd should be catered for in a sport museum or hall of fame facility? There are no definitive answers as yet on this topic from the academic literature.

The seasonality of museum visitation and sport competition does pose some interesting implications for marketing and cross-promotional strategies. Event attendees (particularly locals) might be encouraged to return visit to the museum at non-event times. Tennis Australia might consider incorporating cross-promotional strategies with the neighbouring National Sports Museum that identifies the seasonal nature of the other sports within the museum, and works with those accordingly. While schools have been the target of off-season or non-event time group promotional strategies to increase visitation to museums (Mercer, 2006), lessons from other tourist attractions must be incorporated. For example, the Melbourne Aquarium hosts catered corporate functions, celebrations, parties and weddings, in each of its different aquarium spaces (MFS Living and Leisure Group, 2006). Sport stadia already have the capacity to cater for such events and consideration for such elements could be designed into other sport heritage sites at the stadia, such as museums and halls of fame. Who wouldn't want to boast about the night they had dinner with their favourite tennis hero?

Conclusion

Sport heritage tourism is an exciting and rapidly expanding industry. The heritage collection poses some interesting opportunities and challenges for Tennis Australia in presenting heritage items of international significance. Although the academic literature that explores sport heritage and related heritage sport tourism and nostalgia sport tourism is in its infancy, there are some useful lessons from which Tennis Australia can draw. The sport heritage industry is burgeoning, with museum and heritage facility planners, designers, architects and managers providing high-class facilities that allow nations, sport organizations and fans to celebrate the rich history and culture that sport offers. Scholars have yet to 'catch up' with practitioners in detailed studies of the consumers and consumption of sport heritage sites and experiences. However, with continued dialogue between scholars and practitioners, our knowledge of sport heritage, and all that it offers society, will move forward and important lessons will continue to be learned about the management and marketing of sport heritage.

References

Fairley, S., Kellett, P. and Green, B. C. (2007). Volunteering abroad: motives for travel to volunteer at the Athens Olympic Games. *Journal of Sport Management*, 21(1), 41–57.

Farrell, J. M., Johnston, M. E. and Twynam, G. D. (1998). Volunteer motivation, satisfaction, and management at an elite sporting competition. *Journal of Sport Management*, 12, 288–30.

Frost, W. (2005). The sustainability of sports heritage attractions: lessons from the Australian Football League Hall of Fame. *Journal of Sport Tourism*, 10(4), 295–305.

Gammon, S. and Ramshaw, G. (2005). Editorial: placing heritage in sport tourism. *Journal of Sport Tourism*, 10(4), 225–7.

Higham, J. (2005). Sport tourism as an attraction for managing seasonality. *Sport in Society*, 8(2), 238–62.

IOC (2006). Museum news. <http://www.olympic.org/uk/passion/museum/events/full_story_uk.asp?id=1883> (accessed 1 September 2006).

Mason, D., Duquette, G. H. and Scherer, J. (2005). Heritage, sport tourism and Canadian junior hockey: nostalgia for social experience or sport place? *Journal of Sport Tourism*, 10(4), 253–71.

Mercer, D. (2006). Tennis on display. *International Tennis Federation*, Summer, 28–31.

MFS Living and Leisure Group (2006). Five star functions. <http://www.melbourneaquarium.com.au/content.asp?itemid=18> (accessed 1 September).

Ramshaw, G. and Gammon, S. (2005). More than just nostalgia? Exploring the heritage/sport tourism nexus. *Journal of Sport Tourism*, 10(4), 229–41.

Sanderson, K. (2006). Mather serves up tennis museum. *Design Week*, 6 April, p. 6.

Shilbury, D., Deane, J. and Kellett, P. (2006). *Sport Management in Australia: An Organisational Overview*. Bentleigh, VIC: Strategic Sport Management.

Tennis Australia (2004). *Tennis: Serving Up Strategy*. Melbourne: Tennis Australia.

Wood, J. (2005). Olympic opportunity: realizing the value of sports heritage for tourism in the UK. *Journal of Sport Tourism*, 10(4), 307–21.

Part C

Marketing, revenue and retail

5

Major case study: Welcome to our house— satisfying visitors to the historic house museum

Linda Young

The first image conjured up by the idea 'historic house museum' is probably a grand mansion filled with antique furniture, à la National Trust. The second might be a humble vernacular cottage, perhaps the birthplace of a hero of the nation. Further images might include a magnate's extravagant country house, a famous artist's apartment and studio, a reconstructed prehistoric house or a village of folk houses from far-flung regions.

Historic dwellings constitute a numerous and significant type of heritage site throughout the Western world, old and new, and are being increasingly developed in Asia. Though house museums are as various as described above, they share characteristics that make them a special marketing challenge. The primary condition of the house museum is that it comes as is—a fully formed product. House museums are almost never developed in response to a customer focus. Rather, they exist in a genteel miasma of expectation that audiences will recognize the virtues of house museum visiting and will naturally want to be enlightened and educated by exposure to their fascinating histories. There is a kernel of truth here, but it is by no means always the case. Some famous destinations-in-themselves—such as the palace of Versailles or George Washington's house, Mt Vernon—are sufficiently well known to be at least somewhat meaningful to all potential visitors. But the majority of house museums are much less self-explanatory.

Enticing sufficient paying visitors to maintain their operations, is a major challenge of institutional survival for many house museums. Some close; some revert to private ownership with occasional open days; many struggle to find sponsorship and grant funding. The majority get by on minimal resources. Other options available for house museums are to shift their focus to the market and develop their specialist heritage resource in ways that accord with what the public wants to see and do when it decides to visit the homes of the past.

The nature of the historic house museum

From the marketing point of view, historic houses (and other heritage buildings preserved as museums of themselves, such as courthouses, schoolhouses, shops and workshops) are a particularly obdurate species of cultural product. The house is in and of itself the resource, the attraction, the heritage. Its historic fabric, internal furnishings or collections, and grounds or gardens amount to a substantial physical presence that usually require intensive conservation in the first place, followed by ongoing maintenance and perhaps a continuing programme of further conservation. But once conserved, the house is a closed, complete world, generally frozen in time. Thus historic houses have developed among many people a poisonous reputation for static boredom.

Further constraints in opening a house museum follow from the special value that makes them worth keeping as places of heritage. It is necessary to protect fragile elements such as frescoed walls and precious carpets (or decaying mud-bricks and fragmentary wallpaper) by not permitting visitors to exert pressure which could damage the fabric. It is not that visitors are dangerous, but that they are numerous: one person or five walking on a parquet (or old linoleum) floor won't damage it, but 50 or 500 a day, every day, has the potential to damage. For example, a crowd can push individuals against panelled walls or cramped furniture. Where a chateau may be big enough to absorb busloads of visitors, it's very difficult to introduce a busload safely into a more modest house originally designed for family use. Hence it must be recognized that some houses are so small or vulnerable that visitation must be limited to allow any sustainable public access at all.

Thus constrained by conditions for safe access to house museums, visitors experience what is essentially a walk through a house, usually interpreted by guides, labels or perhaps an audio device. They see the spaces, the rooms, the décor, the furnishings, and with the information and perspectives offered by whatever interpretation is available, they are encouraged to understand why this house is historically or aesthetically important. It may be that the intricate mouldings and old master paintings demonstrate the lifestyle of the rich and powerful and the artistry of specialist craftsmen. Or the few, small rooms filled with simple furniture and a piece-worker's bench in the kitchen-cum-parlour shows the opposite lifestyle of a poor family. If a famous figure grew up here, or lived in such circumstances, the visitor is expected to ponder the connections between a great mind and his/her everyday environment.

It has to be said that a walk through a house, looking at furniture, listening to a guide or an audio device, is a passive mode of experiencing heritage. What visitors get out of it depends on what knowledge resources they themselves bring: the well informed can probably find what they want and expect. But the less informed can only wonder, and either enjoy fantasizing about historic life or feel frustrated and alienated by their ignorance and distance. In one respect, both groups often come to the same conclusion: once you've been to a house museum, you've done it—there's no need ever to make a return visit.

Who visits historic houses and why?

More than a decade of visitor studies around the English-speaking world now shows that museum visitors are a discrete but segmented group. Excluding the input of large foreign tourism, about 40 per cent of domestic US and UK populations visit 'occasionally' and about 15 per cent visit 'several times a year'. The latter possess high educational qualifications and therefore tend to be well off; they visit many types of museums, because they understand and enjoy the kinds of essentially intellectual experiences that museums tend to offer. The occasional visitors are also in the same demographic, but they use the museum visit as a social environment for family and friendly interaction; they see museums as 'good' places to take the children, or the out-of-town visitors, for an interesting experience, a pleasant café, a walk in the grounds. They may value the cachet of in-group knowledge by being au fait with famous works and keeping up with the latest exhibitions, or they may feel that visiting cultural institutions is among the things good family citizens ought to do.

House museum visiting appears to fit these parameters, with no startling exceptions. Houses that are essentially aesthetic experiences, such as the art-collector Isabella Stewart Gardner's house in Boston and the arts-and-crafts designer William Morris's Red House at Bexleyheath, London, attract mainly the same, highest-educated group that visits art museums: knowledgeable about art history and its movements, aware of the role of famous collectors and designers.

The houses of famous characters appeal to a wider span of visitors, but often for idiosyncratic reasons. Some will make a personal pilgrimage to a favourite author's or composer's house: highly emotional responses are frequent at John Lennon's childhood house in Liverpool, and small, romantic sighs punctuate visits to Walt Whitman's house in Camden, New Jersey. Others will go to considerable efforts to take their children to the house of a famous patriot or key historical figure, because it is part of their moral or educational development, for example, Martin Luther King's birthplace in Atlanta (part of a national trail of historic places of the civil rights movement). In the old, authoritarian cultures of Asia, houses associated with national heroes such as Mao Zedong (birthplace in Shaoshen, Hunan province) and Ho Chi Minh (residence in Hanoi) were opened as shrines where the populace could revere the great leader. Today, they continue as popular domestic tourist destinations. The same spirit of patriotic civil religion motivates visitors to the John F. Kennedy National Historic Site (his suburban birthplace in Boston), and the birthplace and ancestral home of Mahatma Gandhi (in Porbandur, Gujarat).

In the UK, Europe and Asia, aesthetics and fame are often blended in the palaces of royalty. Few visitors have deep historical knowledge of kings and queens, but everyone has a fantasy of a royal palace, and the splendid furnishings and artworks that can be viewed in situ (as opposed to the relative sterility of an art museum) satisfy, and sometimes surprise, most kinds of culturally aware visitors.

This observation shifts the focus directly to the idea of the cultural tourist, conceived as interested in heritage in all its manifestations. At the same time, as the examples above suggest, people are motivated to visit particular house museums for experiences which relate to their personal interests. If there is any type of house museum that could be claimed to be attractive to all, it may be the combination of a grand house and a famous personage. Even a little familiarity with a great name seems to ease occasional visitors' resistance to grandiosity: examples are Monticello, Virginia, Thomas Jefferson's self-designed house, now accompanied by detailed reconstructions of slave houses and farm outbuildings; and Blenheim Palace, Oxfordshire, trophy home of the first Duke of Marlborough and birthplace of Winston Churchill.

Monticello and Blenheim are both splendid houses, opulently decorated (on different scales), in which they express the most characteristic form of British (and ex-British) house museum, mockingly known as stately homes and more correctly described as country houses. Yet the mockery points to the tension between educated appreciation of, and ignorant ogling at, aristocratic taste, which is palpable (though difficult to pinpoint) in the UK, and not unknown in the USA. It colours the image of the National Trust and other custodians of such houses, and shapes the suspicion that grand house museums are not suitable for 'ordinary' folk. A technique to extend appeal that satisfies museologists, (museum specialists who might be unaware) it could be called re-branding) is to add a broader historical context to the great house by presenting the 'below stairs' servant or slave dimension of house life. The social history perspective that helps to express the heritage significance of the site is simultaneously perceived by less aesthetically confident visitors as an intelligible entrée into the historic house experience.

Market research suggests that visitors prefer not to be overawed by their heritage visiting experiences. This makes the houses that represent historic periods or regional geography without particular association to heroes or events the most generally user friendly. They tend to focus on the similar-but-different minutiae of daily life set in various periods and places: medieval peasant, pion-eer frontier, urban Victorian, immigrant German, Chinese ethnic minority or whatever. Demonstrating how fluent is the house museum crossover between cultures is the Jim Thompson House, Bangkok: an American silk merchant's 1950s construct of several traditional Thai houses, the house is adapted to Western taste but displays local culture and products. Visitors to this kind of site are specially open to perceiving personal connections with life in the past in a process that may stretch from the delighted nostalgia of 'we had one of those!' to the Gothic horror of 'how'd you like to cook/wash/live in that?' At the same time, the appetite of most visitors for such experiences is finite, and the large number of these generic historic house museums can dull the taste and spoil the appetite.

Non-visitors to museums of any kind comprise about half the population. Is it worth trying to lure them in? Famous examples of offering alternative attractions to the British stately home have changed the nature of house museum visiting at some sites. To attract a new audience to Longleat House, Wiltshire, the Marquess of Bath introduced a lion enclosure which by 1966 grew into the UK's first safari park. Visitors now choose to inspect the house and/or the safari park (by car or boat), the children's adventure castle and maze, the butterfly garden, the miniature railway and further attractions. It is impossible to call such a tourist complex merely a house museum, just as the Palace House at Beaulieu, Hampshire, has been overtaken by the National Motor Museum in its grounds—a magnet for the kind of boys who wouldn't be seen dead in a country house. Nevertheless, some audiences will never be tempted to enjoy visiting a historic house.

The marketing perspective in house museums

It is a rare house museum that doesn't want or need to increase visitation, whether to cover costs or to fulfil its public mandate. Despite the constraints of heritage significance, fragile fabric, passive presentation, sometimes limited space and sometimes grandiloquent image, most house museums could develop their audiences by choosing to focus on visitor wants and needs as well as con-servation. The heritage integrity of the site must always be paramount—it is the brand of every house museum—but most houses have sufficient potential to encompass a much wider span of possibilities than is usually envisaged.

In some opinions, the Longleat example crosses the boundary of integrity, but it must be said that the house itself remains one of the finest specimens of Elizabethan design in the UK open to the public. A smaller estate might not be capable of offering alternative experiences to those who do not fancy historic houses, yet few open range zoos also offer a notable historic house visit. If this is a problem, it is likely to be a consequence of how core business is defined!

The range of further typical aspects of house museums includes gardens, farms and farm animals, historic collections such as artworks, musical instru-ments and horse-drawn carriages, and the whole topic of heritage conservation.

Among this range is a multitude of possibilities to satisfy visitors who might not be very interested in domestic presentations or highly decorated galleries of family portraits.

Gardens constitute a huge attraction at many house museums. Gardening is cited as the most popular hobby (after watching TV) in the suburban world, and visiting well-kept gardens is an agreeable variation on doing real gardening. Strolling around a garden with friends or picnicking with family brings a larger audience to many house museums than those who actually pay to enter the house itself. In fact, some gardens are more famous than the houses they surround, such as at Giverny near Paris, where Claude Monet planted the water lilies which he painted for 40 years. Monet's house is part of the ticketed visit, but it is clearly the garden walk that enchants most visitors. Enhancing the garden experience therefore makes good sense from the points of view of both the heritage manager who wants visitors to appreciate the significance of the site, and of the marketing manager who wants visitors to be so satisfied that they will spend in the café and shop, spread positive word-of-mouth reports to their friends and revisit the museum.

Animal attractions to historic houses do not have to stretch to lions, as at Longleat. More historically appropriate animals such as ornamental birds, horses and farm animals fascinate visitors because they have largely disappeared from our world. Such animals make good sense in interpreting the historical meanings of the site, and can be seen, smelled and sometimes touched to great effect in re-created village settings such as Old World Wisconsin, where 14 original historic farmhouses, plus associated outbuildings, have been relocated to demonstrate the flavour of pioneer settlement from many parts of Europe to the USA. Keeping animals introduces further management challenges in safety and hygiene for animals and humans, but offers a sure recipe for child-visitor happiness: a cost–benefit analysis for each site to consider.

To curators and connoisseurs, the great strength of collections in house museums is their authentic connection to the structure: artworks, furnishings, decorative schemes, or even humble kitchen settings and home–workshop equipment such as looms, can be perceived in their intended human environments. Reflecting an irony of the success of the conventional museum, much of the public is now more accustomed to seeing these relics of other ages and cultures detached and made into specimens, hung on an institutional wall. One of the aims of such exhibition-style display is to enable more interpretive explanation of objects, and this advantage can sometimes be introduced into the house museum as well. For a while the house constitutes a total environment, it lacks the humans who once made it a functional living site within particular social and economic contexts: dimensions that can be addressed via the exhibition medium. A stimulating example was the cooperative exhibition 'Maids and Mistresses' on women's lives, upstairs and downstairs, presented at seven house museums in Yorkshire in 2004. Exhibitions can also be a means of presenting the larger collections which would once have been cycled around the house by season or event, or kept in reserve.

The theme of the physical conservation of heritage houses is of interest to a wider audience than might be expected. A spectacular example is the case of Uppark, a National Trust house in Sussex which almost burned down in 1989; it was rebuilt, based on post-fire archaeology and the re-invention of many traditional building and decorating techniques. A visit to Uppark now commences at the interpretive centre to introduce its destruction, rescue and rebuilding; in the house, guides help visitors to recognize the original and the reconstructed. In a less drastic perspective, displays of materials, conservation of walls, paintings, textiles and so forth meets the interest of technically minded visitors at many a house.

Targeted activity programmes are the way to exploit historic house resources, shaped by a clear focus on market segments. The Historic Houses Trust of New South Wales, for instance, offers 'convict transportation' on a sailing ship across Sydney Harbour, followed by a sleepover in the convict barracks in Sydney; and 'dawn chores' with the farm manager at Rouse Hill House, helping to feed the cows and collect the eggs before a pancake breakfast. Such programmes are demanding to operate and not cheap, but they are regularly sold out because they offer the balance of heritage content, interactivity and parent–child experience that a certain market wants. Responding to a different demographic, the Historic Houses Trust holds an annual 'Fifties Fair' at the modernist Rose Seidler House, featuring 1950s music, dance and fashion, car displays, stalls and memorabilia, in which retro-style meets historic modernism—a long way from mahogany and old lace.

Engaging the attention of visitors via living history interpretation of houses is a colourful but resource-intensive technique: the quality of accuracy is central to the brand image of historic houses and must be upheld. As noted above, the absence of historic people from the halls and kitchens of house museums can make them seem impersonal, however friendly and informative the guide is. Costumed interpreters tending the fireplace, grooming a horse or making tea add colour to the atmosphere as well as a further dimension of understanding how people interacted with the historic domestic environment. The impression of 'life' can be an important stimulus to visitors who are suspicious of history as the dead past, enabling them to enter into human relationships across time. Yet they can also be startled by the experience, as in engaging with a black man dressed in elegant eighteenth century costume at Colonial Williamsburg, Virginia: the clothing seems aristocratic to the modern eye, not what is expected of a slave character. Colonial Williamsburg has trod a sometimes difficult path in presenting the evils of the past. Even well-informed visitors were shaken by the re-creation of a slave auction in 1994, and it has not become a regular event: some elements of history should not be trivialized by presentation, even for so-called edutainment.

Yet new audiences are not the be-all and end-all of house museum audience development: 'core' house visitors need continuous nurturing with reasons to make regular revisits. Seasonal events offer opportunities: Easter egg hunts, Christmas carols, garden festivals, summer music, winter book talks, weekend workshops and so on. The loyalty of core visitors is often concentrated by membership schemes offering specialist programmes and social gatherings, all of them opportunities for fund raising. Members or 'friends' can also be strategic advocates for the house when a non-management voice is required to defend or build its resources.

Now standard at most house museums is the café and shop, understood by marketers as the kind of comfort and satisfaction that caps a success-ful museum visit by providing sustenance and relaxation, and enabling the memory to live on via a souvenir. The educated heritage house visitor might once have sneered at early retail efforts in house museums, but the present popu-larity of museum shops is proof that museum retailers can accurately pinpoint the tastes of visitors. Books and postcards were the original stock-in-trade, and they remain important, but the house museum shop of today focuses on domestic and garden lifestyle products with a historical or artistic edge, sometimes including reproductions of special items such as china and textiles. House museum visiting is predominantly the sphere of better-off seg-ments of society, and their disposable income can be happily converted into profits for rarely well-off institutions.

Cafés are often volunteer-operated tea-and-scone operations, but as historic house management professionalizes and visitor numbers grow, the need for industrial catering skills and equipment has converted the café into an out-sourced business. Locating services such as café and restrooms, and the con-comitant retro-fitting of modern plumbing and electrics, can challenge the integrity of the historic house site, specially when required on a large scale. Sensitive design by heritage-aware architects and builders is critical to main-tain integrity while meeting contemporary visitor needs.

But having achieved the necessary conveniences, house museums can become prime venues for social and commercial events, and for filming advertisements and feature films. Such venue hire is an increasingly valuable income stream for many historic houses, capitalizing on their essence as unique places. By meeting the demand for imaginative settings, special events such as weddings can be enhanced in the fantasy experience of, say, medieval grandeur or neoclassical elegance; the market for this kind of colour at big events is substantial.

Futurologists observe that the long trend of growing middle-class afflu-ence and values typical of the West, and now spreading in the huge nations of Asia, provides a ready audience for museums of all kinds. This is the context in which heritage sites and museums offer the blend of culture-as-leisure that motivates cultural tourism. As promising as it sounds for marketing house museums, the taste for museum visiting is still tinged with an elite cultural aura that makes some potential visitors uneasy. Reassuring such doubts and transforming them into expectations of satisfaction via provision of a wide and various span of experiences that appeal to heritage beginners as well as the cognoscenti, is the quest of today's house museum marketing.

Retailing and the museum: applying the seven 'P's of services marketing to museum stores

Sandra Mottner

In the past, museums have often only ventured into retailing by selling post-cards, books and rolls of film at the admissions desk. The 'shop' was seen as a minor source of revenue and a convenience for visitors but had little import-ance in the overall life of the museum. Today, museum retailing operations often have multiple stores in a variety of formats including catalogues, off-site stores, licensing programmes, as well as sophisticated websites. The trans-formation from a small 'afterthought' to an important museum function has resulted in major revenue production in many cases. Successful museum stores that make a significant financial contribution to their museum are also dedi-cated to extending the museum's mission, the museum's identity and the vis-itor's museum experience. In these cases, visitors to the museum are able to continue their museum experience through the purchase of books, reproduc-tions, collection-inspired products and meaningful gifts that help to further the museum's overall mission of learning, experiencing and building a relationship with the museum's collection.

The extended museum experience offered by museum stores is most suc-cessful when it is an integral part of the museum's overall marketing strategy. Since the objective of most museums is to provide an educational experience, to maintain and preserve the collection, and to enhance the collection (McLean, 1997), then museum stores can help achieve these objectives in two major ways: by raising funds through the sale of merchandise, and by furthering the educa-tional/experiential mission of the museum through retailing marketing strat-egies (Mottner and Ford, 2005). Museum stores with effective marketing plans can produce financial contributions to the museum itself as well as provide visitors with products and other experiences that aid in education, enjoyment and an extension of the visitors' relationship with the museum (Theobald, 2000). Because shopping is very familiar to most people, and indeed is often viewed as a recreational, and even a leisure time experience, the museum store stands in a unique position to extend the museum visit in a familiar type of environment. Further, the museum store also provides another point at which the customer and the museum can form a relationship, often through the personal assistance of the museum store staff. The Colonial Williamsburg Foundation case later in this chapter provides an example of how relationships are formed between costumed historical museum store staff members and visitors. These relationships often both enhance the historical knowledge the visitor acquires and result in increased financial contributions both in museum store purchases and in donations to the foundation.

Development of a strategic marketing plan for a museum store operation can be done using the principles of services marketing (McLean, 1997). Since services marketing is concerned with the marketing of intangibles, it is an extremely useful model for museums in general (McLean, 1997). For example, while museums house tangible collections, the visitor leaves with only a memory or an experience rather than an object. The museum store, while selling tangible objects, is also an extension of the museum itself. So, while the services marketing field offers a number of different dimensions it also offers an expanded set of marketing tools that extends beyond the four 'P's of product, price, promotion and place, with which to implement a marketing strategy. Consequently, a service marketing strategy using the seven 'P's of service (Booms and Bitner, 1981) is an appropriate marketing tool for retailers and particularly for museum stores. The seven 'P's of services marketing—namely product/service, price, promotion, place, people, physical evidence and process—can be used to realize both financial objectives as well as education objectives. This chapter will utilize the framework of the seven 'P's of services marketing to identify specific marketing strategies critical in developing tools to implement an effective marketing strategy for museum stores, and then offer a method for evaluating the strategy itself.

Product strategies

The key marketing decision for retailers is that of product. For-profit retailers make the product decision based on the needs of their target market which in turn allows the retailer to maintain a particular image and forms part of their overall competitive positioning strategy. However, in the museum store setting, the product decisions may be both customer (market) driven as well as mission (educational/collection) driven. In the case of most museums, some form of constraint also plays a role in product decisions. The most common constraints are those related to non-profit tax issues, the influence of powerful stakeholders such as major donors or board members for example, and limited resources for product development. The US Internal Revenue Service, for example, maintains that products sold by non-profit organizations such as museums must be related to the mission of the organization. The judgment as to what is related or not is made on a case-by-case basis. In the USA, a museum's mission must be primarily educational in order to maintain non-profit tax status.

Today's museum visitors are a varied group and, depending upon the type of museum (art, history, zoological, scientific, industrial, etc.), the visitors represent a variety of demographic and psychographic configurations. Each visitor segment has differing needs in terms of products and it is the museum store's challenge to provide products that appeal to the key customer segments, while operating within the constraints of the particular museum. Often the customer profile changes seasonally thus compounding the product preferences.

In order to maximize financial revenues, a museum store needs to use some market research to determine the product needs of their visitors. Useful information may be obtained from market research undertaken by the museum, such as target market profiles, seasonal visitation patterns, and perceptions and preferences for different collections and special exhibitions. In addition, specific museum stores data about visitors' purchase patterns, preferences, product needs and particularly purchasing motivations, will help the store develop a product mix that fits the needs of visitors.

Another source of information that will help museum stores make more financially rewarding product decisions is the use of a POS (point of sale) merchandise management system that tracks sales at the SKU (stock keeping unit) level. Drawbacks of these systems are that the initial investment may be onerous for a very small museum and that the information obtained from the system is only as good as the information put into it when product is received, sold, lost or damaged, or adjusted for physical inventories. A good POS merchandise management system aids product analysis by providing sell-through rates by individual SKU which can aid in more accurately forecasting future product needs. Historical sales information is usually the best predictor of future best sellers, unless a major category of merchandise has not previously been carried in the museum store or a product was chronically out of stock so true demand was unrecorded.

While making as much financial return as possible it is also important for the museum store to contribute to the overall mission of the museum. This translates in most cases to making sure that the product in the museum store is in some way related to or reflective of the museum's collection. While some product can be found on the open market that reflects the museum's collection, best selling products are often adaptations or even reproductions of museum pieces. Product development with input and assistance from the curatorial staff has been shown to be an effective way of helping museum stores meet mission-related objectives. The product development process also yields unique and often custom-made products that form part of the museum's competitive advantage over ordinary gift stores, tourist shops or other retail outlets.

The product development process can be formal or informal but is often best performed if there are a number of people involved, including retail management, curatorial staff, educational staff, suppliers and other key players, depending upon the museum (Theobald, 2000). By involving a number of key players in the development and selection of new products, certain standards for product quality may be determined and agreed upon. Similarly, minimum sell-through rates, or return on investment levels can be determined. Some museum staff from non-retail areas may offer suggestions as to possible product sources. A collaborative process helps to insure that the retail operation is meeting both its mission and financial objectives while fostering

Table 5.1 Product development options (adapted from Theobald, 2000, pp. 65–6).

Product development option	Process	Example
No adaptation needed	Product that relates to the museum's collection is bought from manufacturers	Book about the museum's collection
Manufacturer's product development	A manufacturer develops a product that relates to the museum's collection but they also sell it on the open market	Tricorn hats are sold to a number of historically related museums, sites and tourist shops
Interpretation	An element of a piece in the museum's collection or an element from the museum's building(s) is used to develop product that may be totally unrelated to the original collection item	A stained glass window in a historic building is used as a design element in a silk scarf
Adaptation	An item in the collection is reproduced with an adaptation for colour, size or fabrication	Pottery is reproduced from the collection but in new colours
Reproduction	An item in the collection is reproduced often using the same processes used to make the original	A piece of glass stemware from the collections is reproduced

more cross-disciplinary discussion, sharing of information and a sense that all museum staff are there to achieve the same objectives.

Product development can follow a variety of paths, which range from fairly simple to very complex. Table 5.1 outlines a progressively more involved set of product development options open to the museum store.

The perception of product quality increases for the visitor as the level of adaptation or product development increases. Visitors generally value uniqueness. Consequently, commanding higher prices becomes possible with adaptations and reproductions which helps to defray development costs as well as realize greater gross margins. Indeed, a museum may develop a line of products that are unique and the products are saleable outside the museum venue. The museum may decide to implement a licensing programme, whereby the manufacturer can sell the reproduction on the open market while paying a royalty for the design to the museum.

Price strategies

Pricing is critical for maximizing financial contributions and museum retailers can choose from a number of pricing methods. Most museum retailers use a cost-based method of pricing as opposed to a demand-based method. However, while cost-based is very appropriate, unique products that are highly desirable and in limited supply can handle demand-based pricing (in this case a higher than normal markup over the cost), as long as the product's sales in units do not decrease as the price goes up. Most for-profit retailers are concerned about pricing compared to competitors. A unique product assortment often means that the museum store does not need to be as concerned about competition but rather about offering a perceived value to the museum shopper. Therefore, the marketing research described in the previous 'Product strategy' discussion should also collect information regarding value perceptions for various visitor segments. Because multiple visitor segments usually shop at a museum store, most successful stores develop a product and price assortment plan. A product and price assortment plan allows the museum store manager to plan for the needs of each visitor segment. For example, the Colonial Williamsburg case study in this chapter demonstrates how one museum meets multiple needs.

Promotion strategies

Promotion of the museum store is best achieved through an integrated marketing communications strategy where a number of promotional tools are used synergistically. The promotional tools can be broken down into two major categories: promotional tools such as catalogues, direct mail pieces and Internet websites that communicate information about the museum store at the same time as providing a vehicle for shopping; and promotional tools such as public relations, advertising and direct mail that are used to encourage traffic and hopefully purchases from any of the museum store venues. Just as with product and pricing strategies, an effective relationship between the promotional strategy and the museum collection and overall mission, creates and fosters a unique image and identity for the museum and museum store in the visitor's mind.

Excellent retail websites, such as those run by the Metropolitan Museum of Art and the Smithsonian Institute, reflect the identity of their museum. Catalogues from Winterthur Museum, for example, do the same. Effective catalogues and websites reflect the collection and the museum's identity in their products as well as in the graphics, colour choices, typefaces and copy. In fact, the text offers bits of educational information for readers on the history of the product, the artist or the time period represented. So, like the product and price strategies, the promotional strategies can be designed to achieve two objectives—financial and educational.

Tools used to encourage traffic in the museum store are often less educational but should reflect the museum's image through font style, design, colour choices, paper choice and graphic details. These tools include signage, direct mail pieces and print advertising. Collateral material such as brochures for the museum should also mention the store. Unique bags often serve as promotional tools or even educational devices. For example, the historic stores at Colonial Williamsburg bags carry an eighteenth century design.

While all of the tools in a promotional communications strategy can be effective, the most effective means of promoting the museum store is word of mouth. Positive word of mouth is achieved through consistent, superior product quality and quality experiences in the store, through the website or when ordering through a catalogue. Managing word of mouth can be part of a service marketing strategy for a museum store when the staff of the museum is hired and trained and reinforced to provide exceptional customer service. This will be further discussed under 'People strategies'.

Place strategies

Museum traffic patterns combined with the placement of the museum store are critical in maximizing financial contribution. Stores that are next to the museum's *exit* are the most financially successful. Visitors naturally continue their museum experience in the museum store. Finding means to continue the museum experience through the purchase of unique products related to the museum, meets both financial and educational missions of the museum itself. Museum stores located at the *entrance* to the museum are also inviting to customers who are not touring the museum itself and are the second most productive location in terms of sales. Internet-based stores can be integrated into the physical store locations, stand-alone order sites or through normal means of Internet access. On-line museum store shopping opportunities are usually a key link on the museum's website. The link needs to be easy to use and easy to locate.

Many museums have multiple store locations because the museum is extremely large, and different museum stores cater to distinctly different target markets. For example, Colonial Williamsburg has a 'Little Patriots' store specifically geared for children. Many museums add temporary stores to complement a special collection. Some museums even develop off-site stores or kiosks particularly during holiday shopping times. While most museum stores have some degree of separation from the collection, interesting exceptions are the historic stores at Colonial Williamsburg which are mentioned in this chapter's case study. These stores are fully functioning museum stores but are primarily located on the Duke of Gloucester Street in the heart of the colonial city. They serve not only a revenue producing purpose, but also an educational service to visitors as well.

People strategies

While museum stores can employ managers, product developers, buyers, stock people, etc., the key museum store employee, in the visitor's perception, is the person who helps them buy products. Making astute hiring or volunteer choices, and thorough and ongoing training is an essential strategy that will result in positive financial and educational results. Hiring people who have a passion for the collection has an enormous effect when that excitement and knowledge are shared with visitors. Training in collection-based information, as well as store procedures and professional selling skills, means that staff members can become professional and effective members of the museum team dedicated to the mission of the museum.

Museum store managers need to be hired and trained with care as well. Generally, managerial appointments may come from the museum/museum store staff or be hired with experience in retailing. But the professional museum store manager needs to have a strong understanding of retailing as well as an understanding and deep appreciation of the museum and its collection. This means that most new managers will need training in either retailing skills or museum collection knowledge.

Physical evidence strategies

A visit to a museum is an intangible experience. Nothing physical is taken away except perhaps a brochure or a product from the museum store. Visitors form memories of their museum experience through all their senses: sight, smell, sound, touch (sometimes) and even taste on occasion. The atmospherics that trigger those senses can be mostly controlled and the museum store's strategy needs to include a plan that helps the visitor continue to make positive museum memories through the use of their senses.

A simple example is what a visitor sees in a store. If products are positioned in a way that tells a story that reminds a visitor of something they liked in the museum, the visitor might wish to purchase one of the products that allow them to take home a tangible reminder of the museum. Music is another trigger that jogs the memory. The sound of eighteenth century music in the Williamsburg Craft House reminds visitors of what they have seen in the historic buildings.

Visual merchandising and display of products and the layout of the store help to enhance revenues and can assist the educational objectives. Attractive, clean merchandise is more appealing and the traditional retail strategy of grouping-related products together leads to larger average sales per visitor. For example, merchandise grouped by its association to a part of the museum collection helps to remind visitors of what they have seen in the museum and what it meant. Other standard retailing techniques such as placing small impulse items near registers; installing exciting and attractive wall displays which draw visitors further through a store; and providing well-signed and beautifully organized jewellery in a case to encourage visitors to take a closer look at the pieces, will all help to build average sales.

In some museum stores it is possible for demonstrations to take place. This is especially true if hand-made, unique products are in the assortment. Tradespersons demonstrate how something is made and interact with visitors; sales are made and visitors learn about and appreciate the museum even more.

Process strategies

Large crowds pose a 'process' challenge to museums and their stores. Plans for handling lines and crowds result in fewer unhappy visitors to the store. Multiple registers, fast transactions, traffic flow, efficient credit and debit capabilities, and fast re-stocking of best sellers, result in more positive experiences for visitors and more revenue for the store. These seemingly mundane issues have a major effect on visitors' perceptions of a museum store and hence on the museum. This is especially the case if the service fails to satisfy. Behind the scenes, other 'process' issues such as receiving product, shipping out customer orders in a timely manner, re-stocking product, handling and securing money, scheduling staff and housekeeping, all have a significant effect on revenues and profits.

Evaluating museum store performance

Marketing strategies must be evaluated to see if they are successful or need to be changed or eliminated in the future. Financially oriented strategies should be evaluated using financial data. International organizations such as the Museum Stores Association (www.museumdistrict.com) offer excellent tools for measuring and benchmarking financial information, such as sales per square foot, sales by type of museum, sales per full time equivalent (FTE), and so on. It is essential that a museum and its museum store manager know what financial contribution the store is making to the museum.

In order to measure how well a museum store is supporting the mission of the museum itself, more subjective measures are needed, especially if the mission is largely educational because objective measures (pre- and post-tests of learning) are expensive and problematic. The following statements are offered as a visitor post-purchase survey tool based on the seven 'P's of a service marketing strategy, and can be used to gain an indication of the effectiveness of a museum store in meeting non-financial objectives:

1. The products in the store helped me to understand the museum's collection/subject matter better.
2. The store promoted the museum's collection/subject matter.
3. The prices in the store reflected the quality of the products.
4. The store's location was near the museum's collection.
5. When I bought something from the store I felt like I was taking a 'part of the museum' with me.
6. The people in the store helped me to remember my museum visit.
7. The displays in the store helped me to remember the items I saw in the museum.
8. The museum store seemed very organized.

Case study: the Colonial Williamsburg Foundation

Located in Williamsburg, Virginia (USA), the Colonial Williamsburg Foundation manages a large outdoor museum which is the restored colonial capital of Virginia during the pre-revolutionary war period (1770). This museum city includes more than 500 restored and reconstructed buildings, including a group of historic stores which are recreations of stores that actually operated during the eighteenth century. The historic stores are a good example of how the seven 'P's of a service marketing strategy are employed. The historic stores stock and sell products that would have been sold in a colonial store during that period including millinery, stoneware tankards, food products and imported cream-ware china, to name just a few. Curators and product development staff have traditionally developed products for these stores from original store inventories and other historical sources. The products are developed and priced to represent a variety of values to differing customer groups. Fine gold jewellery, pewter reproductions are found in some stores while very inexpensive rock candy and fifes are offered in other stores. The store staff members wear costumes of the period and have historically based training so that they can not only interpret their store and its products but provide information about the town and historical events as well. Store staff members form relationships with many visitors by helping visitors find specific products, corresponding with a visitor after they have left the museum, or having their pictures taken with visitors and their families. The historic stores display goods in the same manner as products would have been displayed in 1770 and sit on the same sites (for the most part) as the stores in that period. Promotional maps have the historic stores indicated by their historic store names—most often the name of the store's original proprietor.

Other retail venues operated by the Colonial Williamsburg Foundation include stores adjacent to the historic town, such as the Williamsburg Craft House which sells reproductions of furniture and interpretations of eighteenth century designs in home furnishings and many other gifts. Additionally, a bookstore at the Visitor's Centre (admissions) has an extensive collection of books as well as a variety of gifts based on items in the vast collection owned by the Foundation. An Internet website (www. williamsburgmarketplace.com) offers a variety of products from all of the retail venues. Further, the Colonial Williamsburg Foundation has developed a licensing programme with key vendors. Williamsburg Shops® are scattered throughout the USA, carrying authentic reproductions and other merchandise reflective of the museum's collection.

Visitors to Colonial Williamsburg represent a vast spectrum of people. International visitors are not uncommon. School children in groups from across the USA come to the museum because of the critical part the city played in the history of the country. In the summer, many families visit, while in the autumn and spring the visitors tend to be adult couples. Merchandise assortments change with the seasons, as well as by store, and during various events. In summer, the hats and caps for young children are in evidence everywhere. During the Christmas and holiday season one is more likely to see pewter and china giftware featured more prominently. A store targeted at school groups, the Little Patriot, located at the Visitor's Centre, has a large assortment of goods that are easy for younger visitors to carry and afford.

References

Booms, B. H. and Bitner, M. J. (1981). Marketing strategies and organization structures for service firms. In *Marketing Services* (J. H. Donnelly and W. H. George, eds.), pp. 47–52. American Marketing Association.

McLean, F. (1997). *Marketing the Museum*. Routledge.

Mottner, S. and Ford, J. (2005). Measuring nonprofit marketing strategy performance: the case of museum stores. *Journal of Business Research*, 58, X, 829–40.

Theobald, M. M. (2000). *Museum Store Management*. AltaMira Press.

Branding museums in the global marketplace

Anne-Marie Hede

Introduction

When I think of the Museum of Modern Art in New York, words such as 'big', 'cutting edge', 'definite' and 'integrity', come to mind. *Why do I associate these words with this museum? How did I come to arrive at these perceptions? What are the forces that have come to make me think like this? And, is this how the Museum of Modern Art wants to be perceived?* The concept of branding is useful when attempting to answer these questions.

While there is some debate as to whether branding, as it has emerged within the context of products, translates to cultural products and in particular to museums, there is much evidence of its application in the museum sector. This chapter examines the concept of branding within the museum sector and employs a traditional marketing approach to branding; the chapter aims to demonstrate how branding can be, and is, used in the museum sector. It is, of course, up to practitioners in the field to consider the value of branding, and the extent of its use, for their museum.

What is branding?

Branding brings together tools of the marketer to communicate a clear message to consumers in an increasingly complex marketplace. Branding is about conveying the philosophical position of the corporation or product to consumers.

Brands are symbols of values and emotions that are experienced and interpreted by consumers (Urde, 1999). Aaker (2004) noted that the brand plays an endorser role, conveys credibility and stands behind products—in spirit and substance.

A number of adjacent terms have emerged from the branding literature. Brand equity comprises the assets that are part of the brand, and include the heritage of the brand, the logo, the people behind the brand, and the brand's values and priorities. Brand equity is generally developed over time because the market must become familiar with the assets of the brand before its equity becomes evident.

Brands exist at the corporate and product levels. The corporate brand is symbolic of what the organization represents and is formed as a result of internal and external forces on the organization:

- Organizations have brand identities, or personalities—which they craft, develop and maintain. Brand identity is created by the organization with a unique set of associations which implies what the organization can deliver.
- Brand images exist in the minds of consumers. Consumers create an image of the brand from marketing communications and other information that they gain about organizations.

> Some museums are able to turn to their history to identify their brand personality. Take, for example, the Smithsonian. The history of the Smithsonian provides a sound basis for its brand personality—its past determines its present and its future. For other museums, however, history is not available in which the brand personality can be identified. In this case, the brand personality must be created. Often, an individual will champion the vision, and the personality, for the museum. For instance, in the case of the Guggenheim Museum the 'insistence of philanthropist Solomon Guggenheim and artist-adviser Hilla Rebay on a wholly new kind of art seen in a wholly new kind of space, set the institution on its unique path' (Anon, 2006).

The challenge for marketers is to promote congruence between the brand's identity and the brand's image. In this way, consumers come to feel more comfortable with the brand and their purchase. The museum can then begin to develop loyalty to the brand which is manifested in things like repeat attendance, purchase and recommending behaviour.

Think of the Victoria and Albert Museum in the UK. *What is the identity of this museum? What is the image of the Victoria and Albert Museum in the marketplace? Are these congruent with each other?*

Branding in the global marketplace

Branding in the global marketplace is challenging. The global marketplace is often quite cluttered. Further, marketing communications are often prolific and brand communications can sometimes be lost in the communications of other competing, and non-competing organizations. The Internet has accentuated these challenges for organizations. To be successful in the global marketplace, branding communications must, therefore, be clear and precise. Organizations need to be vigilant in terms of their own communications and those of competing organizations.

While not in the museum sector, take for example, the vignerons of Champagne. Around the globe, wineries were claiming that their sparkling wines were 'champagne'. The vignerons of the Champagne region in France insisted that only their sparkling wines, made via the 'methode champenoise', could be labelled champagne. The term 'champagne' signifies unique traditions and quality, invoking values of luxury, and emotions of excitement and happiness. By allowing vignerons outside Champagne to also use the label 'champagne', the integrity of the wines of Champagne were being compromised. In response to this, the vignerons of Champagne engaged in a global branding exercise to protect the intergrity of the brand. After a successful campaign, they now enjoy exclusivity of the use of the term champagne, with the product, the values and emotions that champagne represents now protected in the marketplace.

This simple, yet powerful, anecdote about champagne highlights the power of branding in the global marketplace. Indeed, many museums exhibit collections that comprise items from all over the world; they increasingly operate in the global market place. Museums are often the impetus for tourists to visit tourist destinations, particularly in the case of national museums in regional locations. Furthermore, most museums now employ websites to exhibit their collections on-line to communities around the globe. Many museums are incorporating retail shops on their websites to browse and purchase their, often branded, merchandise. The branding challenge, however, for museums is that they are also very often branding local products. Hence, balancing branding on the global and local levels and in a global/local environment requires strategy, and in many cases, sensitivity to cultural and socio-political factors.

Brand museum

The concept of the museum is a brand in itself. In the past 'brand museum' was communicated and perceived as playing an edificatory role in society—*institutions* that 'collect, preserve and interpret material evidence and associated information for the public benefit' (Anon, 1997). While examples of pheasants behind glass cabinets accompanied by a few selected words about the specimen were appealing to visitors of the early parts of the twentieth century, visitors in the twenty-first century are keen to actively explore museum collections. The contemporary identity and image of museums is that of the *attraction*—where people are enabled 'to explore collections, for inspiration, learning and enjoyment'(Anon, 2003). 'Brand museum' of the twenty-first century symbolizes history and modernity simultaneously.

'Brand museum' is organic and has evolved over time to what it is today—in response to changing consumer values, attitudes and preferences. Organizations like the International Council of Museums (ICOM) support the notion of the contemporary museum as it encourages:

- Professional cooperation and exchange.
- Dissemination of knowledge and raising public awareness of museums training of personnel.

- Advancement of professional standards.
- Elaboration and promotion of professional ethics.
- Preservation of heritage and combating the illicit traffic in cultural property (<http://icom.museum/mission.html>).

A sense of standardization emerges from 'brand museum'. There is a sense of comfort for consumers in 'brand museum' as they have become accustomed to what a museum does and should be, through the branding process.

Successful museums have identified themselves with the notion of the contemporary 'brand museum', rather than the museums of the past. Their first task is to be true to today's 'brand museum', just as the vignerons of Champagne must be true to champagne. 'Brand museum' is at the core of all successful museums.

The competitive marketplace

Not only do museums compete with each other for visitors, they also compete against other types of attractions and activities for revenue, funding and sponsorship. When families consider an afternoon's activities, for example, they might think of going to the movies, visiting the park, gardening or visiting a museum. Children might be more interested in visiting an amusement park, an interactive games arcade or surfing the Internet at home, rather than visiting a museum. For 'empty-nesters', a visit to a museum might be considered alongside attending the theatre, or engaging in some 'retail therapy', or just whiling away an afternoon reading the newspapers or weekend magazines at a local café.

Because the competition is fierce and varied, and aplenty, museums need to communicate very clearly to consumers what the museum is about and what it is aiming to achieve. Branding can offer a museum the opportunity to distinguish itself from another museum. Furthermore, branding can assist a museum to position itself in relation to many of its competitors, which can include other attractions and leisure venues such as cinemas, local cafés or even games arcades.

Branding a museum

'Brand museum', however, makes a dull and boring museum sector if it is not accompanied by individualized branding activities. Branding is an important part of realizing the aims of a museum, as it assists a museum to articulate its identity and project its image to consumers. At the very least, branding places the museum into target markets' evoked sets of activity options, and hopefully enables it to become the activity of preference. Branding communications, therefore, must be clear and well defined. The process of branding should also respond to consumer behaviour and, because the brand evolves over time, it is not uncommon that branding exercises are sometimes unsuccessful. There is, therefore, little room for mixed messages in a competitive marketplace.

How then would a museum go about branding itself?

Larger museums with sufficient marketing budgets will very often contract out the branding process. However, the vast majority of museums do not have the funds to contract a branding exercise to external contractors; they have to undertake it in house. Pros and cons exist, of course, for both approaches. A contractor can offer objective independent advice to a museum; a museum may be too close to the situation to 'see the woods for the trees'. However, the contractor may not fully understand the ethos of the museum to adequately assess whether the brand will resonate with stakeholders. Even so, a museum that does contract out the branding process must stay close to the process to ensure that it stays on track. While funds will likely have an impact on who undertakes the branding process, the process itself is a standard one, which can be followed by those museums that elect to undertake it themselves. Either way, the branding process is an important, if not a time consuming, one that should be part of a longer-term museum marketing strategy.

As part of the longer-term strategy, it is prudent that museums involve their stakeholders in the branding process. Stakeholders are entities with the capacity to influence the success of the museum and without whose support, the museum would not survive. These concepts are taken from Freeman's Stakeholder Theory (Freeman, 1984). Stakeholders for museums include, but are not limited to, their benefactors, the governmental bodies that fund them, their visitors and the public, universities and other like institutions, sponsors, artists and employees. By including the museum's stakeholders in the branding process, it is likely that the existing perceptions of the brand are more accurately identified, as well as the museum's competitors. The branding process generally elicits how complex the brand is, and the need to evaluate its strengths and weaknesses. The task of the museum marketer is to simplify the brand for stakeholders.

In the first instance, it is important for a museum to understand its stakeholders' current perceptions of the museum's brand. This might be best explored by asking:

- What are the core attributes of the museum's brand?
- If the museum was a person, how would you describe that person?

It is unlikely that an existing museum will not already be branded in one way or another; hence, gaining information from a broad set of constituents is highly useful. By including the museum's stakeholders in the branding process, the museum is able to gain a more holistic understanding of the museum's brand than would obtained had it not consulted its stakeholders. It is at this point that a museum is able to assess whether the identity of the museum and the image of the museum are congruent with each other.

Gathering this information from stakeholders can be gained using qualitative and/or quantitative methods. The size and nature of the museum, and the funds available, will obviously impact on how information of this type is gained. Importantly, the information gained, whether it be through qualitative or quantitative methods, must be useful and have integrity. That is, it must be valid and reliable. A small museum may not have the funds to undertake a large public survey about perceptions of the museum's brand, but it may be able to undertake in-depth interviews with its stakeholders using existing budgets. A larger museum, however, would likely collect data on this topic using both qualitative and quantitative techniques. Neither set of information is more valuable than the other; it all depends on how it was collected, interpreted and ultimately used by the museum.

By collecting information from stakeholders, a museum should then be able to identify to what extent the brand values are:

- Durable.
- Relevant.
- Communicable.
- Whether they hold saliency (Morgan, et al., 2003).

Armed with this information from stakeholders, the museum is able to ascertain the breadth of the branding process—whether it is in a situation requiring re-branding or one that requires consolidation of the brand in the marketplace. At this point it is worthwhile presenting the findings of the stakeholder inquiries back to the stakeholders for confirmation and validation.

A museum should continue to work with its stakeholders to come to understand the strengths and weaknesses of the brand. It may be that the brand identity, or personality, is not appealing to stakeholders. This situation has major implications for many museums, as they are often put in a situation where they have to be critical of their past. Finding the balance between the past and the future for older museums can be a very difficult process. It may be that the brand identity is appealing to stakeholders, but that the way in which it is communicated to stakeholders is tired and in need of some updating.

Tools of museum branding

A number of tools can be used to communicate the brand identity. We often come to understand what people are about by looking at what they wear, how they speak, who they socialize with and the things that they do. It's really no different for a museum, so think about the museum as a person. Museums have access to a similar set of tools to assist them to brand themselves. Some of these are easier to manipulate and control than others. For example, the layout of the building in which the museum is housed is often out of the control of the museum brander. They may, however, be able to bring the building in line with other parts of the branding strategy through the use of colour and texture, for example. Things like the exhibitions, whether these are permanent or temporary, play a large role in branding a museum. Other variables that come into play when the brand is created, both objectively and subjectively, are:

- Logos, fonts.
- Copy—semiotics, marketing collateral and website design.

- Packaging.
- Décor, architecture and building.
- Retail areas—shops and cafés, style of food.
- Artists and exhibitors.
- Sponsors.
- Philanthropists.
- Funding agencies.
- Directors, curators and staff.
- Ticketing—accessibility, pricing, tangible, ephemera.

To be successful, however, the tools used by the museum need to complement each other. If the messages that the various tools convey are not consistent with each other, the brand identity and its image are potentially incongruent. In this instance, they will serve limited purpose as marketing tools.

How does the Tate convey its values to target markets and consumers? The Tate Online's website provides an indication of its values through the use of the everyday language . . .

'. . . yes, it's a museum, but it's also like a big living room'.
(<http://www.tate.org.uk/>)

By using this style of language, the Tate Online is attempting to communicate with everyone. It's saying that all four museums are comfortable places to be in—and that you will feel at home when you visit them. This aspect of the Tate Online's marketing is reinforcing that it is a museum with contemporary values. Yet, the museums—Tate Britain, Tate Modern, Tate Liverpool and Tate St Ives—are different and it is interesting to note, that colour is the most obvious method used to differentiate them. Furthermore, a standardized template is used for each of the museum's websites—reinforcing that the museums, while different, are part of a family.

Communications on The Russian Museum's website provide an indication of this museum's brand
(<http://www.rusmuseum.ru/eng/museum/>)

The language used on the website is authoritarian; it explains that the museum 'is a unique depository of artistic treasures, a leading restoration centre, an authoritative institute of academic research, a major educational centre and the nucleus of a network of national museums of art'. The graphics used on the website also convey that the museum and its works are imposing, and that they have played, and continue to play, a significant role in Russia's history.

Assessing the brand in the marketplace

Branding is an evolutionary process. Once the museum is clear about its brand identity and comes to understand its brand image in the marketplace, it then needs to devise a strategy that will successfully maintain the brand's presence in the marketplace. The brand, however, needs to respond to its environment to ensure its success.

For example, the National Museum of Australia, in Canberra, opened in March 2001, and while its brand identity embraced the notion that it was the first museum in Australia devoted to the stories of Australia and Australians, its brand image was in crisis by 2003. Through surveys, the National Museum of Australia identified that Australians had very little understanding of what the museum was about. In response to this, the museum launched the 'Land, Nation, People' campaign to re-affirm the National Museum as Australia's premier social history museum. Extensive research on the awareness and creative direction of the museum was conducted to develop the campaign which was aimed at conveying the unusual personality of the National Museum to Australians. The year-long campaign comprised outdoor advertising, including billboards and signage on buses, to target Sydney, Melbourne and Canberra markets.

The future of branding in the museum sector

It is unlikely that any museum is not already using some form of branding. With a seemingly increasing need for museums to diversify their activities and to successfully compete for funding, the notion of 'brand' will play an increasingly important role in marketing communications. Families of museums, for example, are not uncommon. Think of the Tate or the Smithsonian where the Tate has become a corporate brand that acts like an umbrella communicating a core set of values to consumers at each of the four museums—Tate Britain, Tate Modern, Tate Liverpool and Tate St Ives. The corporate Tate brand draws together the four museums and the result is powerful as it creates a synergistic effect. Similarly, the Smithsonian brand conveys the organization's core values and the emotions that it aims to elicit in consumers—the brand is present in the museum and each of the sub-museums and exhibitions. In Canada, Economuseums© have developed a market presence. Craftspeople in Canada are increasingly subscribing to that brand. As such, they buy into the brand, just as the brand buys into them. While this is no different to what has happened for centuries, it is different in the sense that the museum brand is coming to the artisan rather than the artisan coming to the museum brand.

Conclusion

Established museums and newer museums alike must maintain, or re-engineer, their brand in the marketplace. The process of branding is not the same as developing a set of policies and procedures, such as in human resource management. While branding communications must respond to how the market is communicating with the brand, consistency in the brand must also be conveyed. Hence, the line between success and failure is sometimes fine. As such, branding is very much an interactive process that requires the input of its stakeholders for the brand to be truly successful.

References

Aaker, D. (2004). *Brand Portfolio Strategy: Creating Relevance, Differentiation, Energy, Leverage, and Clarity.* Simon & Schuster, New York.

Anon (1997). *Code of Ethics* (Second edition). Museums Association United Kingdom, London.

Anon (2003). Museum definition. <http://www.city.ac.uk/artspol/mus-def> (accessed 29 September 2003).

Anon (2006). Guggenheim. <http://www.guggenheim.org/new_york_index.shtml> (accessed 5 March 2006).

Freeman, R. (1984). *Strategic Management: A Stakeholder Approach.* Pitman, Boston

Morgan, N. J., Pritchard, A. and Piggott, R. (2003). Destination branding and the role of the stakeholders: the case of New Zealand. *Journal of Vacation Marketing*, 9(3), 285–99.

Urde, M. (1999). Brand orientation: a mindset for building brands into strategic resources. *Journal of Marketing Management*, 15(1–3), 117–33.

Museums and merchandising

Stefan Toepler and Volker Kirchberg

Introduction

Museums were among the prime beneficiaries of the cultural policy boom in the post-World War II period that led to significant increases in public support and a substantial expansion of the cultural infrastructure in much of the Western world. This boom was driven both by the realization that market failure in the arts required increased public intervention and by the then-prevailing social-democratic *zeitgeist* that stressed notions of cultural equity and democratization (Toepler and Zimmer, 2002). By the 1980s, fiscal retrenchment, however, led to a reappraisal of the welfare state in the 1980s and also halted the expansion of cultural policy. In the USA, federal arts support began to stagnate in this period, before dropping off in the 1990s; and in Western Europe, many governments initiated the search for ways to reduce public funding by improving legal and fiscal incentives for private giving and the establishment of philanthropic foundations, such as the French 1987 Law on the Promotion of Maecenatism and the German 1990 Law on the Promotion of Culture and Foundations. Fiscal measures to increase private arts support are also evident in other parts of the world (Schuster, 1999).

In the 1990s, moreover, the policy focus increasingly shifted from merely encouraging private support to a more full-blown privatization or de-governmentalization of public cultural institutions—a trend that was particularly evident in Central and Eastern Europe (Schuster, 1997; Toepler, 2000), but likewise took hold in the West (van Hemel and van der Wielen, 1997).

Unfortunately, the meaning, advantages and drawbacks of cultural privatization remain little understood by both policy makers and cultural managers alike. While policy makers embrace privatization as a mantra for injecting management efficiency and new private revenues into public institutions, cultural managers are haunted by the spectre of commercialization. This was borne out on a large scale in the Italian Government's 2001 proposal to privatize the management of state museums. Intended—according to Italy's Minister of Culture—to 'give greater efficiency to the running of the whole artistic patrimony of Italy' (Cocks, 2001), the initiative was also expected to generate millions of dollars for the state (Willan, 2001). This, in turn, sparked some three dozen directors and curators of prominent museums in North America, Europe, Israel and Australia to publish an open letter, urging the Italian Government not to turn museums over to private enterprise (Cocks, 2001), because—as one American official was quoted as saying—there 'is the sense that profit motives could obliterate the [sic] study and scholarly work' (Henneberger, 2001). In response to international and domestic protests, later revisions of the bill stipulated that museums may be managed by 'non-governmental' rather than by 'private' (e.g., strictly commercial) interests (Henneberger, 2001). With this slight change, the Italian Government ceded a symbolically important point that the international group of museum directors had already stressed in their open letter with respect to the American situation: 'Although museums in the USA are mainly non-governmental private institutions, they are not run as private businesses, or put, all or in part, in the hands of private enterprise, and are strictly not-for-profit in their management' (Cocks, 2001). Casting the privatization as a 'non-governmentalization' or 'non-profitization' effectively addresses the concern that commercial interests might override the public interest in the management of cultural institutions.

So far, however, few Western countries are likely to implement privatization measures as far-reaching as those proposed in Italy at the time. Nevertheless, since the 1990s, there has been a discernible trend to loosen administrative and budgetary rules and regulations in an effort to increase managerial flexibility of autonomy of public arts institutions. Greater autonomy over the use of income streams, in particular, is in turn intended to provide incentives for arts managers to increase earnings (Frey, 2000). Arguably, European cultural policies are in this respect beginning to converge towards the American model with its greater emphasis on private revenues and earned income (Toepler and Zimmer, 2002).

Private, non-profit arts and cultural institutions around the world already rely heavily on earnings, as shown in Table 5.2. Interestingly, the key difference between the USA and other countries does not lie in the degree to which private arts institutions rely on earnings, but rather in the relative importance of public subsidies and private donations. Herein lies both the boon and the bane of the prospects for financing the arts through the market. In the USA, low levels of government subsidies were traditionally compensated by high levels of philanthropic support. Greater commercialism was induced by an

Table 5.2 Key revenue sources of private arts and cultural institutions in percentage, selected countries, c. 1995.

	Government support (%)	Private donations (%)	Earnings (%)
Australia	25	0	75
Austria	77	0	23
Finland	51	4	44
France	44	3	53
Germany	59	7	35
Hungary	36	22	42
USA	14	41	45

Source: Salamon et al. (1999).

expansion of the arts sector in the post-World War I period that eventually outpaced the growth of philanthropic support. Particularly in the European case, however, a comparable philanthropic base is non-existent and mostly marginal changes in tax incentives are not likely to substantially increase the incidence of private support. Significant reductions in public subsidy levels thus directly translate into a pronounced commercialization trend that has become increasingly apparent over the past decade in the USA and elsewhere.

Against this background, it is perhaps not surprising that cultural institutions have increasingly sought to develop alternative, and perhaps more stable and dependable, sources of revenue. Key among these is merchandising, which has been particularly visible in public television: merchandise based on popular children shows, such as 'Sesame Street', 'Barney' or the 'Teletubbies', are basic staples of toy stores around the world. Museums have also developed merchandising into an art form. Many museums, such as the Metropolitan Museum and the Museum of Fine Arts Boston, have sold reproductions of works in their collections since their inception and museum book stands or stores selling exhibition catalogues, posters, postcards and related items have long been a staple in most museums. Since the 1980s or so, however, things have changed considerably. Not only have gift shops continued to expand with the museum, but also spilled out to off-site venues, such as shopping malls, airports and department stores. A number of large museums operate catalogue mail order businesses and the e-commerce revolution has enabled even smaller museums to bring their wares to markets outside the confines of the museum's walls. Moreover, museums in Europe and elsewhere have begun to catch up with their American counterparts. Large British Museums have begun to spin-off their merchandising into wholly owned subsidiary companies in order not to endanger their charitable status (Newbury, 1990), and the British Museum opened the first airport shop at Heathrow in 1996 (Burdon, 1996). An up-scale, underground shopping mall was attached to the Louvre in 1993 and the National Museums of France also operate a store at Charles DeGaulle airport.

Complementing Sandra Mottner's contribution to this volume on the specifics of museum shop marketing strategies, we will take a larger view of the longer-term viability of merchandising in the context of the US museum field.

Reasons and benefits of merchandising

US museums began to develop more extensive stores than the traditional counters selling books, exhibition catalogues and postcards during the 1980s, at about the same that marketing management was discovered in the field. However, the modern merchandising boom is largely a reflection of developments at the trendsetting Metropolitan Museum of Art a good two decades earlier. As discussed in more detail elsewhere (Toepler, 2006), the appointment of Thomas Hoving as Director in the late 1960s sets changes in motion that not only changed the Metropolitan but arguably the museum field at large. Hoving (1993) energetically pursued the acquisition of private collections as well as a building expansion that took the Metropolitan to the outer edges of its Central Park location, while beginning to champion education and its inherent focus on the visitor over acquisition. The resulting resource needs soon began to overtax the two traditional mainstays of museum finance—endowment income and city subsidies—which further gave way in the early 1970s due to growing inflation and economic problems in New York City. The museum's response was a steady and significant exploration of merchandising; a strategy that was further validated by the success of the King Tut show of the late 1970s—the first true blockbuster. The Metropolitan's apparent success in generating resources through merchandising proved a useful model for adaptation when the rest of the museum field found itself in much of the same situation in the 1980s.

Accordingly, Anheier and Toepler (1998) noted four main reasons for the growth of the merchandising phenomenon. Firstly, the museum field experienced significant growth since the 1970s, both in terms of new museums and of expansions of collections and buildings of existing ones. While capital support for 'bricks and mortar' capital investments is relatively easy to come by, general support for the resulting increased operating costs is not, paving the way for the exploration of unrestricted income sources, such as store income. Secondly, and relatedly, museums are generally subject to what economists refer to as the 'cost disease', which suggests increases in labour cost (for curators, security guards, etc.) are not generally compensated by gains in productivity. Because technology cannot substitute labour, museums face income gaps over time—even without any expansions. Thirdly, the objectives of funders, such as individual donors, foundations, corporations and government, may frequently conflict with curatorial goals, interests and intentions. Some exhibition projects favoured by curators fail to attract sufficient interest among private donors, which in turn requires unrestricted, internal funding. In addition, museums face difficulties attracting external funding for important, but less public, core activities, such as conservation and research. Finally, government support for the arts has reached its peak. After significant growth in the 1970s, appropriations for the NEA, which have been crucial in stimulating both private and other governmental spending, became stagnant during the 1980s and have decreased since. State support has been cyclically erratic, and while local government support has been increasing, overall public funding has been more or less flat over the past 10 years. Taken together, these factors have greatly propelled the merchandising trend over the past two decades.

If successful in generating resources, museum merchandising is a win–win situation for all stakeholders. Local, state or national government funders—struggling to balance budgets and fund other core services—perceive the possibility to contain, if not reduce, annual appropriations. Private funders can likewise re-direct scarce philanthropic dollars to other needs. Museum visitors have the ability (and by now also the expectation) to obtain manifest mementos of their museum experience while basking in the 'warm glow' of having supported the institution through the purchase. Museum managers, at last, may derive several benefits. Firstly, merchandising profits constitute unrestricted income that is fully under the discretion of the institution (in contrast to gifts and grants that frequently come with strings attached). Secondly, developing this revenue source may help placate corporate trustees demanding efficiency and more business-like operations. Thirdly, merchandising may increase the visibility and profile of the institution and, finally, also educate the general public about works in the collection.

Financial viability of the merchandising strategy

What is more, the fact that merchandising is financially successful, if not highly lucrative, is generally taken for granted, rarely questioned and remains highly underanalysed. So far, only a small cluster of studies approach the issue from an aggregate level. In a first study on this topic, Anheier and Toepler (1998) utilized tax return information from the International Revenue Service (IRS) to study the financials of the largest museums (the Statistics of Income, SOI, dataset contains information for all museums with a budget of $10 million and more and a sample of smaller ones). They found that US art museums had not become significantly more commercial per se during the 1980s and early 1990s. While total revenue from commercial sources grew significantly, the relative share of total revenues attributable to commercial activities did not increase over time. Given the significant expansion of museum merchandising during the 1980s, this finding was counter-intuitive, but situated the growth of merchandising within the overall growth of the museum field. Anheier and Toepler nevertheless found signs of growing commercialization pressures in the 1990s.

In a more recent study, Toepler and Dewees (2005) extended the original analysis into the late 1990s. This study also contrasted the IRS-SOI data of the largest museums to Economic Census data reflecting the museum field at large. Among the main findings was that the growth of sales revenues of the largest museums (represented in the SOI data) had slowed to a standstill by the late 1990s, which in turn suggests the beginning of a potential 'de-commercialization' trend. While among the largest museums merchandising operations may have reached their peak and begun to retrench, the concomitant analysis of Census data still showed relatively solid growth of merchandising revenues for the museum field at large, suggesting that smaller and mid-sized museums were continuing the expansion of shops and retail. Nevertheless, even the Census data showed a marked slowdown in the course of the 1990s. Whereas merchandising jumped from 6 per cent of total museum revenues in 1987 to 11 per cent in 1992, its share was 10 per cent in 1997. Likewise, the annual growth rates of merchandising revenues dropped from more than 10 per cent in the late 1980s and early 1990s to 7 per cent in the mid- to late 1990s.

While all of these suggest that merchandising will not likely remain a major engine for future financial growth of museums, it does not address the question of how much of a contribution merchandising has made in the past to the financing of museums. Media reports have often noted total sales revenues as the contribution, which tends to convey a highly inaccurate impression, since retail in general is a relatively fickle, low-margin business. Relying on annual report information for a small sample of nine large art museums, Toepler and Kirchberg (2002) investigated this issue from 1989 to 1999. Consistent with the other studies, these nine museums show a relatively high average share of total (or gross) merchandising revenues to total museum revenues (other than revenues for capital projects), which somewhat declines from 20 per cent in the early 1990s to 18 per cent at the end of the decade, as shown in Figure 5.1.

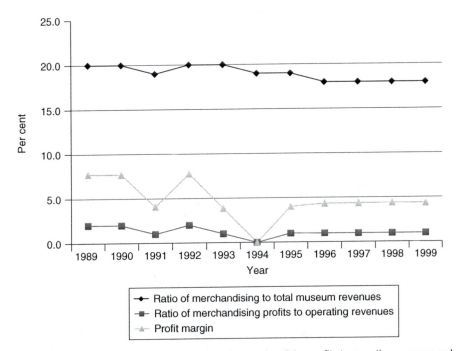

Figure 5.1 Ratios of merchandising to total revenues, merchandising profits to operating revenues and profit margins, nine museum sample, 1989–1999

Significantly, the slight decrease in merchandising gross revenues is accompanied by a similar decrease in net revenues. The share of merchandising net revenues of operating revenues was generally about 2 per cent in the early 1990s, dropped to zero in 1994, and then stagnated at 1 per cent for the second half of the decade. Although merchandising gross revenues in this sample held as high a share of total revenues, the net returns are considerably lower. What is more, while this is not always fully apparent from the annual reports, the majority of museums appear to report only direct expenditures attributable to merchandising rather than also reporting support service (i.e., indirect) charges. To the extent that this is true, the question does arise whether museums—in the aggregate—made any money at all on merchandising in the last half of the 1990s. Likewise, as also shown in Figure 5.1, the profit margin (i.e., net as per cent of gross revenues) across the sample dropped from close to 8 per cent at the beginning of the 1990s to just above 4 per cent from the middle to the end of the decade—a relatively low rate of return that would probably not be acceptable in alternative contexts, such as fundraising.

Conclusion

However limited the evidence is to date that merchandising in general is losing ground, museums—large and small—will likely have to re-evaluate retail and merchandising operations as part of their overall marketing mix in the near future. As a business, retail is characterized as volatile, involving significant investments while providing small margins. While the standard argument is that even small amounts of unrestricted funds provide much-needed relief when it comes to supporting exhibitions or other museum tasks without much appeal to outside funders, the flip side is that merchandising does involve risk and will require more than just wishful thinking about future financial windfalls; it will require sound business planning that also takes alternative uses of available resources into account.

Of course, museums might decide to engage in, or expand existing, merchandising operations for reasons only indirectly to do with the material and immaterial benefits that such activities might generate. In fact, it could be argued that museum customers (i.e., visitors) at this stage expect to find gift shops and museum-related merchandise at the time of their visit—leaving the museum little choice, but to provide this part of the 'museum experience'. Nevertheless, in making decisions about how to respond to such demands, it remains imperative to keep an accurate assessment of costs and potential financial risks in the equation.

Perhaps even more significantly, there may also be implicit peer pressure in existence, whereby museum managers feel that they have to engage in merchandising or re-vamping their restaurants because doing so has developed into a standard within the organizational field. Organizational theorists refer to such pressures as mimetic isomorphism (DiMaggio and Powell, 1991)—the tendency of organizations to respond to uncertainty by emulating, or mimicking, successful and legitimate models. In this case, the extent of apparently successful merchandising and other auxiliary activities of large and prominent museums, such as the Metropolitan Museum, the Museum of Modern Art, the Museum of Fine Arts, Boston or the Art Institute of Chicago, might have encouraged other museums to view such activities as a legitimate response to financial uncertainty. That such institutional pressures and forces might indeed be at play and provide an alternative explanation of managerial motivations, is borne out in the way one art museum described its decision to expand its auxiliary activities in its 1991 annual report:

> In pursuing various solutions [the museum] has in one way finally emulated its peers. During the 1980s America's museums aggressively pursued new sources of income to meet mounting operating

costs. Museum stores became a major resource, merchandise based on the holdings of a collection burgeoned, parking fees were justified by the scarcity of space, and then, most dramatically, admissions were charged, at remarkably escalating prices. For the first time, in 1990, [the museum] too joined the parade—but fortunately still with one all-important exception: general admission remains free ... Not surprisingly, given long-established habits, the announcement of parking fees and admission charges for major (i.e., exceedingly costly) exhibitions aroused some distress at the outset; on the other hand, the museum store, with a greater range of merchandise, clearly responded to many visitors' long-expressed desires.

However, these pressures may also work the other way. Recent problems with the merchandising operations of prominent museums, such as the Metropolitan, the Smithsonian Institution, the Boston Museum of Fine Arts or the Winterthur Museum, may signal to the museum field at large that the era of museum merchandising is slowly coming to an end.

References

Anheier, H. K., and Toepler, S. (1998). Commerce and the muse: are art museums becoming commercial? In *To Profit or Not to Profit? The Commercial Transformation of the Nonprofit Sector* (B. Weisbrod, ed.), pp. 233–48. Cambridge University Press, Cambridge.

Burdon, J. (1996). Fly-Past—Museum Shop to open at Heathrow. *Press Association Ltd.*, 25 September.

Cocks, A. (2001). World museum directors oppose privatisation of Italy's museums. The Art Newspaper.com, October.

DiMaggio, P. and Powell, W. (1991). *The New Institutionalism in Organizational Analysis*. University of Chicago Press, Chicago.

Frey, B. (2000). *Arts and Economics: Analysis and Cultural Policy*. Springer, Berlin-Heidelberg-New York.

Henneberger, M. (2001). Italy plans to have private sector run museums. *New York Times*, 3 December, p. E1.

Hoving, T. (1993). *Making the Mummies Dance: Inside the Metropolitan Museum of Art*. Simon and Schuster, New York.

Newbury, R. (1990). A nation of museum shopkeepers. *Financial Times*, 15 September, Weekend, p. IX.

Salamon, L. M., Anheier, H. K., List, R., Toepler, S. and Sokolowski, S. (1999). *Global Civil Society: Dimensions of the Nonprofit Sector*. Johns Hopkins Center for Civil Society Studies, Baltimore.

Schuster, J. M. (1997). Deconstructing a Tower of Babel: privatisation, decentralisation and devolution as ideas in good currency in cultural policy. *Voluntas*, 8, 261–82.

Schuster, J. M. (1999). The other side of the subsidized muse: Indirect aid revisited. *Journal of Cultural Economics*, 23, 51–70.

Toepler, S. (2000). From Communism to civil society? The arts and the non-profit sector in Central and Eastern Europe. *Journal of Arts Management, Law, and Society*, 30(1), 7–18.

Toepler, S. (2006). Caveat venditor? Museum merchandising, nonprofit commercialization and the case of the Metropolitan Museum in New York. *Voluntas*, 17, 2.

Toepler, S. and Dewees, S. (2005). Are there limits to financing culture through the market? Evidence from the US Museum Field. *International Journal of Public Administration*, 28(1/2), 131–46.

Toepler, S. and Kirchberg, V. (2002). Museums, merchandising and nonprofit commercialization. National Center for Nonprofit Enterprise Working Paper. http://<www.nationalcne.org/papers/museum.htm> (accessed 25 November 2006).

Toepler, S. and Zimmer, A. (2002). Subsidising the arts: Government and the arts in Western Europe and the United States. In *Global Culture: Media, Arts and Cultural Policy in a Global Context* (D. Crane et al., eds.), pp. 23–46. Routledge, London.

van Hemel, A. and van der Wielen, N. (eds.) (1997). *Privatization/Deetatisation and Culture: Limitations or Opportunities for Cultural Development in Europe?* Conference Reader for the Circle Round Table. Boekman Foundation and Twente University, Enschede.

Willan, P. (2001). Italian anger at plan to privatise museums. *The Guardian*, 5 November, p. 15.

Branding museums

Carol Scott

Introduction

Branding has come to prominence since the mid-1990s as museums have struggled to maintain audience share in an increasingly competitive leisure environment. Consultants now specialize in museum branding, a nascent literature is emerging and conferences are devoted to the topic.

The focus of all this activity is generally the individual museum and how it can compete effectively for audiences using the toolkit of branding and marketing. This is undeniably important.

This chapter takes a different view of the subject; it explores the role branding can play in positively positioning the overall museum sector at a time when it faces challenges, not only for market share, but for the hearts and minds of bureaucrats and funding agencies.

This chapter is presented in four sections. The first section examines some of the critical issues museums facing today that affect their ongoing sustainability in terms of public relevance and political will. The second section covers branding definitions and processes. The third section explores what audience research offers to museum branding in terms of consumer benefits and sector differentiation. In the final section, some conclusions are drawn about positioning the sector for maximum impact.

Museums and the public sector

Whichever way we look at it, museums face severe challenges to their ongoing sustainability. This section focuses on two of those challenges—the impact of government reforms on the public sector and the increasing competition for time-poor audiences in a leisure-rich environment.

From the late 1970s, most Organization for Economic Co-operation and Development (OECD) countries embarked on an agenda for major government reform to rein in the expansionist spending that had characterized fiscal policy following World War II and which, by the late 1970s, threatened to bankrupt Western nations (OECD, 2003, 2005).

In an effort to produce balanced budgets, governments redefined their role to focus on policy-making and monitoring, divested themselves of much of the direct service delivery that had been characteristic of Western governments post-World War II and reduced the size of the public sector (OECD, 1997). The reforming agenda commenced and has continued in an environment where discerning and vocal publics demand transparency and accountability of governments.

During the height of economic rationalism in the 1980s and early 1990s, accountability was managed through a system of performance evaluation which required tangible evidence in quantitative form that public monies (inputs) were providing activities (outputs) that produced results (outcomes). From a government perspective, the worth of museums was judged according to fiscal accountability based on demonstrating the efficient and effective use of public grants (OECD, 2004).

In the late 1990s a sea change transformed policy orientation as governments struggled to address mounting pressures to deal with escalating social problems. The dominance of the economic paradigm was challenged and governments sought solutions in social policy, particularly with regard to the need for social inclusion among increasingly diverse populations with multiple value systems (AEGIS, 2004).

The framework of accountability for public sector institutions, honed through years of applying economic rationalism, has remained. Since the late 1990s, however, greater emphasis has been placed on the sector's capacity to achieve the instrumental outcomes of social policy through evidence of inclusion, engagement of marginalized groups, regenerated cities, increased tourism and lifelong learning. Worth is judged by evidence that institutions, such as museums, are contributing to these policy directions (Holden, 2004) and funding agreements are constructed to ensure this (DCMS, 1998; NSW Audit Office, 2006). The Museums, Libraries and Archives Council of England sum up the current situation as a:

> ... commitment to a less ideological age—one more based on 'what works?'. In addition, the need to prove value for money to a sometimes sceptical public, the diminution in the public's desire to simply take professionals at their word, and the greater amount of policy-relevant research that is being undertaken worldwide, have all contributed to the pressure of public agencies to produce evidence for their actions and investments.
>
> (MLA, 2005, p. 2)

However, a growing body of criticism argues that this emphasis on instrumental outcomes and an increasingly output-oriented, quantitative approach to public sector management, down-plays and obscures other, intrinsic benefits of arts and culture (Holden, 2004, 2006a; McCarthy et al., 2004). Further, it questions the appropriateness and capacity of museums to be agents of social change (Bennett, 1989; Matarasso, 2000; Appleton, 2002; AEGIS, 2004).

Nevertheless, being compelled to demonstrate their worth in terms of current policy to maintain ongoing funding has deflected museum leadership from 'articulating certain core functions and responsibilities in a way that is sufficiently compelling to secure the funds to resource them' (Ellis, 2002, p. 8).

In fact, the sector's apparent inability to articulate its worth and value from a position of strength has been a recurring subject of concern (Matarasso, 1996; The Outspan Group and Perron, 1999; McCarthy et al., 2004; Holden, 2004) and one which has critical implications for the future of the sector:

> Unless a common and public language can be found in which to discuss cultural purposes, and intrinsic—alongside instrumental—value, then funders will tend to focus on a partial view of cultural institutions … .
>
> (Ellis, 2003, p. 14)

As we will see later in this chapter, audience research provides insight into the ways in which consumers value museums that can be used to position and brand the sector using a language generated by the public and the professionals with museum experience and expertise.

Audiences and market share

Museums are faced with other challenges in the public domain as they compete with other leisure providers for audiences and market share (Kotler and Kotler, 2000).

MORI's 2004 survey conducted for the Museums, Libraries and Archives Council of England reports that 'just over one third of the population (37%) has visited a museum and/or an art gallery in the past 12 months. This is less popular than visiting a cinema (59%) or library (51%) and matches the proportion that has visited a well-known park or garden' (MORI, 2004, pp. 4–6). Moreover, in spite of the removal of admission charges to national museums in 2001, museum/gallery attendances in England rose only 2 per cent from 35 per cent to 37 per cent.

Australian leisure participation rates are comparable. Almost 70 per cent of Australians go to the cinema, 48 per cent attend live sporting events, 42.1 per cent use public libraries, 41.6 per cent visit botanic gardens, 40 per cent visit zoos and aquaria, and 25 per cent go to museums. Just over a quarter attend popular music concerts while musicals or opera, theatre and dance are attended by less than 20 per cent of the population, respectively (ABS, 2002, 2005).

Attendances to Australian museums have declined from 27.5 per cent in 1995 to 25 per cent in 2002. Attendances to zoos, aquariums, parks and libraries increased 3–6 per cent between 1999 and 2002, while cinema attendances rose from nearly 5 per cent to almost 70 per cent in the same period (ABS, 2002, 2005).

Burton and Scott (2003, p. 61) reported that, based on the National Recreation Participation Surveys, visits to museums and galleries appeared to be decreasing from the mid-1980s while socializing at home, engaging in computer activities, shopping and cinema attendance were all on the increase.

How can we use the tools of branding to promote and market the value of the sector to politicians, bureaucrats and the public alike? The next section of this chapter explores the potential of audience research to contribute to sector branding. Specifically, it looks at the important role of perception in constructing brands and the valuable asset that is provided by audience research studies in discerning the positive perceptions about museums that constitute the sector's defining brand.

The power of brands

Brands create equity and heighten awareness. *Brand equity* is a set of assets (and liabilities) linked to the brand that adds to (or subtracts from) the value promised by the product. Brand equity is affected by the real and perceived quality of the product, its unique value, associations with it and loyalty to it (Gardella, 2002; Hwang, 2002). *Brand awareness* refers to the strength of a brand's presence in the consumer's mind (Gardella, 2002). *Brand quality* 'is usually at the heart of what customers are buying, and in that sense, it is a bottom-line measure of the impact of a brand identity' (Hwang, 2002, p. 13).

Brands provide important benefits to both consumers and firms. For consumers, brands identify the source or maker of the product, clarify costs and enable them to establish which brands satisfy their needs and minimize risk. For the organization, a clear brand simplifies communications and differentiates for both competitive advantage and legal protection of unique features. Most importantly, once brand loyalty has been created it is less costly to retain customers than to attract new ones.

Gardella (2002) and Hwang (2002) conclude that a brand is a mental construct in the minds of consumers. This mental construct is the sum total of the experiences, feelings and perceptions about the product's attributes, its performance and what it stands for. It is 'the promise that exists in the public's mind about who you are and what you do' (Gardella, 2002). Importantly, the distinguishing aspects of a brand are not always rational, tangible or related to product performance. According to Hwang (2002, pp. 11–12), they are just as likely to be 'symbolic, emotional and intangible'.

Kotler and Kotler (2000), Terry (2002) and Gardella (2002) believe that audience research can play an essential role in developing museums brands. Specifically, they advocate the need for data about public perceptions:

> What you need is data, both from the people who use you now and from those who should be using you (i.e., your next most likely audience). What do they see as your strengths? Your weaknesses? What would they like to have from you? What must they have? How are you doing, especially in regard to the must-haves?
>
> (Gardella, 2002)

Audience research, leisure and branding

Audience research illuminates these mental constructs. It reveals much about consumer perceptions with regard to both extrinsic and intrinsic leisure values and positive and negative museum associations. This information can be used to position the sector with consumers in terms of the benefits of engaging with museums.

Extrinsic values

What does the public value in leisure? In 1998, the Powerhouse Museum in Sydney conducted a brand audit to clarify its own brand and develop its positioning (Scott, 2000). Among the objectives for the study, was to clarify the position of museums in relation to other leisure attractions. In one stage of the study, 376 face-to-face interviews were conducted with a cross-section of Sydney residents comprising visitors and non-visitors to the museum. The results were interesting.

When asked to specify the attributes of an *ideal* leisure experience, the respondents told us that the ideal experience would be:

- Entertaining.
- A good place to take family and friends.
- Friendly.
- Fun.
- Exciting.
- Great value for money.
- A place where you can get lost in another world.
- Have a relaxed atmosphere.
- Have plenty of room to move.

The study further found that museums were *not* perceived to share these 'ideal' leisure attributes and were, in fact, linked to a different set of associations that included 'educational', 'places of discovery', 'intellectual experiences', 'challenging', 'thought provoking', 'absorbing', 'fascinating', 'innovative' and 'places where you can touch the past'.

Further research conducted at the Powerhouse in 2002 (Falk et al., 2004) confirmed many of the museum-specific attributes of the 1998 study, but also revealed that museums can be associated with some of the attributes associated with an ideal leisure experience. The 2002 study involved a museum with a science collection and science exhibitions (the Powerhouse Museum in Sydney) and a science centre with interactive displays but without a collection of objects (Sci-Tech Discovery Centre in Perth). At each institution, 100 people were intercepted and 1-hour in-depth interviews were conducted. The first part of the interview asked respondents to say what came to mind when shown either the word 'museum' (for respondents at the Powerhouse) or the words ' science centre' (at Sci-Tech).

Confirming the findings from the 1998 research, this study found that museums were associated with being 'educational places' where one could 'learn' or 'gain knowledge' (53 per cent of people interviewed). A further 20 per cent of respondents associated museums with places where education occurred via collections. For 46 per cent, museums were related to the 'past', 61 per cent associated them with history and 30 per cent referred to objects (often described as 'treasures') when they saw the word 'museums'. Almost half (49 per cent) of respondents associated science centres with interactivity and 'hands on' engagement but only 19 per cent associated these experiences with museums.

However, other data found that museums were perceived to be 'interesting' places (21 per cent of respondents) which are 'entertaining' and where one can 'have fun' (14 per cent). The study also revealed other, less positive, perceptions. Museums can still be associated with being 'stuffy/stale/old/dusty' (6 per cent).

The findings from these studies offer important insights for consumer branding based on real benefits perceived and expressed by the public. Museums can be legitimately positioned as 'interesting' places' which are 'entertaining' and where one can 'have fun' while at the same time 'learning something' and 'gaining knowledge'. Uncomfortably, but necessarily, they also highlight negative perceptions of being 'static', 'stale', 'dusty' and 'old' which we need to counteract.

Intrinsic values

Extrinsic values that people seek in leisure form one aspect that drives choice. Another factor is the nature and quality of the experience, or what is referred to here as the brand's *intrinsic* value. Intrinsic values drill deeper into the impact of a brand through the *quality* of the experience. This is a critical component of a cultural brand because it links it with ' ... strong feelings or even emotions ... as a result of pleasurable past experience' (Hwang, 2002, p. 15).

Holden (2004, 2006a) and McCarthy et al. (2004) believe that encounters in museums result in deeply satisfying experiences such as captivation, pleasure, an expanded capacity for empathy, the creation of social bonds and the expression of communal meanings—values that are intrinsic, intangible and potent. Holden (2006b) asserts that the public are willing to invest time, energy and money into cultural pursuits because of the high importance that they place on the capacity of cultural activities to engender personal experiences of significant intrinsic value.

Primary research by the author for a PhD thesis titled *Museums, Impact and Value* (Scott, 2006, dissertation in progress) tests Holden's theory and finds that the results confirm Holden's argument and are relevant to museum branding. The results of this research demonstrate that the value experiences that museums offer provide another dimension of consumer benefits.

The study involved two cohorts: a group of museum professionals and a public cohort living in urban and regional centres. The 70 respondents in the public cohort ranged across four life stages (18–24 years, parents with dependent children; adults 35–50 years without dependent children; and seniors 55–70 years) and included both visitors and non-visitors to museums.

Research questions sought perspectives on the impact and value of museums from the perspective of both these cohorts. Particularly compelling are the perspectives of the public respondents which revealed an extensive range and depth of value-related experiences associated with museums. Their comments reveal the capacity of the museum experience to engender feelings of inspiration, excitement and awe as well as contributing to the development of perspective, openness and tolerance, to provide opportunities for reflection, discovery, enrichment and insight. For example, a young female respondent (public cohort: 18–24 years) living in a city where she visits museums, was very clear about the *excitement* and *awe* that a museum visit could generate:

> Having a museum in my city means that I don't have to go far to learn and see and touch the history and life style of my culture and many others, past and present. This to me, is an amazing experience. To be able to walk through and see inventions and designs of the world and how much time has changed peoples [sic] perceptions and sense of design. How much technology has expanded with the human mind and how primitive life was in centuries before. I can appreciate life in so many more ways. To me, a museum in my city is a privilege.

An older respondent (a woman 55–70 years living in a city but not a museum-goer) recognized how *inspiring* the museum experience can be: 'Actually "seeing" an original or authentic object can be personal inspiring and bring home to us the size and appearance of many animals (some extinct) that we will probably never see in the flesh'.

For other respondents, exploring the record of human achievement, confronting the vastness of the universe and the myriad complexity and variety of the natural world 'give[s] a perspective of how insignificant the human race really is. Sometimes that is really good when you feel like things happening in your life are overwhelming' (public cohort: female, visitor, parent, urban resident). Perspective also situates individuals and provides 'a chance to view oneself within the fabric of time and space' (public cohort: male, non-visitor, 55–70 years, urban resident). The museum experience encourages reflection for others: '[a museum is] a quiet place to look back over time and reflect on things that have happened over time' (public cohort: female, visitor, parent, urban resident).

A male respondent to this study expressed the impact of museum visiting in terms of 'enrichment': '[The museum] enriches my life by providing me with an opportunity to see/experience/learn about things that I would normally never get the chance to see/experience/learn about' (public cohort: male, visitor, parent, urban resident); while another described the 'valuable insight into unknown subject matter' (male, non-visitor, 35–50 years, urban resident).

McCarthy et al. (2004, p. 48) argue that exposure to and experience of culture draws us out of ourselves through engaging 'our attention on the object, inviting us to make sense of what is before us'. The objects that we encounter in museums present a cognitive challenge 'requiring us to be receptive to new experiences and to relate them to our own knowledge of the world'. Respondents in this study described the cognitive dimension of the museum experience in various ways, one of which was through the term 'discovery':

> [museums offer] possibilities to look at both the familiar and the unexpected. New discoveries among the old friends at every visit (Public cohort: female, visitor, 55–70 years, urban resident).
>
> Museums are valuable educational sources to teach the public about things that are outside the square in which they live (Public cohort: female, non visitor, 18–24 years, urban resident).
>
> [Museums] allow us to be armchair travellers … [they] raise questions about why, how and where without having to travel all around the world! (Public cohort: female, visitor, parent, urban resident).

At a time when issues such as social inclusion and social cohesion feature prominently in public policy, it is confirming to hear respondents express the experience of museums in terms that relate to these goals. One young woman described the impact of museums in these terms: 'being exposed to a greater range of global issues makes individuals more conscious of global events. It makes people more understanding and open' (public cohort: female, non-visitor, 18–24 years, urban resident).

These powerful expressions evoke that intangible, emotional dimension of consumer perception described by Hwang (2002). They are embedded in actual experience, trigger positive memories and promise another beneficial dimension to the potential consumer. They are the words we should be using in our branding of the sector so that branding communication resonates with those with whom we want to engage.

Differentiation

Audience research also provides information for differentiating the museum brand. When the professional cohort in the same study was asked to address the question 'what makes museums different?', they identified four main factors which distinguish museums: objects, freedom, humanity and meaning.

Objects

Museums collect and preserve material culture heritage. 'They are amongst the few places that preserve our material culture and also record our memories' (professional cohort: Senior Exec State Museum resp 9). '[Museums] preserve objects of memory in perpetuity that gives a sense of focus and longevity in an environment of constant shift and emergence and attrition of other organizations/entertainment' (professional cohort: IT Specialist State Museum resp 16):

> The fact that we have 'stuff' sets us apart from other cultural institutions and all the theoretical and practical possibilities and constraints that material culture brings means that we are unique amongst institutions' (Professional cohort: Senior Exec Specialist Museum resp 12).

The presence of objects is defining. Objects are tangible, real things which characterize museums and 'set them apart from other options for education, entertainment or infotainment' (professional cohort: Senior Exec State Museum resp 5). 'The study of objects is both the business of museums and its main communication format' (professional cohort: Senior Curator State Museum resp 15). Snow (2002, p. 3) believes that:

> ... objects are good to think with—they help us think about relationships and issues which we might not otherwise think of. They do not need just to be 'illustrations', but can contribute to analysis by themselves ... . Taking an object as the centre of an analysis and building outwards can make a world of difference.

The recognition of objects is an important factor in self and community identity accentuated by the power of the real and its tangible connection to the past. The 'recognition of artefacts including photographs seems to be an important trigger for self-identity/nostalgia factor' (professional cohort: Support Services for regional museums resp 19).

At a community level, Corum (2002, p. 1) sees the 'immediacy and physicality' of objects providing a reminder 'that history actually happened' and that there is 'a physical link with those other worlds'. 'In this respect, museums are linked more directly to the search for identity in a community' (professional cohort: State Tourism resp 28). 'They help to engender a sense of pride and identity in local communities—especially in regional communities' (professional cohort: Senior Exec State Museum resp 9). They contribute in a unique way by illuminating 'what went before to make the people and place the way they are today' (professional cohort: Support Services for regional museums resp 20). As one respondent summarized it: 'I struggle to find an example of another structured service that like a museum can succeed with time in developing a better sense of place' (professional cohort: Support Services for regional museums resp 21).

Meaning

There are also views that the objects held in museum collections have power because they represent the community's sacred relics and are imbued with the spiritual dimension of socio-cultural value. Museums are places where one can 'quietly venerate the objects, pay homage to the ancestors and sense the spirit of the place' (professional cohort: State Tourism resp 28). One respondent spoke of 'the distinctiveness of the museum' and its 'quasi-religious role':

> With the growth of secular culture, museums have increasingly become the moral equivalent of the church. (How often we describe artefacts as a 'piece of the true cross'.) Events at museums often take on an almost sacrosanct character, whether deservedly or not (Professional cohort: State Tourism resp 28).

Unlike other public secular institutions, museums 'stimulate reflection on the quest for meaning' (professional cohort: IT Specialist State Museum resp 16) and are used by some for 'restorative reasons' and in the quest for 'something sacred, higher order, out of ordinary' (professional cohort: Support Services for regional museums resp 19). Certainly, the combination of inspiration, heightened perspective and awe can create a reverential experience:

> I was 17 years old the first time I entered the American Museum of Natural History in New York. I knew nothing about its layout or holdings at the time, so it was pure serendipity that led me to one of the lower levels on Central Park West. There I drifted into a small, quiet gallery and stood in front of a display of microscopic invertebrates, the creatures that inhabit the minute wetlands of our lives … I felt so startled by joy that my eyes teared. It was a spiritual experience of power and clarity; limning the wonder and sacredness of life, life at any level, even the most remote … I was … feeling saturated by wonder. Only praise leapt to mind, praise that knows no half-truths and pardons all. I felt what Walt Whitman may have felt when he wrote of the starry night, 'The bright suns I see and the dark suns I cannot see are in their place.' His intuition bespeaks the cryptic faith in the unknown and the extrapolation of belief that organized religions require. The part stands for the whole, as it does in natural history museums that say, in effect, 'Here is one wildebeest on the savanna, but there are many more of them, it's part of a species. Trust in it.'
> (Ackerman, in Carliner, 2002)

Freedom

> 'Interaction with museums is by choice and not imposed' (Professional cohort: Senior Exec Commonwealth Museum resp 3).

Museums provide a free or low-cost community resource for recreation, education, entertainment and enjoyment in a physically safe and undemanding space. Importantly, people freely choose to visit museums and this freedom of choice means that people are already somewhat committed to the experience. 'The idea of the visit already means there is a level of commitment to the activity … the fact that visitors are motivated is probably critical to the distinctive role of museums' (professional cohort: Curatorial Division Head-State Museum resp 17).

This freedom is also characteristic of the museum visit during which people self-select from the array of possibilities within the museum environment. It is this exercise of choice in the course of the visit that defines the *type* of learning that occurs in museums. 'Museums allow much free choice as to what and in what order will be encountered by the visitor. An exhibition is a unique form of engaging an audience and allows for multiple readings' (professional cohort: Senior Exec Specialist Museum resp 12). 'Museums provide generous scope for personal learning…. They open windows on a world little understood or appreciated before. The only limit on people enlarging their horizons is really the amount of time and energy they are prepared to put into it' (professional cohort: Support Services for regional museums resp 20).

Freedom of choice has other implications. It defines parameters, permissions and constraints within which museums must operate, particularly in terms of presenting information. In a free choice environment, visitors expect to make up their own minds about subjects and the museum is expected to be an 'honest information broker', presenting multiple sides to an argument:

> Importantly, museums can provide different perspectives simultaneously on an issue, an event. They are not prescriptive in any way. A museum provides an opportunity to learn analytically and at a somewhat disinterested distance from the event, issue or story it represents (Professional cohort: Senior Exec Community Museum resp 11).

The capacity of museums to present varying views on a particular subject simultaneously in a non-threatening environment 'allows a museum to become a subtle but potent social commentator—providing views in contradistinction to traditionally or politically current thinking, challenging the visitor to think more broadly and analytically' (professional cohort: Senior Exec Specialist Museum resp 12).

Museums can often do this successfully because 'in museums, issues of concern or interest to communities can be explored within historic, contemporary or future contexts. In this way, museums can create a forum for debate where even very controversial topics can be addressed' (professional cohort: Senior Exec State Museum resp 8); with the result that 'museums carry a perception of integrity and credibility in the community' (professional cohort: Senior Exec State Museum resp 5). This role as the 'honest information broker' is seen to be an increasingly distinguishing feature of museums. According to one respondent (professional cohort: Senior Exec Commonwealth Museum resp 2), 'museums are respected as truthful and trustworthy, able to provide an objective overview (unlike the media, or individual commentators and authors)' and in the face of change, they 'continue to promote a sense of "trust"' (professional cohort: IT Specialist State Museum resp 16).

Humanity

Respondents to this study felt that museums are distinguished by the place of humanity and human relationship, a quality that permeates every aspect of the museum experience from the position of the visitor, to relationships with communities and to opportunities for sharing with others:

> I think that museums are different in that they are institutions that put a high value on human experiences. Museums give value to the people whose stories are told and to the people who respond as visitors to those stories (Professional cohort: Local government cultural planner resp 27).

At the level of the individual, 'the visitor's own viewpoint is respected and placed in context' (professional cohort: Senior Exec Commonwealth Museum resp 2), 'personal communion with objects is allowed' (professional cohort: IT Specialist State Museum resp 16), a 'person's own direct experience ... enables them to engage in a way that relates to their own interests and is more immediate, personal and intimate' (professional cohort: Support Services for regional museums resp 21) with the result that:

> We are institutions that engage in a dialogue with our audience. (This is increasingly being recognized.) Although linear and didactic communication can have a valid place, museums allow much free choice as to what and in what order will be encountered by the visitor (Professional cohort: Senior Exec Specialist Museum resp 12).

Several of the respondents commented on the valued relationship that museums have with communities. One respondent sees this as based in the concept of 'public ownership' (professional cohort: IT Specialist State Museum resp 16). This may contribute to the perception that museums 'are usually seen as belonging to the community not separate to it' (professional cohort: Senior Exec Commonwealth Museum resp 3), allowing for a level of active engagement: 'Museums also have the potential for community involvement and engagement that is typically hard to achieve in other institutions' (professional cohort: Curatorial Division Head-State Museum resp 17).

The opportunity to share the event with others is an important dimension of the museum experience (Falk and Dierking, 1992). People visit museums in social groups for leisure activities. One can argue that these social group visits to museums are unique because of the group gestalt created by the interaction of the group with the collection content of the museum:

> I think that museums have the ability to provide group education and enjoyment in a way a library cannot. You cannot talk and discuss

items in a library as this would disrupt other visitors. A gallery can be both a private experience or something to be viewed and savoured with others (Professional cohort: IT Specialist State Museum resp 16).

Positioning the 'past'

At a time when the worth of museums is tied to instrumental outcomes determined by government policy, it may come as a surprise to bureaucrats that one of the strongest differentiating attributes of museums in the minds of the public is their position as the 'key to the past'. The majority of public respondents in the 'Museums, Impact and Value' study (53 of the 70 respondents) placed the connection with the past high on their list of the things they valued about museums. This is expressed across several dimensions.

The public believe that museums are unique in their capacity to show what the past looked like. Museums provide '… a graphic and physical way of educating and reminding people of their heritage and history and also of other societies' history and heritage, in a manner that is or should be easily accessible to all' (public cohort: male, non-visitor, 35–50 years, regional resident).

People also value the lessons of history because history's lessons can 'show the way'. 'It is important to remember history to help guide us into the future' (female, non-visitor, 18–24 years, urban resident). 'What is the quote? "a people that knows no past has no future"' (public cohort: female, visitor, 55–70 years, urban resident).

A connection with history is the prism through which other important values, such as *identity* and *belonging*, are realized. 'They can make people feel like they have something to belong to, a type of heritage' (public cohort: female, non-visitor, parent, regional visitor); '[museums provide] a sense of where we came from. Which in turn develops a sense of pride and belonging' (public cohort: female, visitor, 55–70 years, urban resident). 'Museums mean a "living" link to my history, where I came from, how I developed and how my city was formed (public cohort: male, visitor, 55–70 years, urban resident)'.

Other things that people value about the access to history provided by museums, is the opportunity for cultural transmission from one generation to the next and the provision of cultural continuity. It is perceived to be particularly important that children are introduced to the past. Museums offer parents an opportunity for 'showing children what has gone on before them' (public cohort: female, visitor, 55–70 years, urban resident). This is a form of social bonding across generations for 'a father or mother to show the child their experiences of our life and others' (public cohort: female, visitor, 35–50 years, urban resident).

If museums no longer existed:

> Perhaps we as a community would lose our sense of where we came from. Our triumphs and mistakes, as a community would no longer be on display (Public cohort: female, parent, non-visitor, regional resident).

The community would lose its past—I realise that we must progress into the future but we must also value and appreciate what has gone before and follow our story from its inception' (Public cohort: female, visitor, 55–70, regional resident).

Conclusion

Museums face challenges to win the 'hearts and minds' of policy makers, bureaucrats and the public (Holden, 2004, 2006a).

In relation to consumers, the sector must communicate the value and uniqueness of the museum experience to a public which has many options for its scarce leisure time. It must build loyalty through promises that it can deliver and through extrinsic and intrinsic benefits that it actually provides. Audience research enables the sector to explore the benefits that consumers are seeking in leisure and the values that they attribute to the museum experience. This is the basis for a branding communications strategy.

Holden (2006b) believes that the public is as interested in the intrinsic values inherent in cultural experiences as it is in immediate, extrinsic benefits. Hwang (2002) argues that a brand is distinguished by consumers' perceptions and feelings about a product's attributes. Through audience research, consumers' perceptions and feelings about museums reveal the symbolic, emotional and value-rich nature of the experience.

Encounters with museums provide perspective, inspiration, reflection, awe, insight, enrichment, discovery, understanding, openness and enlightenment. The 'promise' that museums offer is a positive one that has the power to attract and engage people's hearts and minds.

The museum experience is one which is freely chosen and mediated visually through 'real' objects. But it is what happens as a result of that experience that sets museums apart from other educational, cultural and leisure experiences. Museums are about relationships. There is the obvious fact that the museum experience can be shared in the company of others. But museums encourage our relationship with ourselves; through stimulating self-reflection, visitors can relate to their personal past, reflect on individual interests and become inspired. Museums enable communities to relate to their 'place', their history, 'who they are and why they came here', grounding their sense of identity. Museums enable people to relate to the wider world, to other phenomena and to the cosmos. Museums help people find their place in relation to the past, in relation to the world at large, in relation to what it means to be human.

If brand equity 'is affected by the real and perceived quality of the product, its unique value, associations with it and loyalty to it' (Gardella, 2002; Hwang, 2002), then the positive equity of museum experience is an under-utilized asset that should be a part of the overall branding of the sector to consumers and bureaucrats alike. Through confidently stating the unique brand that is museums, we as a sector, will have found the voice to speak from our heart and purpose, to those whom we want to hear us.

References

Appleton, J. (2002). Distorted priorities are destroying museums. *The Independent*, 29 May, p. 16.

Australian Expert Group on Industry Studies (AEGIS) (2004). *Social Impacts of Participating in the Arts and Cultural Activities: Report on Stage Two—Evidence, Issues and Recommendations.* Confidential report to the Cultural Ministers Council via the Department of Communication, Information, Technology and the Arts. University of Western Sydney.

Australian Bureau of Statistics (ABS) (2002). *Attendance at Selected Cultural Venues and Events*, Australia, 23 October 2004 (cat. no. 4114.0).

Australian Bureau of Statistics (ABS) (2005). *Year Book Australia: 2005*, Canberra (cat. no. 1301.0).

Bennett, T. (1989). Museums and public culture: history, theory and politics. *Media Information Australia*, 53, August, 57–65.

Burton, C. and Scott, C. A. (2003). Museums: challenges for the 21st century. *The International Journal of Arts Management*, 5(2), 56–68.

Carliner, S. (2002). Reflections on learning in museums. Kappa Delta Pi Record. <http://saulcarliner.home.att.net/museums/inspirearticle.htm> (accessed 19 November 2004).

Corum, T. (2002). Speaking Up for Objects. Paper given at *Objects of Research* (inaugural seminar of the Centre for Heritage Research). University of Leeds. <http://www.leeds.ac.uk/heritage/timtalk.htm> (accessed 30 April 2002).

Department for Culture, Media and Sport (DCMS) (1998) A New Cultural Framework, London, 23 October 2003.

Ellis, A. (2002). *Planning in a Cold Climate*. Lecture at the Getty Leadership Institute, July. The Getty Center.

Ellis, A. (2003). Valuing Culture. Paper presented at the Valuing Culture event held at the National Theatre Studio on 17 June 2003 (organised by Demos in partnership with the National Gallery, the National Theatre and AeA Consulting). <http://www.demos.co.uk/catalogue/valuingculturespeeches/> (accessed 5 October 2004).

Falk, J. and Dierking, L. D. (1992). *The Museum Experience*. Whalesback Books, Washington, DC.

Falk, J., Dierking, L., Rennie, L., Scott, C. A. and Cohen-Jones, M. (2004). Interactives and visitor learning in curator. *The Museum Journal*, 47(2), 171–92.

Gardella, J. (2002). Promises to keep: making branding work for science centers. *ASTC Dimensions*, May/June. <http://www.astc.org/pubs/dimensions/2002/may-jun/branding.htm> (accessed 22 June 2006).

Holden, J. (2004). Capturing cultural value: how culture has become a tool of government policy. DEMOS. <http://<www.demos.co.uk> (accesed 21 November 2004).

Holden, J. (2006a). Cultural value and the crisis of legitimacy: why culture needs a democratic mandate. DEMOS. <http://www.demos.co.uk> (accessed 16 May 2006).

Holden, J. (2006b). Cultural value and the crisis of legitimacy. Presentation at the *Australia Council for the Arts*. Sydney 1 August.

Hwang, J. (2002). *Study of Branding Strategy in New Media and Brand Identity. Development for Short Film Channel*. MFA Thesis. Parsons School of Design and Technology <http://www.mfadt.parsons.edu/thesis_archive/m2002/ Jia_Hwang/JiaHwang_Thesis.pdf> (accessed 22 June 2006).

Kotler, N. and Kotler, P. (2000). Can museums be all things to all people? Missions, goals and marketing's role. *Museum Management and Curatorship*, 18(3), 271–87.

Market and Research Opinion International (MORI) (2004). Visitors to Museums and Galleries 2004. Research study conducted for the Museums, Libraries and Archives Council. <http://www.mla.gov.uk/documents/ mori_visitors_v2.doc> (accessed 1 September 2005).

Matarasso, F. (1996). Defining Values: Evaluating Arts Programmes (Social Impact of the Arts. Working Paper 1). Comedia, Stroud.

Matarasso, F. (2000). Opening up the china cabinet: Museums, inclusion and contemporary society. Paper by François Matarasso for the Museums Association conference, Jessey, 16 October 2000 (unpublished).

McCarthy, F. et al. (2004). Gifts of the Muse: reframing the debate about the benefits of the arts. Rand Corporation. <http://www.rand.org/pubs/ monographs/2005/RAND_MG218.pdf> (accessed 12 February 2005).

Museums, Libraries and Archives Council (MLA) (2005). New directions in social policy: developing the evidence base for museums, libraries and archives in England. Museums, Libraries and Archives Council. <http:// www.mla.gov.uk/documents/ndsp_developing_evidence.doc>   (accessed 1 September 2005).

New South Wales Audit Office (NSW) (2006). *Performance audit: agency use of performance information to manage services. The audit office of New South Wales.* <http://www.audit.nsw.gov.au/publications/reports/performance/2006/ performance_information/performance_information_june2006.pdf> (accessed 12 August 2006).

Organisation for Economic Co-operation and Development (OECD) (1997). In search of results: performance management practices. <http://www.oecd. org/dataoecd/18/12/36144694.pdf> (accessed 22 March 2006).

Organisation for Economic Co-operation and Development (OECD) (2003). Public sector modernisation. Policy Brief Series. <http://www.oecd.org/ dataoecd/63/23/15688578.pdf> (accessed 18 April 2006).

Organisation for Economic Co-operation and Development (OECD) (2004). Public sector modernisation: Governing for performance. Policy Brief Series. <http://www.oecd.org/dataoecd/52/44/33873341.pdf> (accessed 22 March 2006).

Organisation for Economic Co-operation and Development (OECD) (2005). Public sector modernisation: The way forward. Policy brief series. <http:// www.oecd.org/dataoecd/40/33/35654629.pdf> (accessed 22 March 2006).

Scott, C. A. (2000). Branding: positioning museums in the 21st century. *International Journal of Arts Management*, 2(3), 35–9 and *Open Museum Journal*, 2.

Scott, C. A. (2006). *Museums, Impact and Value*. PhD thesis. Dissertation in progress.

Snow, D. (2002). Object Lessons. Paper given at objects of research (inaugural seminar of the Centre for Heritage Research). University of Leeds, 30 April. <http://www.leeds.ac.uk/heritage/timtalk.htm> (accessed 15 January 2006).

Terry, C. J. (2002). Management and marketing—A Director's Perspective. Keynote Case Study presented at the INTERCOM Conference Leadership in Museums: Are our Core Values Shifting, October 16–19.

The Outspan Group and Perron, L. (1999). *Socio-Economic Benefits Framework Applied to the Cultural Sector*. Report prepared for National Arts Centre, National Capital Commission and Department of Canadian Heritage, March. Ontario, Strategic Research and Analysis (SRA). Strategic Planning and Policy Coordination, Department of Canadian Heritage.

6

Major case study: Rethinking Tate Modern as an art museum 'brand'

Martha Phillips and Daragh O'Reilly

Introduction

The art historian Julian Stallabrass, discussing contemporary art museums in the 1990s, asserts that their 'activities … became steadily more commercial as they internalized corporate models of activity, establishing alliances with business, bringing their products closer to commercial culture, and modelling themselves less on libraries than shops and theme parks' (2004, p. 14). Part of this corporatization process is an increasing use of branding by arts marketing practitioners and scholars. In this short case study, we explore, in particular, the development and application of museum branding by London's Tate Modern in partnership with Wolff Olins, the branding consultancy.

Museum branding

Interest in branding among arts and heritage marketing scholars is increasing. However, current marketing textbooks do not deal in great detail with the application of branding to the contemporary art world. Nor in those books which focus on arts or heritage marketing does the specific topic of museum branding receive a very extensive treatment, see Maclean (1997), Kotler and Kotler (1998), Colbert (2001), Chong (2002), Hill et al. (2003) or Kolb (2004). More recently, however, Sargeant's textbook on non-profit marketing management (2005) does write at some length about branding in relation to non-profit organizations, dealing with issues such as brand attributes, benefits, culture, values and personality. In the research literature, Caldwell and Coshall's study (2002) examined consumers' personal constructs of museums, treating the brand essentially in terms of its image in the mind of the consumer. A recent working paper by Evans and Bridson (2006) focuses on brand orientation within museums, conceptualizing it as based on distinctive capabilities, functional benefits to customers, value added and symbolic capabilities. The existing publications, however, arguably seek to apply or explore the application of mainstream managerial marketing ideas about branding to arts, heritage or non-profit organizations. Their writers are principally concerned to ensure that branding concepts are applied to those organizations in a way which does justice to the particularities of the arts and heritage, and also with a view to informing mainstream marketing theory with insights from those sectors.

Brands and social context

It has been argued that managerial marketing theory fails to fully account for brand functionality. Lury (2004), for example, combines cultural, media and marketing theory to explore brand ontology beyond mainstream branding theory. From her work, a variety of constructions of brands emerge which provide a useful alternative to the usual marketing-theoretical notions of brands as intangible assets or differentiation devices. For example, brands can be loosely understood as a medium of exchange between company and consumer, and a rationality that organizes consumption. A brand may be regarded as an object, not fixed in time or space, that generates a patterning of social relations activity (Lury, 2004, p. 2). A brand is also an object of the economy, mediating the supply and demand of products through information. And brands are also a way of considering economic circulation as a culturally structured process (Lury, 2004, p. 4). According to Lury, brands can also be understood as new media objects, since they are reliant on media as a vehicle for their performative role (p. 6) and brands enable the conversion of economic capital to symbolic capital (p. 10). Lury's analysis suggests that that art or 'cultural' brands are a late twentieth century phenomenon that mediate the consumption of art, the art brand being a conceptual 'interface' that encases the exchange of information. In the often confusing realm of art production and consumption, the organization of the subject via the conceptual shorthand of a brand enables the attempt to produce more straightforward patterns of consumption.

The consumption of art through brands, and their creation, is motivated and supported by a contemporary system of social signification. As social constructions, brands are necessarily only meaningful within a social context, and their methods of 'meaning control' operate within predetermined systems of social signification. Therefore, the signified value is key, and profitability lies in engaging with and emphasizing this collective sign system. According to Bourdieu (1986), the consumption of art and culture is a power relations mechanism, with the distribution of a society's symbolic capital being mediated through a classificatory system of 'taste'. Recently in the UK, the idea of 'cool', which has been applied to the production and consumption of (for example) art, design and music, mediates symbolic capital in this way. This is relevant to this case study because the Tate was designated 'Cool Brand Leader' in 2003. This is an award by the Brand Council and its results are heavily promoted by the British Council—coincidentally, like the Tate, also the client of Wolff Olins at the time of writing. An institution such as Tate Modern is in a position of significant power to affirm and promote certain selected aspects of cool symbolic capital. Its open embrace of corporate partnerships and the practice of branding permits business organizations ready access to a key cultural site where certain kinds of symbolic capital are privileged for production and consumption. This can also function as a method of inclusion and exclusion of some art consumers in relation to circuits of symbolic capital.

Branding Tate Modern

The Tate is a group of four galleries (Tate Britain and Tate Modern in London, Tate Liverpool and Tate St Ives), funded by a mix of government grant, lottery funding, admissions charges, corporate sponsorship, donations, fees and trading income. According to the organizational website, the organization employs no less than 20 staff working on marketing communications, as well as the assistance of external marketing communications agencies. Apart from the usual battery of promotional mechanisms, the key elements of the Tate's marketing strategy are the management of its visual identity, sponsorship, the Turner prize, its loudly trumpeted hanging innovations and its commissioning strategy.

The Tate Modern component of this 'brand architecture', the gallery of contemporary art, was an early convert to the idea of the 'museum as brand'. The gallery has attracted large numbers of visitors since its opening on London's South Bank in 2000. Instead of seeking independently to grow their own brand, the organization engaged the help of external consultants, Wolff Olins. This consultancy firm is a subsidiary of Omnicom, a global media conglomerate based on Madison Avenue, New York. In 2005, Omnicom's revenues came to $10.5 billion, with profits of $791 million. It describes itself as 'a strategic holding company of the top creative talent from around the world that it can connect to meet any of a client's marketing and communications challenges'.

Corpwatch has reported (Raphael, 2005) that companies owned by Omnicom enjoyed almost a monopoly (89 per cent) of Bush administration public relations (PR) contracts awarded between 2001 and 2004, totalling nearly a quarter of a billion dollars in revenue. Omnicom's subsidiary, Wolff Olins, is not of course in the contemporary art museum business. It is, according to its website, in the 'reinvention business'. They assist their clients to 'reinvent their organizations, *and the markets they work in*' (emphasis added).

Brand heritage

Wolff Olins' branding strategy required 'the' Tate to drop the definite article, so that, strictly speaking, one should speak of 'Tate' and not 'the Tate'. This of course constructs the organization in much the same way as one might refer to a person. This brings to mind the Tate's 'brand heritage', for Tate was originally a real person, none other than Sir Henry Tate, who made a fortune from shopping and sugar. The shopping origins of Tate Modern are so elided by the brand makeover that the citizen might tend to forget where the founding funds came from. However, Wolff Olins were ever mindful of the Tate's grocery store heritage—as the *Daily Telegraph* once commented (Smee, 2003): 'It was the Tate's own image consultants, Wolff Olins, who notoriously acknowledged their ambition to make going to Tate Modern less like a "museum experience" and more like a "shopping experience"'. The connection between department stores, brands and museums also featured in two UK exhibitions already this century, namely 'Brand.New' an exhibition at the V&A in 2000 and 'Shopping: A Century of Art and Consumer Culture' at the Tate Liverpool in 2003, featuring a replica Tesco store (see Szmigin, 2006, for an analysis from the point of view of the aestheticization of consumption).

Continuing the grocery brand heritage connection, Unilever has been a major sponsor of the Tate Modern's yearly commissions since 2000. The brand owners of 'I Can't Believe It's Not Butter', 'Colman's Mustard', 'PG Tips', 'Vaseline' and the 'Lynx Effect' (among many other leading shopping brands) offer a snug brand fit with Tate's shopping-to-sugar brand heritage. It also helps to align Unilever's creativity with that of the commissioned artists, as 'creativity' is one of Unilever's core brand values. After all, it takes creativity to make shopping brands (e.g., 'Vaseline' by Unilever) and it takes creativity to make art (e.g., Louise Bourgeois's 'I Do, I Undo, I Redo', or 'Double Bind' by Juan Munoz, or 'Marshals' by Amish Kapok, or 'The Weather Project' by Olafur Eliasson). Therefore, just as there is a basic commonality between consuming art and consuming grocery brands or shopping experiences, so also is there a fundamental lack of difference between producing art and designing jars of 'Vaseline'.

Sponsorship and celebrity

Much of the activity in which the Tate engages to renew its brand image is driven by corporate sponsorship. Apart from the funding of the annual commissions series by Unilever, the Tate Modern also relied on sponsorship for its recent rehang, courtesy of UBS. Sponsorship also plays a role in relation to the Tate's annual Turner Prize, currently Courtesy of 'Gordon's® Gin'. The prize's strategy of attracting media controversy through its short-listing of innovative artistic talent generates extraordinary publicity. Televised awards ceremonies have been one of Britain's major growth industries in the past 5 years, particularly in the areas of TV soaps and popular music. The Turner organizers also invite celebrities, such as Madonna, to present the awards, making the event a mediatized celebrity spectacle. The late twentieth century celebrity fixation and the cult of the celebrity artist clearly contribute towards the branding process. This is a culturally rooted influence, documented in detail in Walker's 'Art and Celebrity' (2003), where it is argued Picasso and Dali were the first artists to master the publicity game (p. 47). Contemporary artists engage in extensive self-promotion, and their notoriety derives from their attributes of youth, eccentricity, radicalism and shock. Furthermore, in cases such as Hirst and Emin, their cult of personality is inextricable from, and accentuated by, their work. Stallabrass argues that Hirst and Emin's work, by its very nature, necessarily has a life as mass media objects (2006, p. 43). Underlying all of these, for some observers, are questions about the value of this circus. Artists and institutions appear to exploit the transgressive trend of modern art as part of the brand building process. Tate Modern's 'Blockbuster' shows feature high-profile individuals such as Frida Kahlo, whose 2005 exhibition was accompanied by a visual spectacle of Mexican culture. These efforts might be read as attempts to build brand power and identity by hijacking fetishized, romanticized public attitudes to modern art and 'celebrity' artists in the collective public consciousness.

The uses of museum branding

It is clear that the Tate is an important reference site for the Wolff Olins consultancy. It features as one of only three brands mentioned in a short narrative at the top of the agency's client list (see <http://www.wolff-olins.com/tate.htm>), the others being First Direct and Orange. There is even a downloadable case study about the Tate on the website. A claim is made in this case study that part of the Tate's motivation for re-branding itself 'was to establish a distinct brand appeal through accessibility and a forward-thinking approach to art' (Wolff Olins, 2006). The consultancy's experience with Tate is used as a means of selling to other prospects, and this is explicitly attempted by means of a piece entitled 'To brand or not to brand? How can cultural organisations benefit from branding?' written by a senior Wolff Olins' consultant (Wentworth, 2006). The writer states that 'there can hardly be a business in the developed world that doesn't understand the contribution a powerful brand makes to its market value'. The writer mentions the case of Orange and attributes its increased value on acquisition to its 'brand success'. It would be interesting to know what relevance this has to leaders of cultural organizations which are not usually traded on the stock exchange and therefore do not usually deliver large capital gains to their equity shareholders. The writer asks 'Should [cultural organizations] concern themselves with branding?'. The answer is that 'To achieve their goals of diversity, accessibility and education, they need money. Lots of it. Unfortunately, they can no longer rely on the state to provide it' (Wentworth, 2006). Branding is then offered as a means of competing in the markets for funding, sponsorship, staff, artists and visitors. Seeking to pre-empt any prospective client's objection to the idea of branding cultural organizations, the writer constructs directors and curators as associating branding with 'selling out, dumbing-down, loss of integrity—an open door for commercialism and theme-park culture' (Wentworth, 2006); and of course how wrong they are! This is where a key thread in recent brand thinking is used to warrant the branding of contemporary art museums, namely the notion of the affective power of brands and their generation of, or association with, emotional consumption experiences. Museum visiting is seen by Wolff Olins as an emotional experience and social occasion, 'an experience that is defined *as much* by [...] what's on sale in the shop, the architecture [...] or the atmosphere in the café, as by the objects or paintings on display' (emphasis added) (Wentworth, 2006).

Traditionally, museums demanded effort and engagement from the visitor, but 'postmodern theories of leisure [...] suggest that contemporary leisure activities are increasingly fragmented and superficial and demand little commitment from the participant' (Burton and Scott, 2003). This moves the debate about museums' role into the area of the experience economy (Pine and Gilmore, 1999), and the society of the spectacle (Debord, 1992). Some years before the Tate brand makeover, Nicholas Serota, its Director since 1988, wrote a book entitled '*Experience or Interpretation: The Dilemma of Museums of Modern Art*' (2000). It seems that there has been a happy marriage between the director's thinking and contemporary brand ideology.

Conclusion

It is clear that the Tate Modern is a major tourist attraction, an example of what George Yudice calls the 'the expediency of culture' (2003), and therefore of major economic value to London, much as the Olympic Games have the potential to be in 2012. On the other hand, Tate Modern is also a key reference site for Madison Avenue on London's South Bank and an example of the cooptation of a certain kind of artistic aesthetic by global media and business conglomerates. It is an opportunity for business organizations to associate themselves with a 'cool' art–cultural brand and to inject their values into the contemporary circuits of art consumption and symbolic capital. This is part of the wider corporatization and consumerization of the arts and heritage through co-branding deals such as product placement, sponsorship and celebrity endorsement—deals in which, it has to be said, many artists and museums are enthusiastic partners. On its website, Wolff Olins describes the Tate Modern as being 'brand-led, rather than institution-led'—a clear indication of a shift away from traditional cultural institutional values to a commitment to commodified offerings, and a sign that the Tate has become a 'cultural corporate'.

References

Bourdieu, P. (1986). *Distinction: A Social Critique of the Judgement of Taste.* Routledge.

Burton, C. and Scott, C. (2003). Museums: challenges for the 21st century. *International Journal of Arts Management,* 5(2), 55–68.

Caldwell, N. and Coshall, J. (2002). Measuring brand associations for museums and galleries using repertory grid. *Management Decision,* 40(4), 383.

Chong, D. (2002). *Arts Management.* Routledge.

Colbert, F. (2001). *Marketing Culture and the Arts.* Presses HEC.

Debord, G. (1992). *Society of the Spectacle.* Rebel Press.

Evans, J. and Bridson, K. (2006). Brand Orientation and Retail Strategy within the Australian Museum Sector. Working Paper. Academy of Marketing Proceedings, July. Middlesex University.

Hill, E., O'Sullivan, T. and O'Sullivan, C. (2003). *Creative Arts Marketing.* Elsevier.

Kolb, B. (2004). *Marketing for Cultural Organisations: New Strategies for Attracting Audiences to Classical Music, Dance, Museums, Theatre and Opera.* Thomson.

Kotler, P. and Kotler, N. (1998). *Museum Strategy and Marketing: Designing Missions, Building Audiences, Generating Revenue and Resources.* Jossey Bass Wiley.

Lury, C. (2004). *Brands: The Logos of the Global Economy.* Routledge.

Maclean, F. (1997). *Marketing the Museum.* Routledge.

Pine, J. and Gilmore, J. (1999). *Experience Economy: Work Is Theatre and Every Business a Stage.* Harvard Business School Press.

Raphael, C. (2005). Spinning Media for Government, Corpwatch. 10 February. <http://www.corpwatch.org/> (accessed 28 June 2006).

Sargeant, A. (2005). *Marketing Management for Nonprofit Organisations.* Oxford University Press.

Serota, N. (2000). *Experience or Interpretation.* Thames and Hudson.

Smee, S. (2003). He turned a river green and reversed a waterfall: so what does Olafur Eliasson have in store for Tate Modern? We could be in for a surprise, he tells Sebastian Smee. *Daily Telegraph,* 30 September <http://www.telegraph.co.uk/arts/main.jhtml?xml=/arts/2003/09/30/baolaf30.xml> (accessed 10 December 2006).

Stallabrass, J. (2004). *Art Incorporated: The Story of Contemporary Art.* Oxford University Press.

Stallabrass, J. (2006). *High Art Lite: The Rise and Fall of BritArt.* Verso.

Szmigin, I. (2006). The aestheticisation of consumption: an exploration of brand.new and Shopping. *Marketing Theory,* 6(1), 107–18.

Walker, J. (2003). *Art and Celebrity*. Pluto Press.

Wentworth, J. (2006). To brand or not to brand? How can cultural organisations benefit from branding? Wolff-Olins. <http://www.wolff-olins.com/tobrandornottobrand.htm> (accessed 10 December 2006).

Wolff Olins (2006). Tate: look again, think again. <http://www.wolff-olins.com/files/Tate_case_study_web.pdf> (accessed 10 December 2006).

Yudice, G. (2003). *The Expediency of Culture: Uses of Culture in the Global Era (Post-Contemporary Interventions)*. Duke University Press.

Part D

Museum marketing culture

7

Major case study: Museum of contemporary art markets itself

Ruth Rentschler

About non-profit art museums

Non-profit art museums are a genre of institution that typically depends on a mix of funding sources for survival. This case concerns a university art museum. University art museums are a particular type of non-profit art museum: they are part of a university whose mission is education, not cultural awareness. This leads to a gap in funding opportunities: each level of government sees the funding of the university art museum as the others' responsibility. Universities do not see museums as core to their central mission and therefore often leave museums under-resourced. This underscores the importance of initially establishing the purpose of university museums (Arnold-Foster, 2000). It also underscores the importance of university museums marketing themselves.

About the museum of contemporary art

The Museum of Contemporary Art (MCA) opened in 1991 as a university art museum. It is located in a twentieth century maritime building on Sydney's harbour front at Circular Quay. It was converted in order to house the contemporary art collection created by the Power Bequest, which was left to the University of Sydney by John Power, a graduate of the university. In 1906, at the age of 24 years, he received a significant inheritance. He left his inheritance to the university 'for the future endowment of the people of Australia, to facilitate the exposition and dissemination of knowledge of the plastic arts' and for the purchase of art works for a collection of contemporary art (Thompson, 1999). The university received the bequest in 1962 after the death of John Power and his sister.

While the first works of art were purchased in 1967, it took some years for the bequest to reach fruition in the form of an MCA. On 24 November 1984, the Maritime Services Building (MSB) on Circular Quay was chosen to house the MCA, with assistance from the New South Wales Government (Murphy, 1993). The stipulation of the Power Bequest meant the MCA's association with its parent university was never going to be a traditional one: it immediately positioned itself as Australia's national MCA focusing 'on achieving a match between the latest in contemporary art and ideas and an adventurous art-going public' (Wallace, 2000). The MCA's site in the heart of the city gave it a profile vital to accessing the wider community and attracting substantial corporate sponsorship while creating a psychological and philosophical distance from the university and its central role as an educational institution (Wallace, 2000, p. 34).

At the time of its opening in 1991, the MCA was the only Australian public art museum linked with a university and it benefited from the university's long history and established reputation as a cultural institution. As well as attracting a wider public audience, the MCA's site helped to attract substantial corporate sponsorship.

The MCA was the first major cultural centre in Australia dedicated to contemporary art. The promotional benefits for such an institution include: the adaptive reuse of a heritage site, with a row of shops facing the tourist-flooded end of inner-city George Street; being the focal point for the promotion of local and international works of art; and becoming a vehicle to facilitate private subsidy of the arts, making it a desirable medium through which cultural policy can be pursued.

When the MCA opened, it had no separate marketing department, but was part of the university's communications department. However, it was realized from the outset that the MCA had great potential to become an icon cultural identity—a brand—in the marketplace, and that through this brand identity it could expand its income from sponsorship and employ public relations (PR) and other innovative fund-raising activities (Thompson, 1999). As a result, the marketing function evolved to become a separate department.

The PR role was the responsibility of a full-time manager. Considerable resources were devoted to it: it is one of very few cultural organizations to dedicate such resources to the PR role. Because the MCA generates some 87 per cent of its own funds, in contrast to other non-profit museums in Australia and New Zealand, PR is an important function. Savings in advertising costs and the likelihood of gaining a high profile in the media were seen as justification for bearing the salary of the PR person (Thompson, 1999).

Despite variable attendance figures, recent market research done by the museum indicates that it can claim 100 per cent recognition throughout Sydney. Furthermore, the museum is able to promote itself as an essential part of Sydney's reputation as one of the great cities of the world.

The MCA once boasted that 89 per cent of its operational income came from private sponsorship, donations, admissions and commercial operations. This is a most unusual position for a non-profit art museum in Australia; non-profit art museums generally receive government funding of up to 70 per cent of income. The funding model adopted follows the English model: a substantive amount of funding comes from government, with additional sources from sponsorship, and audience income from activities such as blockbuster exhibitions, restaurants and bookshops. This differs from the US model of philanthropy and sponsorship, which sees a far greater diversity of funding but with little, if any, deriving from government sources (Rentschler, 2000). As the then chairman of the board stated:

> Although the museum's programs embrace not only familiar and popular cultural forms, but also present difficult, and even confronting subjects, the fact that the MCA is almost self-supporting is unequalled in Australia; moreover it has few parallels abroad.
>
> (MCA, 1995)

In this light, MCA's funding achievements represent truly significant marketing successes. However, while its funding model underlines the importance of marketing to recognition, it also shows the importance of leadership to sustainability.

Non-profit art museums and funding

Non-profit art museums need to market their wares in much the same way as profit-oriented organizations offering experiential products. However, such art museums are different in that they depend on a mix of funding sources for survival, rather than box-office takings alone. The mix of funding sources usually includes government, sponsorship and audience income. University art museums are a particular type of non-profit art museum for they are part of a university whose mission is education, rather than creation of cultural awareness. As mentioned in the introduction, this leads to a gap in funding opportunities, as each level of government sees the funding of the university art museum as the others' responsibility. The university does not see the museum as core to its central mission and therefore may leave the museum under-resourced. Under such circumstances, it is important to establish the reason for the museum's existence right from the outset.

As previously stated, Australian non-profit art museums usually rely on government funding for up to 70 per cent of their income. In the case of the

MCA in Sydney, the funding usually provided by government was supplied by the University of Sydney but did not meet the level of funding needed. Like its counterparts, the MCA has become more entrepreneurial and markets itself externally to the public, as well as internally to its university funding source.

Entrepreneurship and innovation in marketing

The MCA is entrepreneurial in its development of creative programmes and promotes them in ways that ensure it retains its funding diversity. For example, media and annual reports of the MCA since the 1990s indicate a wealth of entrepreneurial and innovative activity associated with creative events scheduling and in the methods used to maintain funding diversity.

While discussion of finance and organizational issues frequently occurs, it is always in the context of the realization of entrepreneurial opportunities from sponsors. The focus of the annual reports is as a marketing communication tool appealing to potential sponsors. The consistent emphasis on funding is thus a major focus of the museum's management. Moreover, the MCA's annual reports constantly stress the organization's innovative activities, particularly as these activities relate to its ability to realize its entrepreneurial goal.

The MCA is innovative in the type of sponsorships it attracts and in the way it cost-effectively uses PR as an integrated marketing communication tool (Thompson, 1999). Funding is seen as a means of realizing market opportunities and audience relevance with innovative presentations to potential sponsors of the ways the MCA can benefit them. The annual reports indicate the ongoing quest for funding from a diversity of sources.

External cross-promotions and internal neglect

On the one hand, the MCA recognizes the strategic necessity of remaining on side with political, government and cultural parties to achieve its funding aims; however, it balances this with important cross-promotions and sponsorships. For example, the involvement by American Express (AmEx) in the quirky 'Plastic Fantastic' exhibition of 1997 shows the value of a partnership that won the MCA/AmEx the Australasian Sponsorship Marketing Association Awards for the Overall Best Sponsorship of 1997 and the Best Small Budget Sponsorship. The show was built around works made from plastic and generated large audiences because it intrigued them as an experiential event. The MCA marketing manager at that time explained that exclusive benefits to card members were provided by free card admission days and the promotions created great memory recall for potential audiences (Thompson, 1999).

However, there is evidence that while the MCA has aimed to stimulate demand from the public, it has possibly ignored its 'parent' organization, the University of Sydney. This may in part have contributed to the difficulties the MCA experienced towards the end of the 1990s and may have led to a complex game of brinkmanship involving the key parties.

Funding stability needed

Raising funds for capital works can be the simple part of establishing a museum, while the difficulties of obtaining support for ongoing operational costs are often underestimated (Cossons, 1999). The MCA boasts that 87 per cent of its operational income comes from private sponsorship, donations, admissions and commercial operations. This is a most unusual position for a non-profit art museum in Australia.

Since 1997, the MCA has enjoyed the largest ongoing cash sponsorship for visual arts in the country from its $2 million deal with Seppelt Wines. This equates to more than 10 per cent of MCA's funds regularly being sourced from individual donations and membership. Corporate sponsorship accounts for the largest proportion of its revenue, and means that the MCA continually faces challenges in this regard, but the MCA's determination to pursue the controversial—in particular the $1 million venture to display Jeff Koons' 'Puppy'—is the root cause of much of its financial woes.

MCA had had rising staff costs and falling audience numbers, complicated by ongoing bickering with the University of Sydney about funding obligations. In 1999, the New South Wales State Government was forced to bail out the MCA with a $750,000 donation to stave off imminent insolvency, augmented by a one-off gift from AmEx of $250,000. Telstra also dug into its pockets, allowing the scrapping of admission fees in the light of the Olympics and the MCA's potential role in the celebrations. By 2000, new Director Elizabeth Ann MacGregor attributed a small profit to tight cost controls and near record attendances, but still faced looming cash flow problems after the Power Bequest funding was lost in 1999. Stable, ongoing funding is vital to secure major corporate or private pledges and MacGregor summed this up by saying: 'We should never be dependent on private income, which should be the cream on the top' (Turner, 2000, p. 13).

Looking to the future

The MCA is recognized as a valuable cultural institution. The combination of contemporary arts development and display, heritage preservation, and cultural tourism opportunity might provide some justification for its subsidization. The MCA is an instrument of cultural policy, which is capable of effectively marketing the benefits it offers to both external and internal markets.

After years of haggling, by the early 2000s, the MCA had secured its future (Sexton, 2001). Numerous pledges from sponsors, government and non-profit organizations came in. The MCA needed between $1.5 and $2 million in recurrent funding to ensure its long-term viability. The premier of New South Wales, representing his government, agreed to contribute to the MCA's running costs for the first time, contributing $3 million each year for 5 years. Through the Sydney Harbour Foreshore Authority (SHFA), it will spend another $7 million over 10 years on capital works. The University of Sydney will walk away from the MCA, writing off a $6.4 million debt. The university will relinquish its lease on the building to the SHFA. The Sydney City Council (SCC) also walks away $1.5 million poorer.

It was originally intended that the University of Sydney, through the Power Bequest, would provide ongoing funding for the MCA, in a similar fashion to that provided to national or state non-profit art museums in Australia. However, that arrangement did not come to fruition and, as it transpired, 10 weeks before the MCA ran out of cash, past funding from the University of Sydney was replaced by government funding from the New South Wales State Government.

The MCA is a cultural icon, recognized for the profile it brings the Sydney Harbour foreshore. The actions of partners and sponsors recognize this fact. The combination of contemporary arts development and display, heritage preservation, and cultural tourism opportunity provide justification to subsidize the institution. But the circumstances of the case provide opportunity to observe how the roles of respective stakeholders can become bogged down in politics, personalities and provision of funds. Once that happens, marketing communications are forgotten.

Hence, the MCA still needs to focus its activities so that it employs integrated marketing communication to market both the experiential events it schedules, and the sponsorship opportunities these present for marketing companies. It cannot be distracted by games of politics, provision of funds or people. How to bring this about remains an ongoing issue.

References

Arnold-Foster, K. (2000). A developing sense of crisis: a new look at University Collections in the United Kingdom. *Museum International*, 52(3), 10–14.

Cossons, N. (1999). United Nations. *Museums Journal*, 99(2), 32–5.

Murphy, B. (1993). *Museum of Contemporary Art: Vision and Context*. Museum of Contemporary Art, Sydney.

Museum of Contemporary Art (MCA) (1993/1994, 1994/1995, 1996/1997, 1997/1998). Annual Reports. Museums and Collections in Australia. Australian Vice-Chancellors' Committee.

Rentschler, R. (2000). Entrepreneurship: from denial to discovery in non-profit art museums. *UIC/AMA Research Symposium*, Chicago, 12–13 June.

Sexton, J. (2001). Premier guarantees museum's future. *The Weekend Australian*, 14–15 July, p. 4.

Thompson, B. (1999). Museum of contemporary art: Harbourside Art Museum. In *Innovative Arts Marketing* (R. Rentschler, ed.), pp. 32–47, Allen and Unwin, New South Wales.

Turner, B. (2000). MCA to Land in the Black. *Australian Financial Review*, 11 February, p. 13.

Wallace, S-A. (2000). From campus to city: University Museums in Australia. *Museum International*, 52(3), 32–7.

The rise and rise of art museum marketing discourse

Derrick Chong

Introduction

As a precursory note, the title of this chapter makes reference to two recent issues of '*Critical Quarterly*' edited by Andrew Brighton (2002): 'The rise and rise of management discourse' offered a series of essays on how the ethos and language of management, associated with Anglo-American business corporations (Wal-Mart, Starbucks, IBM, Virgin, and Tesco, for example), pervades our everyday lives (as expressed in catchphrases like Coca-Cola as 'The Real Thing' and 'Just Do It' with Nike).

The art museum sits at the summit of museum categories as 'temples of the human spirit' and important civic institutions. This recognizes the art museum's 'relationship with modern democratic culture' (Carrier, 2006, p. 15). However, it is recognized that such historical links may be lost on those who seek 'superstar' museums as part of an itinerary of international destination sites. This chapter examines the impact of marketing discourses on art museums in the US and the UK. Different influences appear to be driving marketing developments in the two countries. The issue of art museums and public trust has been raised by the Association of Art Museum Directors (AAMD)—a membership organization which represents 175 directors of the major art museums in the USA, Canada, and Mexico (e.g., Metropolitan Museum of Art, Museum of Modern Art, Philadelphia Museum of Art, and Art Gallery of Ontario)—in several position papers since 2001. This is due to the growing number of commercial exchanges such as exhibition collaborations with for-profit enterprises and other revenue generating schemes, and relationships with private collectors and corporate sponsors (AAMD, 2001a, b, c; 2006a, b). The case of the Solomon R. Guggenheim Foundation is worth noting as it has been the most ambitious promoter (of art museums under the Guggenheim brand) from a marketing perspective. In the UK, the most well-known art museums (e.g., British Museum, National Gallery, Tate Gallery, Victoria and Albert Museum (V&A), and National Portrait Gallery) are designated National Museums and

Galleries (NMGs). With direct funding from central government, NMGs are subject to the oversight—including performance measurement targets—by the Department of Culture, Media, and Sport (DCMS). New public sector management imperatives, in the UK (and elsewhere), put an emphasis on customer-focused delivery.

Case study 1

What does retail marketing offer art museums?

The National Bureau of Economic Research (NBER) organized a conference on the economics of art museums in the early 1990s, with the participation of art museum directors and presidents. In a background paper on the marketing of art museums, Robert Blattberg and Cynthia Broderick focused what they perceived to be the key dilemma faced by art museums—having separate and distinct audiences—from retailing and marketing perspectives. Several ways to serve such audiences were proffered in their background paper:

- Separating the museum into two distinct parts so that each suborganization can serve the needs of its constituency effectively.
- Creating marketing managers who are responsible for understanding the needs of these two distinct segments.
- Redesigning the product so that the general public is given a product that meets their needs (more involving and more entertaining) while at the same time serving the other audiences which like and appreciate more sophisticated art exhibits.
- Requiring the curatorial staff to think more the way retail buyers do, who not only worry about the quality of the merchandise but also about the appeal to the product to each segment.
- Creating profit centres to analyse and manage the two distinct museums just as companies manage different products (Blattberg and Broderick, 1991, p. 345).

Anne d'Harnoncourt, Director of the Philadelphia Museum of Art, objected to marketing as applied:

> I was quite disturbed by the background paper for this conference that posited the possibility or the necessity of museums' addressing two very different kinds of audiences. The paper argued that there is the collector–donor, sophisticated audience, and there is the general public audience, and museums ought to divide what they do and divide their resources to serve those two audiences quite separately. It seems to me that that may possibly undermine the whole mission of a museum, which is to bring as many people as you can to a kind of experience that they can only get in an art museum: direct contact with a work of art. ... So I think that the idea of dividing our resources to cultivate donors on one hand, and to please a general public on the other, is dangerous.
>
> (d'Harnoncourt, 1991, pp. 36–7)

d'Harnoncourt continues:

> The issue of marketing is a fascinating one, and one that raises every museum hackle that I know. It is an issue that we keep coming back to because no curator and no museum director wants to hang a gallery full of objects or install an exhibition and have nobody there. However, marketing has to do with products, and if you say, let us change the product to fit what the audience wants, that makes everybody nervous.
>
> (d'Harnoncourt, 1991, p. 37)

Discussion: Retailing and catering opportunities have expanded throughout the museum space since the 1990s. It is no longer deemed sufficient to have a shop at the entrance and a café in the basement. Does this mean that d'Harnoncourt has 'lost' the marketing debate? Is the permanent collection next?

Case study 2

An 'ace caff' versus the Modern

In 1988, the Victoria and Albert Museum was rebuked for its promotional campaign 'an ace caff with a rather nice museum attached', produced by Saatchi and Saatchi, to launch the opening of the Henry Cole Wing. The reference to the new restaurant was supposed to make the museum more inviting to 'twenty-something' Londoners. Rather than being viewed as whimsical and urbane, the advertising copy was interpreted as a crass attempt to make the museum more popular.

The reopening of New York's Museum of Modern Art in 2004 included many comments, not least of them, on the availability of up-market food and drink. With a separate street-level entrance—not requiring museum entry and offering access beyond MoMA's opening hours—the Modern is marketed as a fine-dining restaurant featuring French-American cuisine. Adjacent to the Modern is the Bar Room and a further two private dining rooms are available. According to the Director, Glenn Lowry, 'The art and the food are utterly complementary. The better the food, the more intense the museum experience. ... I would love it if the Modern emerges as one of the great restaurants in New York' (Lowry, in Collins, 2004). The Modern is a partnership with Danny Meyer's Union Square Hospitality Group.

Discussion: What separates the reception of the two museum restaurants?

Maintaining public trust: art museums in the USA

Roberta Smith (2000) writing in the *New York Times* sparked a national debate among art museum directors when she challenged them to ensure that objects on display are treated as works of art. Two exhibitions, both from 2000, were cited by Smith as being seriously flawed to the point of compromising the aesthetic mission of art museums: 'Giorgio Armani' at the Guggenheim Museum had the effect of turning the Frank Lloyd Wright building into a department store; and the Los Angeles County Museum of Art was turned into a historical society with 'Made in California: art, image and identity 1900–2000'. Leading members of AAMD replied with 'Whose Muse?', edited by James Cuno (2004) now President of the Art Institute of Chicago Art museums, claiming art museums must retain the public trust:

> For in the end, this is what visitors most want from us: to have access to works of art in order to change them, to alter their experience of the world, to sharpen and heighten their sensitivities to it, to make it come alive or new for them, so they can walk away at a different angle to the world.
>
> (Cuno, 2004, p. 73)

The institutional reputation of art museums as a class is at stake.

Managing relationships with key stakeholders—such as private collectors, the single most important source for accessioning works of art as part of a museum's permanent collection (AAMD, 2001c), and business corporations— is viewed by the AAMD as essential to maintain public trust. The importance of revenue generation is posited as a means to subsidize the cost of entry: 'Charging admission fees comparable to their expenses would create an economic barrier to the public and undermine the museum's role as a public institution' (AAMD, 2001a, p. 1). Various revenue streams are identified (e.g., endowment income, membership dues, museum store sales, private philanthropy, corporate sponsorship, and public agency funding), 'as well as new forms of public-spirited entrepreneurship and innovative non-profit business development' (AAMD, 2001a, p. 2).

The AAMD recognizes that corporate sponsorship arrangements generate high publicity for business corporations and art museums:

> American businesses have increasingly viewed art museums as venues for sponsorship both to serve the public interest and to address corporate relations and marketing goals. This circumstance provides obvious opportunities to art museums that seek to expand and diversify their base of financial support and to reach new audiences. At the same time, it presents challenges to ensure that the museum's educational mission is not compromised by external commercial interests.
>
> (AAMD, 2001a, pp. 1–2)

Of course, some critics feel that the balance has already tipped in favour of Fortune 500 firms. Chin-tao Wu (2002), for example, is critical of the growing influence of business corporations in art (e.g., corporate sponsorship, corporate-sponsored art awards, and corporate art collections). Wu's analysis is embedded in the interventions associated with 'agitprop' artist Hans Haacke (see Bourdieu and Haacke, 1995) to shed light on the influence of business corporations on contemporary culture. It is argued that it has become impossible to mount a major exhibition without corporate sponsorship. This can be interpreted as having an impact on the kind of exhibitions that can be organized. On the other hand, James Twitchell (2004) views corporate involvement as a sign of the times. If high culture is beginning to look more like the rest of our culture, is such a blurring of distinctions to be regretted? Branding, as a form of storytelling that is also applicable to art museums, may be invigorating high culture by bringing it a new audience and, according to Twitchell (2004), making it more integral to our lives. Thus the so-called blockbuster exhibitions may allow familiar paintings to be displayed in a new context such that a new narrative is used to brand the art.

The Guggenheim Foundation's multinational network of museums and cultural partnerships has been the vision of Thomas Krens, since his appointment as Director in 1988. At present, the Guggenheim owns three museums (the flagship New York site built by Frank Lloyd Wright, the Peggy Guggenheim Collection in Venice, and the Guggenheim hermitage Museum in Las Vegas) and provides curatorial direction and management services to two museums (Guggenheim Museum Bilbao and Deutsche Guggenheim in Berlin):

> The mission of the Solomon R. Foundation is to promote the understanding and appreciation of art, architecture, and other manifestations of visual culture, primarily of the modern and contemporary periods, and to collect, conserve, and study the art of our time. The Foundation realizes this mission through exceptional exhibitions, education programmes, research initiatives, and publications, and strives to engage and educate an increasingly diverse international audience through its unique network of museums and cultural partnerships.
>
> (Guggenheim, 2005b)

Krens has pushed the boundaries of what it means to be an art museum and what can serve as an exhibition. For example, 'Rubens and His Age: Masterpieces from the Hermitage Museum' featured at the Guggenheim Hermitage Museum at The Venetian (a resort–hotel–casino complex) in 2006. (Of course, other Las Vegas casinos, such as Steve Wynn's Mirage Resorts, have used Van Gogh, Renoir, Picasso, and Monet as star attractions, though not in partnership with art museums.) An exhibition devoted to a fashion designer was criticized as a form of product placement. Yet it was not a singular example: 'Art of the Motorcycle' (sponsored by BMW with BMW motorcycles in the lobby) and the motion picture Star Wars have been other controversial exhibitions mounted by the Guggenheim.

The Guggenheim's business model is admired by Twitchell (2004), who views franchising as a way to think of the museum as a brand that can be leveraged for commercial advantage. In examining what the art museum might become, art historian David Carrier believes that Krens should 'be praised for understanding that only when high art is as popular as mass culture can it compete' (2006, p. 217). On the other hand, the Guggenheim is deemed aggressive, even reckless, in its treatment of the permanent collection as trading capital (i.e., art as assets to be used to expand institutional presence and enhance financial stability). Rosiland Krauss (1990) was one of the first to challenge the 'leveraging' of art by the Guggenheim. Though not being sold (or de-accessioned), art is being asked to perform an additional role as credit for the Guggenheim's expansion, nationally and internationally, to take place. 'The notion of the museum as a guardian of the public patrimony has given way to the notion of the museum as a corporate entity with a highly market-able inventory and desire for growth' (Philip Weiss, in Krauss, 1990, p. 5).

The Guggenheim's most ambitious proposal, in response to the West Kowloon Cultural District (WKCD) in Hong Kong, was announced in 2005 as a partnership bid with the Centre Pompidou and property developer Dynamic Sun International.[1] The WKCD is part of a 40-hectare waterfront site being developed by the government of Hong Kong to create 'an integrated arts, cultural, and entertainment district' that offers 'an exciting possibility for cultural exchange, sharing, and dialogue' (Guggenheim, 2005a).

The current Director of the Museum of Modern Art is unimpressed with the Guggenheim's conduct and behaviour:

> What distinguishes the Guggenheim is that rather than keeping a fine balance between the museum as school and theater, a place of learning and a place of enjoyment, it has focused its energies on becoming an entertainment center and appears to be no longer interested in or committed to the ideas and the art that gave birth to the museums at its founding.
>
> (Lowry, in Cuno, 2004, p. 138)

Without making explicit reference to the Guggenheim's Hong Kong proposal, the AAMD has raised concern that 'several joint exhibition ventures with for-profit companies have received an increasing level of attention. These newly emerging collaborations with for-profit partners to organize, travel and pro-mote museum exhibitions are high-profile exceptions to traditional museum approaches of organizing and funding exhibitions' (AAMD, 2006b, p. 1). A more rigorous approach, with consideration of the long-term consequences for art museums from revenue-generating private–public partnerships, is advised by the AAMD:

> Proponents of exhibition collaboration with for-profit enterprises often make their case by citing changes in our global culture. Their argument is that 'education' and 'entertainment' as well as 'art' and

[1]At the time of writing, in summer 2006, the Guggenheim Foundation announced a joint project in Abu Dhabi, the capital of the United Arab Emirates, to establish a museum, the Guggenheim Abu Dhabi designed by Frank Gehry (Guggenheim, 2006a). At 30,000 square metres, the Abu Dhabi museum will be the only Guggenheim museum in the region and will be larger than any existing Guggenheim worldwide. It is expected that the museum will be constructed within 5 years.

'experience' are becoming more and more fused. Moreover, the growing sense of cooperation between for-profit and not-for-profit ventures in many other aspects of daily life has further broken down traditional barriers between these kinds of organizations.

(AAMD, 2006b, pp. 1–2)

Krens on the Guggenheim's model

In a 2006 interview with Charlie Rose, Krens accepts the criticisms from MoMA's Glenn Lowry as part of the competitive rivalry that exists in New York 'among the various institutions for audience and identity' (Guggenheim, 2006b). MoMA is the leading museum of modern art in the world, according to Krens, so the Guggenheim needs to develop methods to compete against the other top modern art museums such as London's Tate Modern, Paris's Centre Pompidou, and Amsterdam's Stedelijk.[2] With five venues, the Guggenheim is able to say that total attendance—used by many as one measure of a museum's success—surpasses 2.5 million per year.

Krens objects to critics whose perception is that the Guggenheim exporting a commodity is somehow the same wherever the Guggenheim is situated. The notion of franchising, with its fast food connotations, is not a word Krens uses. Rather Krens talks about mutual exchange:

> The whole idea here is about a free exchange of commentary and ideas. It's a discourse on an international scale. In a contemporary society, for contemporary art, with everything becoming ever more interconnected, I think it's an essential aspect of how museums have to confront the world.

(Guggenheim, 2006b)

'Pioneering' is how Krens describes the various mutual exchanges (or partnerships) with other institutions: 'The fact that these institutions would choose to work to work [sic] with us and enter into a long-term agreement to share

---

[2] The high reputation that has been accorded to Tate Modern (which opened in 2000), as a museum of modern art, is in part due to (now Sir) Nicholas Serota's role as Director in 1988 of what was then called the Tate Gallery. He was able to make the argument that the original Millbank site (now Tate Britain) was too small to display the permanent collection. His first major project was to re-hang the permanent collection on an 'annual' basis under the banner New Displays. But physical size can only take an art museum director so far. More significantly, Serota made the conceptual argument that the then Tate arrangement of historical British and modern international art under one roof was an anomaly by international standards. Serota (1996) cited New York's MoMA and Paris's Centre Pompidou as 'urban' examples he had in mind; at the same time, he was interested in Copenhagen's Louisiana and Amsterdam's Rijksmusems as 'rural' and 'humanistic' examples that the Tate should learn from. Why did London, as a comparable international city, not have a museum of modern art?

collections, to share staff, to share programming, in effect, to regard ourselves as a kind of—how would you say—free trade zone or strategic alliance of some kind I think is significant' (Guggenheim, 2006b).

In addressing the WKCD proposal in Hong Kong, Krens alludes to Bilbao (the most successful Guggenheim project):

> The Hong Kong government has created a site that is now called the West Kowloon Cultural District. It's about 110 acres. And this will be almost in the center of Hong Kong. It's hugely valuable commercial property and real estate development, but they're calling it a cultural district, and the Hong Kong government is mandating that the developer must create five museums and three performing arts centers, and fund these cultural activities for thirty years. Now this is a colossal scale. This is probably four or five times the scale of Bilbao.
>
> (Guggenheim, 2006b)

That the Centre Pompidou is a partner in the WKCD proposal is used to justify the Guggenheim's strategy of international expansion: 'And more and more, you see the French museums adopting this direction as a matter of national policy' (Guggenheim, 2006b).[3]

Performance management and consumers: NMGs in the UK

The art museum environment in the USA is different from the situation in the UK on at least two counts. First, the corporate scandals associated with Enron and WorldCom led to the more stringent corporate governance thresholds in the USA, as illustrated by the Sarbanes-Oxley Act of 2002, and this has had an impact on all types of organizations in the USA. Second, the funding arrangement for UK's NMGs, with a majority share of operating revenues from direct government subsidy and a less generous taxation regime to encourage private giving, has meant much less attention (until quite recently) to American-style forms of revenue generation.

The UK has excelled at introducing forms of performance measurement to public services. Auditing principles have been applied to gauge the value for money in terms of the three 'E's of effectiveness, efficiency, and economy (Power, 1994). In doing so, there has been a displacement from first-order experts (such as curators, educators, and conservators in the case of art museums) to second-order verificatory activities monitored by overseers (such as bureaucrats at public funding agencies). More significantly, performance

---

[3]Krens cites the Tate as an example of doing nationally—with two museums sites in London and one in each of Liverpool and St Ives—what the Guggenheim is doing internationally: 'it has an opportunity to use its collection and to reach a wider audience, and that's essentially what is driving us' (Guggenheim, 2006b).

measurement presupposes a shift in ethos from citizens to consumers. 'Gone are the days when viewers went to galleries, audiences attended concerts or the theatre; they [are] all consumers', according to the Director of London's Barbican Centre (Tusa, 1997, p. 38).

The DCMS/V&A Funding Agreement 2003–2006 is instructive as a contract between a public funding agency (DCMS) and its client (V&A). The DCMS identifies four key strategic priorities:

1. Enhance access to a fuller cultural and sporting life for children and young people, and giving them the opportunity to develop their talents to the full.
2. Opening our institutional to the wider community, to promote lifelong learning and social cohesion.
3. Maximizing the contribution which the leisure and creative industries can make to the economy.
4. Modernizing delivery, by ensuring our sponsored bodies are set, and meet targets which put customers first (DCMS/V&A, 2003, Annex A).

The key goal for the V&A in the funding agreement period 'is to open up the Museum to the widest possible audience' (DCMS/V&A, 2003, para 2.5.1). Quantitative and qualitative performance targets are identified. There are six specific quantitative targets linked to the DCMS's priorities on children and under-represented social class groups:

1. Total number of visitors.
2. Number of visits by children.
3. Number of venues in England to which objects from the collection are loaned.
4. Number of C2/D/E visitors (representing the lower half of the six social class groupings used in the UK) required to achieve an 8 per cent increase by 2005–2006 on the 2002–2003 baseline.
5. Number of website hits (unique users).
6. Number of children in organized educational programmes both on-site and outreach.

Qualitative measures (by activity, outcomes, and measure of success) are developed to support the DCMS's priorities on children and young people, the wider community (to promote lifelong learning and social cohesion), and economic impact.

The increasing instrumentalism of arts policymakers like the DCMS is challenged in a recent Policy Exchange document, 'Culture Wars' (Mirza, 2006). In many respects, it was building concerns raised in Brighton's special issues of *Critical Quarterly* (2002) on the rise of managerialism. For example, according to Sara Selwood, Head of Cultural Policy and Management at City University:

> It is significant that the DCMS has found such measures elusive, and that it is not alone in doing so. Attempting to measure the impact of

museums through outcomes is tantamount to measuring what modernism always cast as unmeasurable. Given that the sector still has to come to grips with such basic outputs as visitor numbers, producing evidence of social impact remains essentially aspirational.

(Selwood, 2002, p. 75)

A similar position is adopted by Grayson Perry, the 'transvestite potter' (to borrow a tabloid press descriptor), who was awarded the Turner Prize in 2003:

New Labour has been pouring money into the arts not just because this is a good thing but because of the belief that the arts will heal communities, reduce crime and raise the aspirations of those not educated enough to know whether they like Bartók or Birtwistle. ... While I appreciate that artistic activities may have a beneficial effect on some groups, I do not believe that thrusting mediocre culture targets will improve health, enliven run-down cities or bring C2DEs into the political 'we'. ... The evidence that art has this power is sketchy and based mainly on research commissioned by arts institutions with the aim of advocacy in mind.

(Perry, 2006)

The main priorities of the DCMS, according to its agreement with the V&A (an illustrative NMG), put an emphasis on two main groups (children and young people; and under-represented groups as measured by social class and ethnicity), the importance of measuring economic impact, and the marketing orientation of public services with citizens reconceptualized as customers. It goes without saying that it is very difficult for NMGs to baulk at the priorities of their main funding agency even if they are deemed dubious. To do so runs the risk of being charged with elitism, catering to affluent, well-educated spectators with public-subsidized funds.

Concluding remarks

At the outset of the twenty-first century, the V&A mounted an exhibition on the rise of brands and branding: 'The brand is a prefix; the qualifier of character. The symbolic associations of the brand name are often used in preference to the pragmatic description of a useful object' (Pavitt, 2000, p. 16). Yet would art museums be wise to follow what is deemed the marketing path of success for commercial enterprises? Is the Guggenheim a harbinger of things to come for art museums? Do the relationships with the Venetian and Dynamic Star International foreshadow other sectors of the leisure industry that can do business with art museums?

Most recently, the AAMD notes that members 'must continually reassess and reaffirm their commitment to good governance' in order to ensure that they remain among 'the most trusted and respected public institutions in the world—resources for education and enjoyment that provide lasting benefit to the people of the world' (AAMD, 2006a, pp. 1, 4). The reputations at stake are even higher for UK's NMGs.

References

(*Note*: For the Association of Art Museums Directors (AAMD), see 'position papers and reports' at <www.aamd.org>; Guggenheim material is available from the 'press office' at <www.guggenheim.org>.)

AAMD (2001a). Art museums, private collectors, and the public benefit, October.

AAMD (2001b). Managing the relationship between art museums and corporate sponsors, October.

AAMD (2001c). Revenue generation: an investment in the public service of museums, October.

AAMD (2006a). Good governance and non-profit integrity, June.

AAMD (2006b). Exhibition collaborations between American art museums and for-profit enterprises, March.

Blattberg, R. and Broderick, C. (1991). Marketing and art museums. In *The Economics of Art Museums* (M. Feldstein, ed.), pp. 327–46. University of Chicago Press, Chicago and London.

Bourdieu, P. and Haacke, H. (1995). *Free Exchange*. Trans. Randal Johnson. Polity Press, Oxford.

Brighton, A. (ed.) (2002). The rise and rise of management discourse. *Critical Quarterly*, 44, Special issues, 3–4.

Carrier, D. (2006). *Museum Skepticism: A History of the Display of Art in Public Galleries*. Duke University Press, Durham, NC and London.

Collins, G. (2004). A destination for food (and some art, too). *New York Times*, 27 October.

Cuno, J. (ed.) (2004). *Whose Muse? Art Museums and the Public Trust*. Princeton University Press, Princeton, NJ.

Department of Culture, Media and Sport/Victoria and Albert Museum (DCMS/V&A). (2003). Three year funding agreement (2003–2006) between the Department for Culture, Media and Sport and the Victoria and Albert Museum.

d'Harnoncourt, A. (1991). The museum and the public. In *The Economics of Art Museums* (M. Feldstein, ed.), pp. 35–9. University of Chicago Press, Chicago and London.

Guggenheim (2005a). Centre Pompidou and the Solomon R. Guggenheim Foundation announce partnership for Hong Kong proposal. *Press Release*, 28 October.

Guggenheim (2005b). The Solomon R. Guggenheim Foundation: mission, overview, director. *Press Release*, September.

Guggenheim (2006a). Abu Dhabi to build Gehry-designed Guggenheim Museum. *Press Release*, 8 July.

Guggenheim (2006b). Thomas Krens, director of the Solomon R. Guggenheim Foundation, talks about the role of museums and the mission of the Guggenheim. *Charlie Rose Show*, 3 January.

Krauss, R. (1990). The cultural logic of late capitalism. October, 54, Fall, 3–17.

Mirza, M. (ed.) (2006). *Culture Vultures: is UK Arts Policy Damaging the Arts?* Policy Exchange, London.

Pavitt, J. (ed.) (2000). *Brand.new*. V&A Publications, London.

Perry, G. (2006). Cheap art won't make poverty history, Tony. *London Times*, 8 March.

Power, M. (1994). *The Audit Explosion*. Demos, London.

Selwood, S. (2002). What difference do museums make? Producing evidence on the impact of museums. *Critical Quarterly*, 44(4), 65–81.

Serota, N. (1996). *Experience or Interpretation: The Dilemma of Museums of Modern Art*. Thames and Hudson.

Smith, R. (2000). Memo to art museums: don't give up on art. *New York Times*, 3 December.

Tusa, J. (1997). For art's sake. *Prospect*, January, 36–40.

Twitchell, J. (2004). *Branded Nation: The Marketing of Megachurch, College Inc., and Museumworld*. Simon and Schuster, New York.

Wu, C. (2002). *Privatizing Culture: Corporate Art Intervention since the 1980s*. Verso, London.

'The social museum' and its implications for marketing

Fiona McLean and Mark O'Neill

The twenty-first century museum is increasingly analysed in terms of its impact on society, taking its place alongside other cultural institutions which both define and are defined by contemporary society. This means that '[museums] must consider their impact on society and seek to shape that impact through practice that is based on contemporary values and a commitment to social equality' (Sandell, 2002, p. 21). Social inclusion in museums is not just a response to government rhetoric, particularly in the UK, as some have argued, but has been long in the making. As Rhiannon Mason has documented in her historical analysis of the discourses which have informed debates about the idea of the socially inclusive museum, social inclusion has been manifest in museums since their inception in the Victorian era (Mason, 2004). Since the 1980s in particular, museums have increasingly been adopting socially inclusive approaches to representation and participation, which predated any central government agenda which, it is claimed, is forcing museums in this direction (Appleton, 2000). The turn to what has been termed 'new museology', where the Victorian rhetoric of inclusion has been given substance by a focus on the public, heralded a sea change in the museal engagement with society. This new approach has become implicit in the processes of more and more museums, in seeking to perform their function of acting, according to the UK's Museums Association's definition of museums, 'for the public benefit'.

Museums are operating in a context where the material and the social have a mutual relationship, where 'physical heritage acts as the material substance of identity' (Macdonald, 2006, p. 11). In material culture studies, in particular, the turn has been towards the relationship of materiality with identity. Recent research has suggested that the museum is a place where people actively make and remake their identities (McLean and Cooke, 2000), a view supported by Lee, who states that 'people invest a certain amount of their self in material objects as a way of managing their sense of place, social position and identity' (1993, p. 26). The mechanisms through which identity is constructed in the museum is not always clear, although memory, in particular memories based around the experiences of family members, provides important reference points (Newman and McLean, 2006).

Museums which are making attempts to develop their audience, by trying to attract new segments which are drawn from those who do not currently visit the museum, need to be aware of the implications of identity. Equally, the museum which is developing a new product and attempting to diversify and attract new audiences requires an appreciation of the identity-conferring status of the museum's representations. Ways to understanding the representation and construction of identities through museums are becoming increasingly sophisticated, with new research suggesting ways forward in approaching audience and product development. See, for example, recent special journal issues on 'heritage and identity' and 'museums and national identity' in the *International Journal of Heritage Studies* (McLean, 2006) and *Museum and Society* (McLean, 2005b), respectively.

This chapter argues that the 'social museum', which takes an interventionist approach to social inclusion and the representation of identities, is inclusive for all. The case study of Kelvingrove Museum and Art Gallery in Glasgow, Scotland, illustrates how the refurbishment of a museum can adopt a social justice agenda encompassing the whole audience, which is underpinned by acknowledgement of the diversity of identity. It offers insights for marketing on the approach that Glasgow City Council has taken 'based on an underlying commitment to equity in the distribution of cultural services and to a citizenship which everyone shares' (O'Neill, 2006, p. 45). Kelvingrove demonstrates how the museum of the twenty-first century is reflecting the values of the new millennium. It demonstrates how the 'social museum' can be successful in attracting and retaining both existing and new audiences, while making a positive impact on society.

The museum audience and identity

Museums are social constructs, which meet social needs; since 'the museum is socially derived, its artefacts are social creations and manifest social relations. Decisions on its artefacts are socially constructed, and the purpose of the museum is social utility' (McLean, 1997, p. 22). The relevance of the museum's artefacts and society's needs are constantly changing and evolving (Fitzgerald, 2005, p. 134), which, by implication, suggests that museums need to reflect these changes. The rapid and accelerating pace of social change means that one of the most pressing issues for contemporary museums is the relationship between museums and their audiences (Witcomb, 2003).

Among many changes in society, a pattern of development can be seen which is increasingly focused on equality, where diversity and difference are manifest globally. The challenge for the twenty-first century is difference according to Stuart Hall (1997), referring to the proliferation of identities, many of them previously repressed, which individuals and communities express. While nineteenth century museums did often have radically inclusive ambitions, these were limited both by imperial perceptions of identity and by an intellectual focus on categorizing and collecting artefacts. In the second half of the twentieth century, museums became better informed about and more focused on their audiences, including those identities which emerged with feminism, decolonization, anti-racism and gay rights. Museums have 'an identity-conferring status' (Urry, 1996, p. 61), where through representation of 'self' and 'other', they give immediacy to the challenge of 'difference'. Identities are manifest through the individual who shares those identities with an imagined community (Anderson, 1983). The challenge for twenty-first century museums is not just to embrace the many identities which are emerging, but at the same time to create a sense of democratic society in which they can all find a place. This requires far more than the bolting on of some additional functions to a museum (e.g., outreach departments) or exhibitions targeted at specific groups: it requires the transformation of the museum. Andrea Witcomb argues that to adopt a community perspective in museums, 'would be to think of museums themselves as communities' (2003, p. 81). This would require an interrogation of the processes of museum work and how these processes manifest the relationship of the museum with its audience.

Audiences are not monolithic, they come from a range of backgrounds and cultures, and to engage their members as individuals in any meaningful way, museums need to reflect or at least acknowledge that diversity. Few museums, apart from those art museums where an 'art for art's sake' ideology still holds sway (Ryan, 2000), would dispute this. Some, though, are better than others at adopting what inevitably 'requires an ability to construct policy and implement practice which makes real connections across all sectors and spheres of life' (Mason, 2004, p. 66). This requires significant change not only in attitude to the audience, but also to the processes within the museum which ultimately impact on the individual. It requires the whole museum service to adopt an audience approach.

We have chosen to refer to the 'audience' of museums rather than the 'customers' or 'consumers'. This is deliberate, not because of the possible negative connotations that such marketing terms may hold in the museum sector, but because often those who deal directly with the public in museums are the education staff who adopt an audience approach, undertaking for example, audience analysis and evaluation, which in marketing parlance would be referred to as consumer analysis and evaluation (McLean, 2005a). This is an interesting fact in itself, in that it does not belie the role of the marketing function, but suggests that marketing for whatever reason, whether because it is more acceptable as an education remit or that marketing tenets have been enthusiastically adopted, permeates museum activities in unexpected ways.

Museum audience development

Throughout the world there is a correlation of museum visiting with higher social class and economic status, and with majority ethnicity. Museums have been associated with privileged access to knowledge, as 'sacred places' open to those who know how to read their rituals and texts (Duncan, 1995). There is an even closer correlation with education—not due to the efficacy of museum visits by schools, but because of the social and cultural capital which accompanies success in the education system (Newman and McLean, 2004). Those who are disadvantaged are unlikely to have a familial, community or cultural tradition of museum visiting and are therefore very difficult to convert into regular visitors. All museums have a cut-off point at which it becomes more difficult than it is worth to try to attract such visitors. This cut-off point varies by country, museum type and by individual museum, and can be defined by two measures. The first is the percentage of its resource that the museum is prepared to invest in attracting audiences from excluded groups. The second is the degree to which it is prepared to change the museum to make it relevant and accessible to these groups. In marketing terms, most museums accept the need to use modern methods of communication to reach their audiences, and to mount popular—ideally blockbuster—exhibitions. Most, however, would not accept the degree of influence on the museum implied in commercial concepts of product development, where audience testing would have a significant influence on the nature of the provision.

In parallel with the evidence about the relationship of the museum to its 'natural' demographic, considerable evidence also exists that non-visitors among the less educated (less well-off, lower class) sections of the community (unlike educated well-off people who simply do not like museums) have perceptions of museums which, even if not true, exclude them. Thus when residents of the public housing estates near Glasgow's prestigious Burrell Collection were asked why they never visited, they said it was too expensive. Admission to the Burrell Collection has always, as it has for all of Glasgow's museums, been free. This is not just misinformation that could be changed by communicating better through traditional marketing techniques (though that might help), but a reflection that they perceived the Burrell as belonging to a different world; 'not for the likes of us' is the recurrent phrase.

Within the parameters of traditional marketing, these demographics and perceptions are mutually reinforcing, and would indicate that museums wishing to (or under pressure to) increase visitor numbers should focus on getting existing or lapsed visitors to return, and at most aim to recruit new visitors from among groups with similar characteristics to the core audience. For example, Keith Diggle summarizes the situation in *Arts Marketing* as follows:

> The Available Audience consists of those people who, for reasons to do with education, upbringing, and any number of other influences which could include for example, things seen and heard in newspapers, magazines, books, radios and television programmes, have already experienced the art form you and your organisation are presenting and include such experiences in their regular diet of activities ... The Unavailable Audience is made up of those people who do not attend events of the type you are presenting, do not feel

any particular need to attend such events and, in many cases, are antipathetic to the notion that they might attend them—this section of the your community is beyond your reach within a realistic times-cale using the methods that will enable you to reach, persuade and ultimately sell to the Available Audience. But do not give up all hope, some potential does lie within this group.

(Diggle, 1994, pp. 33–5)

Many museums, however, do not share these perceptions, do not share the view that museums are for the already educated, and that persuading them to avail of the experience being offered is simply a matter of technique. Instead they believe that museums in themselves are educative (defined in a much broader way than contributing to children's schooling) and that they should be accessible as a matter of social justice (O'Neill, 2006). They see the phrase 'not for the likes of us' as reflecting a general sense of not being entitled to use the amenities which are provided through public or voluntary sector investment, not a reflection of a lack of interest in museums. This view of museums goes back to the Victorian philanthropic ideals which led to many of them being established, predating the conversion of the UK Government to 'social inclusion' as an objective of cultural institutions (Mason, 2004). No doubt, however, motivating visitors from 'unavailable audiences' are more difficult and more complex than working within the traditional demographic, requiring not just investment in targeted marketing campaigns, but a fundamental change in the culture and public programme of the museum. This can be very easily conceptualized within traditional marketing—to target a particular audience, product development and service delivery need to take them into account—but museums are very reluctant to take on this aspect of marketing. Even the most traditional museums now agree with the importance of communicating with the public through high-quality professional marketing campaigns, and, acknowledged or not, take public taste into account when selecting themes for temporary exhibitions—these are too expensive to mount without consider-able visitor income. However, only museums which are really committed to attracting non-traditional audiences explicitly acknowledge that to do so means changing not just the image, but the reality of the museum.

Museum product development

Recognizing that the museum is a social construct is crucial in product development, from utilizing audience analysis as advocated by, for example, Falk and Dierking (1992), but more fundamentally, to change in approach to exhibition design. If it is acknowledged that material culture is inherently social in all its meanings, then it is only one small step to reflecting the social culture in the design of the exhibition. The presentation of objects needs to reflect real people because ultimately it is the objects' connections to people which give them meaning. This requires a much more sophisticated approach to audience

participation in exhibition design than is currently the norm in most museums, as well as a more people-oriented approach to representation. Acknowledging and reflecting the identities of those being represented, as well as
those to whom the objects are being represented, enable connections to be
made by the audience.

The refurbishment of Kelvingrove Museum and Art Gallery has been chosen as a case study to demonstrate this shift in museums to re-conceptualizing
their processes which are equitable and enabling. It serves to demonstrate that
an inclusive approach can enhance the museum experience for all; without
exclusion, both the traditional museum (available) audiences and new emerging audiences. Glasgow City Council did 'not give up hope', but recognized
that 'potential does lie within this group', and that by harnessing this potential, the museum ultimately becomes more meaningful for the available audience and for society as a whole.

The evaluation studies which were undertaken during the development
phase of the Kelvingrove refurbishment have been documented by Maria
Economou (2004). Economou argues that the strategy (designed in 1999):

> ... was a real step forward for the Museum and the field as a whole,
> as it outlined a wide range of evaluation activities and examined the
> issues that these raise for the whole of the institution, and not just
> for small independent projects or services ... the strategy addressed
> evaluation holistically, and planned extensively and in-depth how it
> could be used as a useful tool to support the key activities through-
> out the organization (2004, p. 31).

Economou further explains how the evaluation systematically recorded quantitative and qualitative information about the visitors' demographic characteristics, needs and preferences. The evaluation combined various methods
at different stages of the design process: the formative testing of information technology exhibits; the involvement of different visitor and community
groups and the use of education, community and access advisory panels in
an effort to improve physical and intellectual access to the collections and the
building; developing relationships with non-visitors and involving them in
the exhibition creation process; and the involvement of members of staff with
evaluation work and communication with visitors (Economou, 2004, p. 42).

This evaluation process took cognisance of the articulation between production and consumption, enabling the 'active' role of the audience in making
meaning and constructing their identities in the museum context (Macdonald,
2002). Rather than merely conducting market research, which inevitably
assigns a passive role to the museum audience, the evaluation approach allows
for the participation of a number of actors, ranging from a number of audience communities, through other stakeholders in the museum, to the museum's staff. It allows for the dynamic between production and consumption,
or more usefully when considering representation, the encoding and decoding of the museum exhibition (Hall, 1980; Dicks, 2000). That is, as Newman

and McLean discovered in their studies of socially inclusive exhibitions and community-based development projects 'contests of identity are engaged in by all involved, from those who directly or indirectly were responsible for the exhibitions and museum-based community development projects to the respondents who consumed them' (2006, p. 64).

Kelvingrove is an example of how a combination of socially inclusive practices, sophisticated evaluation strategies and a holistic approach to process has enabled the creation of a museum which reflects and is reflective of the communities it serves. In doing so, it has created opportunities for identity negotiation and construction in the museum for all its potential audiences. It has attracted both its available audience and previously unavailable audience, and has demonstrated that by reaching out to all it can appeal to all.

Case study: Glasgow Museums—Kelvingrove Museum and Art Gallery

Glasgow Museums work on the assumption that roughly the same percentage of any group in society, including working class people and minority ethnic communities, as middle class people would be interested in museums, given the right opportunities. The city has a unique tradition of museum visiting, in which people from traditional 'respectable working class' communities feel a sense of belonging to and ownership of the museums—but as many as a third of the population do not visit museums, not because they find them boring, but because they feel they 'are not for the likes of us'. However, the wide social base provides cultural, community and political support for the development of museums as explicitly and inherently inclusive, rather than regarding the core displays of museums as having a fixed essence, on to which marketing and temporary exhibitions are bolted as a means of keeping visitor numbers up. The redevelopment of Glasgow Museums in these terms since 1989 has led to extensive experimentation in integrating a philosophy of access at all levels within the museum's practices and structures. Thus the largest education and access team of any museum in Britain enables the museum service to engage with people in a variety of ways. Key projects have included a biennial programme on Contemporary Art and Human Rights and the creation of a museum of world religions—one of only four in the world (O'Neill, 2006). The most extensive development in these terms has been the restoration and redisplay of Kelvingrove Museum and Art Gallery, completed in 2006. Built in 1901 at the height of the city's Victorian wealth and confidence, the renewed museum, with 10,000 square metres (100,000 square feet) of public space, constitutes the largest experiment in radically rethinking museums since the opening of Te Papa in Wellington, New Zealand, and the National Museum of Australia in Canberra.

The project included building the £7.4 million Glasgow Museums Resource Centre (GMRC) to house 200,000 objects formerly stored in Kelvingrove and free up the basement for new public facilities. GMRC reflects the integration of access as an organizational ideal. Rather than being a traditional store used mostly by staff and by knowledgeable visitors who make requests to see objects, GMRC provides behind the scenes tours 7 days a week for anyone who might be interested. On the basis that the objects are public property, interest or curiosity is all that is required to see the collection. Education programmes build on this to take people into study of the collection or museum visiting.

On the basis that the museums represent civic values, Glasgow Museums' programme targets hitherto excluded groups, and reflects their culture. Along with traditional subjects exhibition topics have included: Homelessness, The Veil in Islam, Gay History, Women and War, Voodoo. As well as celebrating human creativity and the diversity of cultures, the museums regard it as their role to challenge negative heritage, including racism, sectarianism and domestic violence, all of which have been the subject of exhibitions and education programmes.

Kelvingrove was the last and largest museum created by Victorian Britain's civic museum movement. Encyclopaedic in its ambitions, it housed internationally significant collections of Dutch and Italian Old Masters, French Impressionists and Charles Rennie Mackintosh, alongside Scottish and world natural history, European Arms and Armour, Scottish History, Anthropology and Scottish and Mediterranean archaeology. Creating new displays involved a complete rethink of the philosophy of the museum, not just updating the old galleries. The 'product development' involved a radical return to first principles, with the display approach informed by a thorough and extensive process of visitor (and non-visitor) consultation. The new displays were based on the ideal of providing a way in to even the most difficult subjects for novices, while at the same time providing something of interest to knowledgeable visitors. Evolved over decades, the key elements of the vision for the new Kelvingrove are that the displays are: object based, enable stories to be told, audience centred and flexible.

Object based

The essence of museums is that they inspire and enable appreciation and learning through real things. Kelvingrove seeks to retain this museum Unique Selling Point, while introducing the best modern display methods. The result of this was a commitment to double the number of objects on display, from 4000 when it closed to 8000 at re-opening.

Storytelling

Rather than summarize museum disciplines (like Art History, Archaeology or Geology), the museum focused on telling the most interesting stories about the most interesting objects in the collection. By using narrative rather than the structure of these subjects, the displays are able to function at many different levels—accessible to the novice, but resonant for the knowledgeable visitor. Storytelling is conceived of as fitting more closely with how people really make sense of things, with their meaning-making capacity. Curators proposed over 200 stories which, through the process of consultation, were eventually whittled down to the 100 on display. Each object forms part of a story which needed to be written to rigorous standards of research and accessibility—the displays involve more than 250,000 words. No single display method was chosen—every story used the communication method which worked best for its content and its envisioned audience. Key elements and innovations were tested on target groups to ensure that they worked.

Reflecting the task of envisioning a society of many identities held together by democratic values, the greatest challenge facing Kelvingrove was organizing the vast range of material and display approaches into a coherent whole, to ensure that the museum had a sense of unity. This was done by grouping the 100 stories into 22 themes in ways which reflected visitors' interests and perceptions. Traditional museum disciplines were retained where they genuinely reflected the nature of public interest in the collection, thus 'French Art' and 'Charles Rennie Mackintosh and the Glasgow Style' were retained. However, 'Arms and Armour' was replaced by 'Conflict and Consequence', which focuses on the reality of the impact of the weapons on display, rather than fetishizing them as most museums do, as well as exploring areas of the collection which were plundered by Scottish soldiers during the Empire period. Similarly, the museum celebrates local hero, James Watt, whose modification of the steam engine triggered the industrial revolution. But the same gallery includes stories on domestic violence and on sectarianism.

Audience centred

The museum aims to welcome every visitor, no matter what their background or prior knowledge, and to provide them with a way in to understanding the wonderful objects on display. Education, community and disability advisory panels, along with a junior board, focus groups, visitor surveys and building usage surveys, informed the story development. Even the most basic traditions of museum presentation were re-assessed through empirical experiments. For example, pilot displays revealed that when paintings were hung below rather than at eye-level people looked at them for longer—presumably because it is less tiring on the neck muscles. Lessons were drawn from learning style theory and retail psychology as well as from other museum experiments (e.g., the Art Institute of Chicago's education gallery) to ensure a museum which worked with how people really are.

Flexible

Because each of the 22 galleries shows four to eight separate stories under a broad theme, individual stories can be changed without having to redisplay entire galleries. This is one of Kelvingrove's major innovations; it is a genuinely flexible museum. By changing three or four stories a year, the programme will be able to evolve over time, remain up-to-date, and respond to new discoveries and public interests. This responsiveness and the epistemological and practical flexibility it requires are essential features of the social museum.

In the first 5 months after re-opening, Kelvingrove received nearly 2 million visits. While detailed breakdown of these visitors' characteristics is not yet available, it is clear that they are, overwhelmingly, local. To generate these numbers, many people must be making multiple repeat visits. In the first regular MORI poll about the efficacy of council services taken after re-opening, the percentage of people who responded 'yes' to the question, 'Have you or a member of your family visited a museum in the past year?', increased by 9 per cent and for the first time ever was above 50 per cent of the population. This popularity was combined with rave reviews from broadsheet newspapers, traditionally hostile to popularizing 'high culture'. 'Welcome to the Future of Museums' wrote *Scotland on Sunday*, while the (London) *Observer* said, 'The new museum, so imaginatively and empathetically redesigned, deserves as much and more love as the old ... Not so much a museum of culture as of life itself' (Cumming, 2006).

References

Anderson, B. (1983). *Imagined Communities: Reflections on the Origin and Spread of Nationalism*. Verso, London.

Appleton, J. (2000). Social inclusion: a sustainable illusion? In *Museums and Social Inclusion* (GLLAM), Institute of Ideas Ltd, pp. 9–15.

Cumming, L. (2006). Ready heights. *The Observer*, 9 July.

Dicks, B. (2000). Encoding and decoding the people: circuits of communication at a local heritage museum. *European Journal of Communication*, 15(1), 61–78.

Diggle, K. (1994). *Arts Marketing*. Rhinegold, London.

Duncan, C. (1995). *Civilizing Rituals: Inside Public Art Museums*. Routledge, London.

Economou, M. (2004). Evaluation strategies in the cultural sector: the case of Kelvingrove Museum and Art Gallery. *Museum and Society*, 2(1), 30–46.

Falk, J. H. and Dierking, L. D. (1992). *The Museum Experience*. Whalesback Books, Washington DC.

Fitzgerald, L. (2005). Building on Victorian ideas. In *Reshaping Museum Space: Architecture, Design, Exhibitions* (S. MacLeod, ed.), pp. 133–45. Routledge, London.

Hall, S. (1980). Encoding/decoding. In *Culture, Media, Language: Working Papers in Cultural Studies* (S. Hall, D. Hobson, A. Lowe and P. Willis, eds.), pp. 128–38. Unwin Hyman, London.

Hall, S. (1997). The Spectacle of the 'Other'. In *Representation: Cultural Representations and Signifying Practices* (S. Hall, ed.), pp. 225–79. Sage, London.

Lee, M. J. (1993). *Consumer Culture Reborn: The Cultural Politics of Consumption*. Routledge, London.

Macdonald, S. (2002). *Behind the Scenes at the Science Museum*. Berg, Oxford.

Macdonald, S. (2006). Undesirable heritage: fascist material culture and historical consciousness in Nuremberg. *International Journal of Heritage Studies*, 12(1), 9–28.

Mason, R. (2004). Conflict and complement: an exploration of the discourses informing the concept of the socially inclusive museum in contemporary Britain. *International Journal of Heritage Studies*, 10(1), 49–73.

McLean, F. (1997). *Marketing the Museum*. Routledge, London.

McLean, F. (2005a). Creating a synergy between the museum's collection and audience. *Museum Ireland*, 15, 42–7.

McLean, F. (ed.) (2005b). Special issue: museums and national identity. *Museum and Society*, 3(1), 1–4.

McLean, F. (ed.) (2006). Special issue: heritage and identity. *International Journal of Heritage Studies*, 12(1), 3–7.

McLean, F. and Cooke, S. (2000). Communicating identity. In *Heritage and Museums: Shaping National Identity* (J. F. Fladmark, ed.), pp. 147–60. Donhead, Shaftesbury.

Newman, A. and McLean, F. (2004). Capital and the evaluation of the museum experience. *International Journal of Cultural Studies*, 7(4), 480–98.

Newman, A. and McLean, F. (2006). The impact of museums upon identity. *International Journal of Heritage Studies*, 12(1), 49–68.

O'Neill, M. (2006). Museums and identity in Glasgow. *International Journal of Heritage Studies*, 12(1), 29–48.

Ryan, M. (2000). Manipulation without end. In *Art for All? Their Policies and Our Culture* (M. Wallinger and M. Warnock, eds.). Peer, London.

Sandell, R. (2002). Museums and the combating of social inequality: roles, responsibilities, resistance. In *Museums, Society, Inequality* (R. Sandell, ed.), pp. 3–23. Routledge, London.

Urry, J. (1996). How societies remember the past. In *Theorizing Museums* (S. Macdonald and G. Fyfe, eds.), pp. 45–68. Blackwell, Oxford.

Witcomb, A. (2003). *Re-Imagining the Museum: Beyond the Mausoleum*. Routledge, London.

Museum architecture and visitor experience

Jonathan Sweet

Introduction

Across the globe, architects of museums are encouraged to consider economic imperatives and, consequently, to design buildings accordingly. In the USA alone, at least 50 new museums or large-scale additions were under construction in 2000 (Kim, 2000, p. 12). Existing museums and galleries have had their interiors substantially reconfigured or their exteriors dramatically altered. Museum interiors now feature greater entertainment facilities and non-gallery spaces, including shops, cafes and 'all occasions' function facilities. The funding of contemporary museums allows architects to incorporate these resources in boldly emblematic or signature buildings, which seek to express a unique identity and to differentiate a product.

Both public and private museums are acutely aware of competition in the leisure marketplace, and are responding to this through addressing the desires of potential visitors and through seeking a competitive edge. The trend for constructing bold and innovative museum buildings designed by prominent architects is a striking element of this strategy. It coexists with other practices. First, in the central positioning of museums within local, regional or international tourism strategies. Second, in exhibition programming, which often places a high priority on revenue generation through corporate sponsorship and ticket sales. Third, in acquisition policy, which, particularly in the case of art museums, often targets objects of international significance, so-called 'destination art'. Fourth, in the provision of more responsive and diverse on-site and off-site visitor services, and lastly, in the integration of sophisticated merchandising plans. All of these elements have impacted on the way museums look and feel.

The apparent commercialization of museums may be in conflict with the ability of museums to deliver on their traditional roles, to preserve, research and interpret cultural and natural heritage material, something recognized by the current British and US definitions of 'museum'. If museums are designed according to the principle of form and function, it follows that design planning begins with thinking about how visitors are going to engage with the collections on display, which is their core business. It makes little sense to observe of recent museum architecture as Kim has, that 'one can experience and appreciate many diverse and attractive exhibition spaces', as if that experience is the end product (Kim, 2000, p. 12). What about engagement with collections and the knowledge we can create from them?

While exhibitions spaces can provide an ambience they also have a functional role, which is primarily as places for display. In institutions as varied as art galleries and natural history museums, collections may be very complex and vary considerably in dimensions and materials. They are often very precious and their presentation in galleries requires consideration of a range of issues, including the need to provide optimum security and environmental conditions. Most sharply, these requirements distinguish museum display from the display of merchandise in a retail business; museum display techniques function to provide access to collections and information, but also to provide necessary barriers to some forms of more active engagement, often epitomized by the saying 'look, but do not touch'.

A polarization of views is reflected in the discourse about the role of museum architecture. On the one hand, it is held that museum architecture ought to provide a neutral space where nothing distracts the attention of the visitor away from the opportunity to engage with the exhibit. As Hebditch wrote of nineteenth century museum buildings, 'the needs of the scholar and the generally curious were met in one totally displayed collection wrapped in an appropriate architectural envelope' (Hebditch, 1984, p. 498). On the other hand, however, it is held that museum architecture is privileged with another purpose; it should be aesthetically significant, and the process of its design should clearly engage with the historical trajectory of architectural theory and practice, applying new materials and new technologies. A recent example of this is the Groninger Museum, the Netherlands, of which a former curator wrote that the architecture of the museum 'clearly declares its intention of being considered an artwork itself' (Welkamp, 1999, p. 12).

A museum can be cast as a product, a service or an identity, and it can incorporate multiple functions. Above all, however, it is a place where visitors engage with culture and, seen in these terms, the discussion of museum architecture and interiors cannot be limited to style. As Barker reiterated recently, because museum design and the display is central to the way in which museums shape knowledge, museums can never just be 'neutral containers offering a transparent, unmediated experience'; museum display, according to Barker, 'colours our perception and informs our understanding' (Barker, 1999, p. 8). Museum architecture combines aesthetic, ideological and ethical considerations, expressing a position on the role and function of museums, and how they seek to mediate the experience of visitors. As museums have necessarily responded to changes in society, these issues have been more comprehensively addressed, with much greater awareness of visitor behaviour. Sophisticated interior design considers a range of psychological, physical and intellectual issues that affect the quality of visitor experiences. This is reflected in the configuration of galleries, passageways and services within museums. A recent theoretical model, for example, incorporates four primary elements: reception and visitor services, 25 per cent; display and exhibitions, 25 per cent; collections storage, 25 per cent; and support services, 25 per cent (Ambrose & Payne 2006, p. 209). This means that half the public space in the museum is reserved for visitor activities other than engaging with exhibits. The exterior too is a critical dimension in the orientation of visitors. Ravelli, for example, has described how the architectural practices of 'framing' and 'coding orientation' work to define the particular 'face' of a museum, and to actively prime visitors for their experiences within (Ravelli, 2006, p. 142).

Architecture and interior design now shape museum visitor experiences within a more market sensitive paradigm. Museum architecture often expresses the desire of societies to broaden audiences and to embrace programmes other than those for which they were traditionally distinguished from other organizations. In this chapter, therefore, we examine some aspects of the history of museums to gain insight into the relationship between architecture and marketing, particularly through the construction of museum identity and the shaping of visitor experiences.

Museum architecture, International Exhibitions and visitor experience

Early public museums evolved from enlightenment principles and were designed to express a scholarly purpose. Archetypical examples are the Altes Museum, Berlin (1830) or the British Museum of the same period. These buildings were influential in establishing a European taste for grand museum architecture in the classical style. This representational type spread to the new world, becoming a convention that, among other things, often reflected the values of scholarship and nationhood. In the 1960s, however, the facade of the venerable British Museum was a target of criticism. An architectural critic considered the severe classical colonnade to be insufficiently inviting to visitors. The mid-twentieth century modernist, Summerson, looked at architecture in terms of form and function, and infamously stated in a 1963 BBC radio broadcast that the British Museum was 'all colonnade'. He suggested that 'there is not a single architectural clue to the building behind it, which so far as the onlooker from the outside is concerned, might almost as well not be there' (Summerson, 1964, p. 42). The architecture of the British Museum was seen to have more in common with a classical temple and where once this was applauded, the appropriateness of this museum archetype was under review, because it failed to project a face, which responded to an increasing concern to broaden museum visitation. It followed that the museums of the twentieth century needed a new identity, one which responded to contemporary concerns.

However, in 2006 (nearly two centuries after it was commenced) the British Museum is a global icon and one of the most visited attractions in London. Underpinning this is the reputation of the organization and its universal attitude to collecting and research. The facade remains as a recognizable symbol of this reputation. Even so, the museum has embraced a new attitude to visitor experience with gusto. This is evident in the substantial interior remodelling of the museum, designed by Sir Norman Foster and finished in 2000. Among other things, visitor experience is now enhanced by an astonishing atrium referred to as the 'Great Court', which has been described as 'a light and airy serene courtyard'. This provides an orientation area for visitors, and gives 'a sense of order and clarity to a once confusing museum experience' (Barreneche, 2005, p. 67).

The new 'Great Court' at the British Museum is perhaps one of the latest examples in a long tradition where the design of museums has been influenced by the International Exhibition movement of the second half of the nineteenth century. International Exhibitions were mega-events, leaving deeply ingrained values that have underpinned both the approach of architects to the framing of visitor expectations in museums and the ways in which visitors may read museum architecture. The influence of International Exhibitions is also relevant because they developed in the same cultural, economic and technological networks, which provided the conditions that also nurtured museums around the world. The results show some of the same characteristics as the contemporary global museum discourse; bearing out Osterhammel and Petersson's contention that, 'globalization' is clearly visible in earlier historical periods (Osterhammel and Petersson, 2005). Most significantly, however, in recognition of the global significance of the International Exhibition movement, The Royal Exhibition Building (1880), Melbourne, is listed as a UNESCO World Heritage Site (UNESCO, 2004).

One of the ways that the International Exhibitions movement influenced attitudes and expectations in museums was through consciously embracing the public. In part this was achieved through consistently showing a fondness for innovative, or at least imposing, architecture. Standing against the more refined tradition of museum architecture, event-oriented International Exhibitions favoured extravagant architecture conceived for popular delight. For example, the 1849 exhibition building in Paris was 'a specially built "Vast parallelogram" of a palace painted outside to look like stone' and was noteable in an English report because 'the gigantic scale of the building necessarily elevates the general effect into something of impressiveness' (quoted in Bonython and Burton, 2003, p. 116). English observers paid close attention to their competition and their response in 1851 was the 'Crystal Palace', the centrepiece of the 'Great Exhibition of the Arts of All Nations', which eclipsed the Paris building in an impressive show of industrial strength and global ambition. The innovative architecture utilized a modularized system of iron and glass on a mega-scale, creating a humungous light-filled greenhouse in Hyde Park, in which, as Hudson later appreciated, the displays were presented 'on a scale and in such a manner which would ensure a large attendance, both from home and abroad' (Hudson, 1987, p. 48). In the event, the exhibition attracted 6 million visitors and generated enough profits for the organizers to establish the South Kensington Museum (now the Victoria and Albert Museum of Art and Design) (Hudson, 1987, p. 48). The new atrium at the British Museum reveals the influence of this trajectory, but it has also been suggested that in more ways than one, the 'Crystal Palace' is the ultimate antecedent of The

Centre National d'Art et de Culture, Georges Pompidou (the Pompidou), Paris, which was designed by architects Renzo Piano and Richard Rogers and opened in 1977 (Newhouse, 1998, p. 193).

The International Exhibition movement left a number of legacies relevant to the nexus between contemporary museum design and visitor experience, evident in museums such as the Pompidou. First, these exhibitions helped to shape consumer behaviour, engendering new ways through which the public could directly engage with material culture. The movement enhanced the status of objects and popularized secular mercantile sites for cultural activity. As Richards has written of the Great Exhibition of 1851:

> [it] prescribed the rituals by which consumers venerated the commodity for the rest of the century. It was the first world's fair, the first department store, the first shopping mall ... the commodity became and remained the still center of the turning earth, the focal point of all gazing and the end point of all pilgrimages.
>
> (Richards, 1990, pp. 17–18)

Secondly, because International Exhibitions ultimately achieved a high degree of global intellectual coherence, their influence on consumer behaviour could not be ignored by museums. As Roche has written, museums 'were qualitatively transformed' as the movement introduced 'a new level of popular recognition of, and access to, institutions [museums] which were effectively closed and elite orientated' (Roche, 2000, pp. 70–1). In 1977, the philosophy that underpinned the design concept of the Pompidou reflected both a desire for openness and a changing conception of the museum's role, as according to the idealistic first director, it aimed to be a place where the 'public becomes creative' (Hulton, in Newhouse, 1998, p. 193). The design of the building reflected this ambition, featuring flexible internal spaces rather than defined galleries, and outwardly encouraged connections with the local urban community. By 1997, this relationship between design and visitor experience had coded the museum with a unique identity, apparently quite successfully, as it was reported that 8 million people had visited the museum in that year, making it Paris' number one tourist attraction (Newhouse, 1998, p. 198).

International Exhibitions encouraged popular engagement in the cultural sphere and shaped consumer behaviour both in the significance accorded to objects and in the language of architecture, and each of these threads is evident in the contemporary discourse around the design and commercialization of museums. However, the success of the International Exhibition movement left another profound legacy which resonates in recent developments in the global discourse concerning the role of museum architecture, because in the wake of the 'Crystal Palace', it fuelled a dynamic competition for the next 100 years at least, in which host city after host city around the globe continued to use the International Exhibition system as a means of civic global branding, like the way cities often use museums. Participating in this trend, Thomas Krens, Director of the Solomon R. Guggenheim Foundation, recently argued that the museum of the twenty-first century should not be defined narrowly by the enlightenment concept of the encyclopaedia. A contemporary definition of 'museum' recognizes diversity and this offers opportunities for the decentralization of museum buildings and the possibility of providing very specific visitor experiences, thus facilitating visitation to new destinations, or, in his words, 'pilgrimage' (Krens, in Van Bruggen, 1997, p. 19).

Global positioning

In response to the brashness of International Exhibitions and their effect on the popularization of cultural activities, many museums remained doggedly committed to their core functions through the twentieth century. Visitor experience was primarily visual and silence was the most notable characteristic of museum interiors. Art museums in particular were principally places of *contemplation*, providing a secure and almost private space where a visitor could look at pictures and other objects, largely on a one-to-one basis, an approach that may also have influenced other types of museums (Marshall, 2005, pp. 170–84). Museum designer Michael Brawne was an exponent and advocate of this approach and, in a seminal book of 1965, he proffered the view that galleries had a sole purpose, which was to 'sharpen the encounter between object and observer, to make possible a communication between artefact and individual'. This orthodox view held that it was the responsibility of museum architecture and display 'to exploit this unique sense of immediacy, this direct encounter between viewer and viewed' (Brawne, 1965, p. 7).

One of the most interesting and clearly articulated architectural expressions of this view was the mid-twentieth century Solomon R. Guggenheim Museum, New York, designed by Frank Lloyd Wright (1956–1959). Wright focused on the relationship between design and visitor engagement. Unlike the British Museum, the extraordinary exterior of this building reveals its internal logic such that according to the architect the 'Walls slant gently outward forming a giant spiral for a well defined purpose; a new unity between beholder, painting and architecture'; the building as a 'frame' in which the internal ambience was created by 'clean beautiful surfaces … all beautifully proportioned to human scale' (Wright, in Brawne, 1965, p. 142). The Guggenheim purposely presented art as a precious commodity and it paid attention to the physical needs of visitors, who were transported to the top of the spiral by elevator:

> Comfortable low seats of the same character are placed conveniently at the base of the structural webs forming the sides of the alcoves. The gentle upward, or downward, sweep of the main spiral-ramp itself serves to make visitors more comfortable by their very descent along the spiral, viewing the various exhibits: the elevator is doing the lifting, the visitor the drifting from alcove to alcove.
>
> (Wright, in Brawne, 1965, p. 142)

Wright was guided by the desire to minimize the effects of 'museum fatigue' and to thereby enhance visitor engagement, one role of museum design. He was however, minimally, if at all, directly concerned with facilitating the interaction that might take place between visitors, something that is now regarded as one significant measure of visitor satisfaction and one thing which has driven change in museum design.

Due to its rational conception and expression of modernity, however, the spiral form of the New York Guggenheim has made it one of the most iconic museum buildings of the twentieth century. This status is something the Guggenheim Foundation has keenly exploited in recent years in its development of a global brand. The foundation has consolidated a branch in Venice and spawned new satellite museums in Berlin, St Petersburg (with the Hermitage) and Los Vegas. The most famous recent addition to the stable is the Guggenheim Museum in Bilbao, Spain (1997) designed by Frank O. Gehry, which is once again highly distinguished for its contemporary architecture and which, according to a report, has turned the northern Spanish industrial town into 'a destination for the globetrotting cultural set' (Barreneche, 2005, p. 7). However, unlike the New York building, the exterior does not in any way reveal its primary purpose as a place for viewing objects; like the Groninger Museum, Guggenheim in Bilbao is designed to be a significant work of architecture. And the momentum continues, as another Guggenheim is planned for Adu Dhabi, which will apparently 'dwarf' the dramatic architecture of its older sibling in Bilbao (Arts Guardian, 2006).

The global expansion of the Solomon R. Guggenheim Museum, New York, is an exceptional example of museum ambition, where contemporary architecture is used to project the organization's commitment to art. The apparent success of this coding has provoked many cities (and museum governing bodies) into pursuing a strategic advantage through architectural branding as a way, writes Barreneche, 'to remain competitive on the global scene' (Barreneche, 2005, p. 8). In this quest the aesthetic diversity in contemporary architectural projects is valued as a sophisticated and appropriate way of providing both local and global branding and market differentiation, and is driven by the observation, as Barreneche writes, that 'crowds come for the building as much as for the objects on display inside' (Barreneche, 2005, p. 8).

The observation that the contents of a museum may not always be the prime attraction for visitors is to some extent born out by evaluation. For example, in 1998, a study found that 19 per cent of visitors to the Pompidou Centre in Paris were solely interested in the views of the surrounding district from the building (Newhouse, 1998, p. 198). In the case of the Guggenheim Museum, Bilbao, the expressive distinctiveness of the building has perhaps exceeded all expectations and, more than any other museum, has fuelled the belief that architecture alone can act as a strong commercial brand and as a primary attraction for museum visitors.

Other new museum projects have benefited from confidence in the global positioning strength of museum architecture and this has offered new opportunities for museum planners to incorporate other kinds of visitor experiences in their designs. This is evident in projects included in a current architectural survey of recent museum buildings. The exhibition 'Museums in the 21st Century: Ideas, Projects, Buildings' opened at the K20 Kunstsammlung Nordrhein-Westfalen, Dusseldorf, in 2006, and will tour in Europe and the USA until mid-2009 (Greub and Thierry Greub Prestel, 2006). It includes 26 recent museum projects from around the world and it is evident in this work that contemporary museum design recognizes the galvanizing social role that museums can have for local communities. For example, the catalogue describes one project included in the exhibition as notable, in part, because it has successfully engendered a space where people meet each other socially (van Schaik, in Greub and Thierry Greub Prestel, 2006, p.64). The privileging of signature museum architecture as the primary face of an organization has been adopted as a global positioning strategy, and although this may have dimmed the visibility of collections, it has offered museum planners the opportunity to provide commercial opportunities, which often seek to respond to more general kinds of consumer behaviour.

Commerce and culture

The International Exhibition movement demonstrated that commerce and culture were successfully integrated, however, in the twentieth century, museums were mostly resilient to mercantile operations, tending to maintain their allegiances to their status as publicly funded and scholarly institutions, with associated core functions. Since the mid-1980s, however, public museums have been forced to become more economically self-sufficient, to be more awake to their competitors and to the varied needs of consumers. As well, however, critical thinkers have also gone further and defined the role of museums in more social terms, asserting that the museum has a responsibility to enhance the wellbeing of society and to nourish communities. An attempt to incorporate these objectives has been reflected in some museum design and marketing projects.

An early response to government pressure in Britain to shift financial responsibility from the public purse to museums themselves is the 1988 watershed 'Ace café' advertising campaign conceived by Saatchi and Saatchi for the Victoria and Albert Museum (V&A). The V&A is a largely government-funded art and design museum, originally established with a mission to use its collections for educational purposes. In this campaign, however, advertisements peppered the London underground, which boldly ignored the collections, stating instead that the V&A had 'an ace café, with quite a nice museum attached'. The campaign subverted expectations; and, for some stakeholders and citizens, both outside and within the museum profession, it was heretical, not only because the museum was seen to be advertising its wares like a commercial business, but also, more importantly, because the campaign was seen to cynically challenge the sanctimonious air with which the museum had become associated. It questioned current museum operations both in terms of the narrow visitor profile and the narrow range of experiences that were on offer. In the museum's defence, Bayley responded in 1989 that *commerce* was, and always had been, part of culture and not something alien to it, observing that:

> Shops and museums have a great deal in common. Urban, predominantly middle class, dedicated to exhibition, committed to consumption, either of images, ideas or goods. Once separated only by the availability of their contents, new attitudes and new technologies tend to erode this distinction between merchandise and collections.
>
> (Bayley, 1989, p. 5)

Indeed, this distinction was further eroded at the time when, in partnership with Conran department stores, the newly constituted merchandising arm of the museum, V&A Enterprises, released a range of bed linen based on William Morris designs held in the collection.

Under this kind of pressure, the core functions of public museums have increasingly been shaped in reference to measures of visitor satisfaction and of economic outcomes, as has been their design. Theorists such as Gurian have recognized these key driving forces, characterized museum visitors as consumers of a cultural experience, and looked with profit at the way in which the design of shopping centres seeks to engage consumers (Gurian, 2006, p. 123). In this respect, she formulated a number of key principles. However, when it comes to the design and function of museum buildings Gurian identified a central problem derived from the responsibility museums have to preserve and display cultural heritage material: she concluded that 'the mission aspired to by many art museums to create a temple of the contemplative ... has an easier correlation with both traditional and contemporary architecture than does the mission to create a welcoming, inclusionary museum' (Gurian, 2006, p. 116). This recognizes the inherent tension between traditional and more diverse museum functions, particularly those seeking to engage with communities in new ways, and reminds us that in order to deliver on all the unfolding expectations, museum planners may be charged with developing quite radical and innovative architectural briefs and designers may be challenged to realize them.

While museums may need to be more responsive to the needs of a broader range of consumers, some people are unsettled by a common approach adopted by museum planners, which is to update physical entrances, the face of the organization. This is often controversial. Core stakeholders, the regular museum visitors, are often sceptical of change, particularly where they see a risk to heritage values, and they demonstrate their strength of feeling in newspapers and magazines. In this example, a letter writer to the *New Yorker* magazine comments on a new addition to the Morgan Library & Museum, designed by Renzo Piano:

> The building may indeed be aesthetically pleasing, but where is the human element? The entryway is cramped, the once agreeable

cafe has disappeared, and while Piano's addition may be no taller, its imbalance in scale overwhelms the intimacy of the older space. Perhaps the conceptual approach to architecture would overlook these criticisms, but only at the expense of the client the design was meant to serve.

(Pomery, 2006, p. 5)

Cultural consumers are often passionate and diverse in their concerns. Their opinions, however, are an ever-pertinent reminder that museum operations have an impossible task if they are aiming to deliver on the entirety of society's expectations.

One way, however, that Gurian has identified of reconciling some aspects of the tension between the traditional core functions of museums (and the audiences associated with these) and the desire to be more open to more diverse visitors and more social forms of engagement is modelled on the idea of 'livable-cities' espoused by Jane Jacobs in the 1960s. Gurian has suggested that people from different segments of the community may use the museum as a site for interaction and creativity if mixed-use spaces were integrated into both museum and precinct design (Gurian, 2006, pp. 99–114). This is a strategy, which was flagged in the philosophical perspective of the Pompidou in the 1970s, and which, in various ways, has been applied more recently to new museum developments around the globe. At Federation Square, Melbourne, for example, signature contemporary architecture dominates the design concept and the site has a bold presence in the central business district. It houses publicly funded museums dedicated to Australian art and to new media; a corporate museum dedicated to horse racing; and a large open air broadcast screen facing onto a large piazza fringed with restaurants. The concept resembles a shopping centre, in that it provides a range of consumer attractions nestled together under one umbrella and designed to appeal to a broad range of audiences. The overall design also seeks to facilitate an interaction between people and the museums, and by providing for the functional needs of consumers in other components of the development, it enables the museums to concentrate on their core functions, the interpretation of cultural heritage material.

An 'inclusionary museum' welcomes visitors to use spaces for experiences other than just for the contemplation of the objects, and it is closely aligned with both social needs and consumer behaviour. It is sensitive to potential audiences both in the services offered and the architectural interventions that are made. A well-considered application of these principles offers opportunities to increase visitation through attracting non-traditional museum visitors.

Conclusion

Museum marketing plans may include a new building and more visitor facilities to address the need for increased visitation, and to shape visitor experiences in more effective ways. This is a strategy which has the considerable advantage of being enormously appealing to both government and private patrons, who often prefer capital works programmes to other kinds of less tangible programmes. It is notable, however, that one of the key reference points for this confidence is the Guggenheim Foundation, a private organization with enormous resources and strong global identity, and that despite the success of some other highly publicized projects, it is unlikely that iconic architecture will necessarily guarantee commercial success. It is more likely that other variable museum characteristics have a significant role to play in how potential visitors make their choices about whether to visit a particular museum and, perhaps more importantly, whether to return again. These variable characteristics may include the quality of the architecture and interior design, the status of particular exhibits, the relevance of temporary exhibitions or the reputation of the museum. They may also include the attractiveness and effectiveness of informal social spaces, such as the cafe, or more structured opportunities for social interaction, such as special events. In the end, however, it is the quality of visitor experience that will surely underpin sustainability, perhaps best measured by evaluating how much people learn about the significance of the cultural heritage material that is on display.

References

Ambrose, T. and Payne, C. (2006). *Museum Basics* (Second Edition). Routledge. London, New York.

Arts Guardian (2006). <http://arts.guardian.co.uk/news/story/0,,1816806,00. ht> (accessed 12 July 2006).

Barker, E. (1999). *Contemporary Cultures of Display*. Yale University Press and The Open University. New Haven, London.

Barreneche, R. A. (2005). *New Museums*. Phaidon Press. London, New York.

Bayley, S. (ed.) (1989). *Commerce and Culture: From Pre-Industrial Art to Post-Industrial Value*. Design Museum and Fourth Estate. London.

Bonython, E. and Burton, A. (2003). *The Great Exhibitor: The Life and Work of Henry Cole*. V&A Publications. London.

Brawne, M. (1965). *The New Museum: Architecture and Display*. The Architectural Press. London.

Greub, S. and Thierry Greub Prestel, M. (2006). *Museums in the 21st Century: Concepts Projects Buildings*. Prestel Verlag. Baxi.

Gurian, E. H. (2006). *Civilizing the Museum: The Collected Writings of Elaine Heumann Gurian*. Routledge. London.

Hebditch, M. (1984). The management of premises. In *Manual of Curatorship: A Guide to Museum Practice* (J. M. Thompson, ed.), p. 498. Butterworths. London, Boston.

Hudson, K. (1987). *Museums of Influence*. Cambridge University Press. Cambridge, New York.

Kim, I. (2000). Art or architecture. In *Designing the New Museum: Building a Destination* (J. G. Trulove, ed.), p. 12. Rockport Publishers. Gloucester.

Marshall, C. R. (2005). When worlds collide: the contemporary museum as art gallery. In *Reshaping Museum Space: Architecture, Design, Exhibitions* (S. MacLeod, ed.), pp. 170–84. Routledge. London, New York.

Newhouse, V. (1998). *Towards a New Museum*. The Monacelli Press.

Osterhammel, J. and Petersson, N. P. (2005). *Globalization: A Short History*. Princeton University Press.

Pomery, T. L. (2006). Design Concepts. *The New Yorker*, 26 June, p. 5.

Ravelli, L. J. (2006). *Museum Texts: Communication Frameworks*. Routledge.

Richards, T. (1990). *The Commodity Culture of Victorian England: Advertising and Spectacle, 1851–1914*. Stanford University Press.

Roche, M. (2000). *Mega-Events and Modernity: Olympics and Expos in the Growth of Global Culture*. Routledge.

Summerson, J. (1964). *The Classical Language of Architecture*. Methuen and Co. Ltd.

UNESCO (2004). World Heritage Centre: the Royal Exhibition Building and Carlton Gardens. Justification for Inscription. <http://whc.unesco.org/en/list/1131> (accessed 15 June 2006).

Van Bruggen, C. (1997). *Frank O. Gehry Guggenheim Museum Bilbao*. Guggenheim Museum Publications.

van Schaik, L. (2006). *Museums in the 21st Century: Concepts Projects Buildings* (S. Greub and M. Thierry Greub Prestel, eds.), p. 64. Prestel Verlag.

Welkamp, A. (1999). It's Loud, It's Funky, It's a Museum. *Museum National*, 8(2), 12.

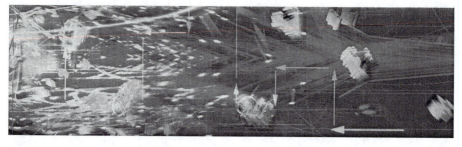

8

Major case study: Internet marketing at Maningrida Arts and Culture, 1995–2006

Megan Cardamone

We are new people. We new people have changed things.
(John Mawurndjul, MAC artist, 2004)

Since 1994, electronic media has unlocked possibilities for marketing Australian Indigenous art. In the 1990s, Aboriginal community art centres in remote locations experienced a renewed demand for high-quality authentic Indigenous art and were ideally positioned to exploit some of the key characteristics of new media tools—speed, reach, interactivity and multimedia capacity. Maningrida Arts and Culture (MAC) was the first Aboriginal-owned art centre to have a website and indeed one of the earliest organizational web presences in Australia. MAC has the characteristics of both cultural museum and art gallery, in that it works to represent artists, preserve performed and material culture, as well as exhibiting, retailing and wholesaling fine art.

MAC's major challenges include overcoming its remote location, maintaining quality and reputation, and maximizing returns to artists. This case study discusses the evolution of that website, the role of e-mail and the instructive experiences of its creators, in the continuing evolution of effective electronic marketing at MAC.

Electronic tools, such as the Internet-based World Wide Web, are most successful when they are used in direct service of an organization's needs and objectives (King and Kramer, 1984). E-tools are also most successful when the correct tool is used for each task (Rice, 1992). MAC objectives are typical of arts organizations in that they include cultural and economic considerations. While MAC had always maintained both sets of objectives, changes in the website demonstrate changing emphasis at different periods. Not only was the first MAC website a pioneering presence on the Web, but evaluation and revision of the site's role and performance has also been an ongoing consideration. The website was established in 1995. It has been revised and upgraded three times; first in 1998, again in 2000 and the third and the last upgrade occurred in 2003.

An important aim of MAC is to generate economic returns for artists. When formally established around 1970, MAC was intended as a source of employment and income, rather than as a cultural or political exercise (Altman, 2004). MAC's 2000 and 2003 business plans advocate 'efficient marketing of art of high integrity ... to ensure optimum returns to artists' as central to MAC's organizational mission, in addition to 'non-commercial objectives'. In 2006, MAC's director, Apolline Kohen, observed that the art centre's performance was important to the Maningrida community because it was almost the only non-government money coming into the community. The current organizational aspirations of MAC are to 'continue the reputation for high-quality art, and maximize economic returns to artists' (Kohen, 2006).

Remote location and distance from markets are key challenges for MAC. The community of Maningrida is located on the Arnhem Coast in Northern Australia. It is 500 kilometres by road from Darwin and accessible only by air during the wet season, between November and March. MAC is housed in a modern building complex in the township of Maningrida, along with its parent organization Bawinanga Aboriginal Corporation (BAC). As an art centre MAC represents more than 700 artists from the Maningrida community and surrounding region of 10,000 square kilometres (Kohen, n.d.). As a cultural research facility, MAC has hosted Australian and international researchers from visual art, music, linguistics and anthropology fields. It also conducts diverse projects to collect and record artefacts, music, cultural practices and oral histories from the region. The main cash influx to Maningrida (other than government subsidy) is through art centre sales.

A permit is required to visit Maningrida. With a low volume of physical visitation, MAC has always needed to find alternative ways of getting the product in front of buyers. One of the earliest strategies was to establish close relationships with dealers and commercial galleries and to ensure that work by MAC artists frequently appeared in major exhibitions.

Throughout the 1980s, the major method for marketing Aboriginal art was through major exhibitions that occurred overseas, such as 'Dreamings' in New York (1988) and through links and programmes forged with Australian institutions, such as NGV, Museum Victoria and the Museum of Contemporary Art in Sydney.

A more recent strategy has been to use emerging technology, such as electronic mail and the Web, taking advantage of the speed, reach and multimedia capabilities of these technologies. The Commonwealth Department of Communications Information Technology and the Arts (DCITA) proposed that '(through electronic media) physical remoteness has ceased to be the predominant issue in marketing Aboriginal artworks' (DCITA, 2004).

Now the Internet is absolutely imperative at MAC. Ninety per cent of sales are via e-mail with images attached. The website has become a key marketing tool, especially for the overseas market. The Internet has 'rapidly changed traditional business strategies and marketing methods' (Clarke and Flaherty, 2002, p. 147). The adoption of e-business tools gives Australian cultural industries the power to develop new markets and deliver their products and services in innovative ways. It also gives the industry 'the means to project Australian culture to a global audience' (Kemp, 2002).

In 2006, marketing priorities for MAC include a continued focus of exhibitions, travel, lectures and publications and the retail outlet. However, the Internet is an important feature too, especially e-mail communications but also the website (MAC Business Plan 2006/2007 to 2008/2009).

The first website: 1995

In 1995, doctoral student Margaret Carew was undertaking research in Maningrida. She had arrived from Melbourne in 1993 to conduct PhD fieldwork about the Gun-nartpa language (Jordan, 2000). Carew 'noticed how much of Maningrida's art was sold to local *balanda* (white people)—up to $10,000 a month'. Carew believed that sales could be boosted further by presenting the artists and their work on a web page (Murray, 1996).

Seeing the potential benefits for MAC, she volunteered to work with Cultural Research Officer Peter Danaja to establish a web presence and e-mail capacity for the art centre. The strong community involvement that occurred in the development of this first website was central to its success and to the acclaim it received.

It was clear from the first MAC website that the medium was more effective for promotional and educational strategies than for hosting transactions. In fact 'only a handful of bark-paintings were sold at all, and turnover from the site was minimal' (Jordan, 2000).

Interestingly, MAC began to use the website to support a personalized approach to major clients. In 1996, Cultural Research Officer Robert Handelsman began to 'customize private web pages for avid overseas buyers'

(Murray, 1996). This action anticipates the success of later 'individualized-marketing' strategies at MAC.

While the website could be customized for separate clients, MAC soon found that this was not particularly efficient. Customized attention is important, but more appropriately delivered to clients in the form of one-on-one relationships maintained particularly via e-mail. Highly personalized client relationships have also been important at Warlayirti Artists, at Balgo in Western Australia—another successful art centre with a strong reputation (Healy, 2006).

Small businesses which can exploit the Internet most successfully are those with non-standard products; and those targeting niche markets (Swatman, 2000). While standard e-commerce is not particularly suited to fine art, the Internet is ideal for reaching a narrow and highly dispersed market, such as the global audience for Aboriginal art. Kohen agrees that a regular e-commerce site wouldn't work 'because it's very much targeted ... if I ask (staff) to do a photo, I know where it's going' (Kohen, 2006). In 2002, Federal Arts Minister The Hon. Rod Kemp observed that 'the focus of e-business is moving beyond the technology and on to how these tools can make business processes and relationships more efficient' (Kemp, 2002).

Websites and e-mail are complementary tools, each with its own strengths. The MAC website is a great drawcard, but after the point of first contact via the site, MAC maintains close one-to-one relationships with most clients usually via e-mail and phone. With MAC's many overseas buyers, e-mail is particularly useful because it is 'asynchronous'. Unlike with telephone communication, efficient communication is possible across different time zones. Both MAC staff and buyers can attend to a waiting e-mail conversation when it suits them, during their own business hours.

The Internet is also ideal for bringing sellers and buyers of art together in a more efficient manner (Clarke and Flaherty, 2002). Aboriginal art centres (and their coordinators) already fulfil a vital role of cross-cultural liaison or 'brokerage' between buyers and Indigenous artists (Altman, 2005). Technology can directly enhance that brokering role.

The first upgrade: 1997–1998

Around 1997, the Commonwealth Government established the Networking the Nation (NTN) Fund. It aimed to boost economic development in remote and regional areas by increasing digital connectivity and access for remote communities.

By this time, business websites were fairly common and simply having a site was no longer an innovation in itself. The MAC website was still a simple static page and needed an upgrade. In 1998, Fiona Salmon, then Director of MAC, and Adam Saulwick, Cultural Researcher, performed a major upgrade of the site.

The new site was heavily focused on the culture of the region and cultural projects at MAC, such as projects to record oral history and song cycles, and an overview of Maningrida's Djomi Museum, including a user-driven virtual tour function. There were also lists of academic publications about Maningrida's languages, music and art traditions. Dictionaries and learner guides for six languages were developed through MAC and available on the website (BAC Annual report, 2003–2004). The upgraded site was very much about presenting a cultural profile of the region and showcasing the unique attributes of Maningrida—in a sense, a culturally based differentiation strategy. The NTN programme was assisting many other Aboriginal art centres to go on-line, and so differentiation through the website became important for MAC.

The second upgrade: 2002–2003

By 2000, MAC had begun to think more strategically about its website (Jordan, 2000). It wanted to test the sales potential of a website for fine art. In 2002, MAC received over $45,000 through the Commonwealth Government's 'OZeCulture: Making IT Work' program. MAC's grant project 'Remote access: Building the Web into the Core of Maningrida Arts Centre' was focused on positioning the site at the centre of MAC's activities and maximizing the on-line sale potential (Kemp, 2002). Therefore, a key goal was the 'development of a "search and find" function on the website, which will interface with MAC's existing off-line Arts Management System database' (Kemp, 2002). The role as a promotional tool and shopfront for on-line sales was also to be maximized. MAC's Web Manager Kellie Austin was in charge of implementing the programme at MAC.

The new MAC website was launched in 2003 with a new 'DillyBag' quasi-e-commerce section, an on-line store with some artworks linked to information. The website was still without facility for on-line payments, but visitors could click on an 'Enquire' button from a specific product which would dispatch an e-mail as a sales lead for MAC staff to follow up. The website continued to present a large amount of information about artistic practices, the region, upcoming exhibitions, news and awards. The site's new functionality was deemed a success. By 2003, the website generated the majority of new sales leads (up to 70 per cent of all enquiries) (DCITA, 2003).

Future plans

In 2006, current MAC Director Apolline Kohen wishes to see the website upgraded further. The main barrier to this is a lack of resources. Web Manager Kellie Austin left MAC in 2004 and at the time of writing MAC was in the process of recruiting for the role of Web and Marketing Manager. Kohen explains 'it's not that we don't have vision; we don't have time' (Kohen, 2006).

Kohen regularly monitors the number of hits (total files viewed by visitors), pages viewed and visits (number of separate visit occasions by each single user). There were over 1500 'visits' in April 2006, which represents about an average of 53 people looking at the site per day (Maningrida.com, server log, April 2006). However, Kohen explains that the website creates only a small percentage of sales by itself. High-end sales which sustain MAC require close interpersonal relationships and client servicing. Kohen also cites MAC's reputation for quality and integrity as an indispensable ingredient, and one which has been earned and established over many decades. One of the weaknesses of electronic media for business is the lack of trust in buyers' perceptions. The Internet is currently a 'low-trust' medium and this is heightened when the product is expensive and non-standard as in fine arts. Trust must be built through ongoing relationships which can be achieved and maintained using electronic communications tools (Olsen et al., 2001). The importance of 'reputation' for successful Australian arts practitioners has been shown (Van den Bosch, 2005) and this is particularly true in an electronic environment.

Optimizing or marketing the website is the next step for MAC. Part of this means broadening the search terms which will return MAC as a search result. Maximizing the website to support MAC's export objectives is also a priority. This will support aspirations to 'develop international markets as a key opportunity for business growth' (MAC, 2006/2007 to 2008/2009, p. 14). 'Maximizing the website, especially for export and access overseas, that's what we want to focus on for the next 3 years' (Kohen, 2006). MAC also plans to use a live digital video link between the art centre and MAC's retail outlet in Darwin. Kohen (2006) believes that 'people would be so happy to see (inside) the Arts Centre, to see Aboriginal people painting ... I think that people would just love it, and feel a connection that they can't have because they're not in Maningrida'.

References

Altman, J. (2004). Brokering Kuninjku art: artists, institutions and the market. In *Crossing Country: The Alchemy of Western Arnhem Land Art* (H. Perkins, ed.), pp. 173–87. Art Gallery of New South Wales, Sydney.

Altman, J. (2005). Brokering Aboriginal art: a critical perspective on marketing, institutions and the state. Kenneth Myer Lecture (R. Rentschler, ed.), Deakin University, Melbourne.

Bawinanga Aboriginal Corporation (BAC) (2003–2004). Annual report 2003–2004, Maningrida.

Clarke, I. and Flaherty, T. (2002). Marketing fine art on the Internet: issues and ideas. *International Journal of Nonprofit and Voluntary Sector Marketing*, 7(2), 146–60.

DCITA (2003). Maningrida e-commerce case study. <http://www.e-businessguide.gov.au/resources/case_studies> (accessed September 2006).

DCITA (2004). Getting started: an Australian guide to doing business online. June 2004. Canberra.

Healy, J. (2006). The marketing of aboriginal art. Seminar, August 3, Burwood campus, Deakin University, Melbourne.

Jordan, M. (2000). Remote access: Maningrida Arts & Culture and the World Wide Web. *Australian Aboriginal Studies*, 1(2), 84–7.

Kemp, The Hon, R. (2002). Government Boosts Cultural E-Business. Media release (Australian Minister for the Arts and Sport), March 12. <http://www.dcita.gov.au/Article/0,0_5-2_4009-4_103994,00.html> (accessed August 2006).

King, K. and Kramer, K. (1984). Evolution and organisational information systems: an assessment of Nolan's Stage Model. *Communications of the ACM*, 27(5), 466–75.

Kohen, A. (n.d.) in 'Maningrida Fibre Art', Promotional pamphlet, Maningrida Arts and Culture, Maningrida.

Kohen, A. (2006). Personal interview with author, 12 May 2006, at Maningrida Arts & Culture, Maningrida.

Maningrida Arts and Culture (2006). Business Plan 2006/7–2008/9, unpublished business plan.

Mawurndjul, J. (2004). I'm a chemist man myself. In *Crossing Country: The Alchemy of Western Arnhem Land Art* (H. Perkins, ed.), pp. 134–41, Art Gallery of New South Wales, Sydney.

Murray, K. (1996). Voices from the Top End. *The Age*, 17 December, Higher Education section, p. 8.

Olsen, M., Keevers, M., Paul, J. and Covington, S. (2001). E-relationship development strategy for the nonprofit fundraising professional. *Nonprofit and Voluntary Sector Marketing*, 6(4), 364–73.

Rice, R. (1992). Task Analyzability, use of new media and effectiveness: a multi-site exploration of media richness. *Organizations Science*, 3(4), 475–500.

Swatman, P. (2000). Internet for SMEs: A New Silk Road? International Trade Centre Executive Forum on National Export Strategies: Export Development in the Digital Economy. Paper, September. <http://www.intracen.org/execforum/ef2000/db4ps.htm> (accessed November 2006).

Van den Bosch, A. (2005). *The Australian Art World*. Allen & Unwin, Sydney.

9

Major case study: Historic museum 'co-opetition'— the case of the James River Plantations

Sandra Mottner

Along the James River in Virginia in the USA, are a number of large historic houses. Some are in ruins, many are still family homes, and a few are open to the public. A cluster of these homes lies on the north side of the river between historic Jamestown (the site of the first permanent settlement made by the British in 1607) and Richmond, the current capital of Virginia. About an hour's drive takes one from Jamestown (or nearby Williamsburg) to Richmond. While most of these historic houses are still privately owned, often by descendants of the original owners, they operate as if they were museums. All are recognized on the National Register of Historic Places.

The motivation for opening the houses to the public is generally to share an important part of US history and to provide funds with which to maintain the historic sites. Guided tours of the houses, and in some cases outbuildings and grounds, are offered by paid and trained interpreters who are knowledgeable in colonial Virginia history. From the late 1980s through most of the 1990s (the period of this case), four major homes were open to the public: Sherwood Forest, Shirley, Evelynton, and Berkeley. Another major colonial home, Westover Plantation, opened its grounds to the public all year but the house itself only periodically. Sherwood Forest, Shirley, Evelynton, and Berkeley had gift shops that were very similar to museum stores. In fact, two of the store managers belonged to the Museum Stores Association. Some of the houses offered part of their sites for hire for weddings and parties. One of the houses offered a garden centre specializing in English boxwoods, one of the hallmark plantings in Virginia plantation home gardens. A number of smaller historic homes also provided an assortment of tours, bed and breakfast facilities, and dining opportunities.

The owners of the various homes were friendly with one another—in fact some of them were even related to one another. However, when marketing their homes, especially to potential visitors, dealings were cordial but somewhat competitive. An example of this type of competitiveness can be found in promotional material for Berkeley Plantation which featured a quote from *Good Housekeeping* magazine which stated, 'if you only have time for one plantation, Berkeley should be at the top of your list' (*Good Housekeeping*, on Berkeley, 2005). The objective of advertising and other marketing efforts for each of the four major homes generally focused on encouraging visitors to come to that specific site. Each of the major homes had their own brochures and paid to have these distributed at key locations. Since the plantations are located near a number of other historic locations such as Jamestown, Yorktown, Williamsburg, and Richmond, Virginia, and are only about 2 hours away from Washington, DC—the US capital—the likelihood of a visitor deciding to tour one, two, or more plantations was very good; especially if they knew that the plantation homes offered something worth seeing and learning about and were relatively convenient to reach. While some cooperative ventures were undertaken, they were generally the exception rather than the norm.

All of the major houses had at one time or another been the home of a family whose primary livelihood depended on farming. The homes are usually referred to as plantations, a term originally used to define a settlement in a new place. However, as time progressed these settlements were more generally regarded as the holdings of one family with a principle large residence and a farm that was worked originally by indentured servants and then later by slaves (National Park Services, 2006). The primary crop was historically tobacco, although today mostly corn, soybeans, and wheat are raised on the remaining farm land. At the beginning of the twenty-first century, as in the past, the region remains mainly rural. The houses generally stand close to the James River which was the historical route of transportation. Many of the houses survived the revolutionary period as well as the US Civil War which was actively fought through the James River area.

Each of the plantations in this region offers a story through its buildings and individual history that reflects different aspects of life in Virginia until the current times. Shirley Plantation, for example, is the home of the Hills and the Carters and has been their home since shortly after Jamestown was settled. The current home, built in 1723, is still home to the family and is much the same as it was originally, including its unique architectural features and its large farm and outbuildings. Berkeley Plantation was the birthplace of a US President, William Henry Harrison, as well as one of his ancestors who signed the US Declaration of Independence from Britain. The family who currently owns Berkeley Plantation are descendants of a man who first saw the home when he was a drummer boy during the Civil War and was encamped on the grounds. Sherwood Forest was the home of President John Tyler and is still owned by his descendants. It has the distinction of being the longest frame home in America. Sherwood Forest has a number of seventeenth century outbuildings forming a complete plantation 'yard' as well as gardens that were laid out in the mid-nineteenth century. Evelynton is unusual among the plantations in that it was originally part of the holdings of William Byrd, who built and owned Westover Plantation. The original house at Evelynton was burned during the Battle of Evelynton Heights, a fierce Civil War skirmish. It is owned today by the Ruffin family whose patriarch, Edmund Ruffin, bought it in 1847. The current house is a colonial revival manor house completed in 1937. Evelynton is arguably one of the most beautiful homes, closest to what visitors imagine an old plantation home looked like; however, although architecturally significant the house does not have a long history. Westover, on the other hand, is an excellent example of Georgian architecture built in 1730 by William Byrd, who founded Richmond. Its classical features, including its gardens, outbuildings, and the house itself form an elegant riverside view of eighteenth century life.

As can be seen from their brief descriptions, each of the plantation houses has a unique 'story'. Each plantation site sought, through their marketing efforts, to exploit their uniqueness thereby maximizing the number of visitors, and thereby admissions, to their location. Revenues were primarily admissions driven in the late 1980s through the early 1990s. Berkeley and Shirley had been open to the public the longest and enjoyed what could be termed a 'first mover advantage' due to longer-term public notice, public recall, positioning in tourist literature, and relationships formed with tour group companies. The other sites had been either open for self-guided grounds tours, not open at all, or sporadically open over the years. As Evelynton and Sherwood Forest reopened their homes to the public they sought to identify themselves with individual visitors and group tour operators as unique properties. The disparate marketing efforts that exploited the uniqueness of each site allowed each of the James River houses to develop a 'brand identity' and a 'brand personality'. Not surprisingly, each of the houses could point to certain key historical personages as key features of their property and personalities with which visitors could identify. Some of these figures had great historical interest such as the presidents associated with Berkeley and Sherwood Forest, Edmund Ruffin at Evelynton (who is purported to have fired the first shot of the Civil War), and the Carter family of Shirley. In addition, some more romantic figures, such as the young bride, Julia Gardiner Tyler at Sherwood Forest; Evelyn Byrd, the tragic daughter of William Byrd of Westover for whom Evelynton is named; and Anne Hill Carter, mother of Civil War hero Robert E. Lee at Shirley, all provided unique personalities as part of the 'brand image' of the houses.

Brochures, the primary marketing tool, were designed independently for each site. Each property worked with various local tourism and visitor centres in Richmond, Williamsburg (adjacent to Jamestown), and Hopewell (across the James River) to differing degrees. The sites did coordinate group tour promotions with the Williamsburg tourism office. Some coordinated advertising efforts were managed in print, although primarily through the efforts of the media. The plantation owners and managers were most interested in garnering the maximum number of visitors to their particular site and pursued mostly individual and somewhat competitive means to attract visitors in the late 1980s.

However, by the early 1990s, the strategies of each of the historic houses began to change. Evelynton, while very beautiful, had less 'history' to offer than others and began to rent out a portion of the house and grounds for weddings and corporate functions while continuing to grow its admissions business. By the mid-1990s revenues from site rentals outstripped those from admissions. Sherwood Forest also diversified into the site rental business but in a more restricted manner. However, the biggest change came when the plantations realized that their combined strength in the marketplace was much bigger than their individual strengths. 'Co-opetition', the joint use of cooperation and competition (Brandenburger and Nalebuff, 1996), allowed the plantations to implement a number of marketing strategies that used their combined strength and allowed the groups of plantations to compete with other much larger historical attractions for visitors. Cooperation, collaboration, and coordination (Brandenburger and Nalebuff, 1996) among traditionally competitive sites leveraged the effectiveness of the marketing efforts of all four of the plantation home sites to a new level.

Cooperative efforts took many forms. One of the first efforts was the production and distribution of a brochure promoting all of the various historic sites in the region including the plantations with their large houses, bed and breakfast sites and smaller plantation homes, and historic restaurants. The synergy of promoting sites to visit, along with places to eat and places to stay, meant that visitors could immerse themselves in the history of the region, often meeting the owners of the properties and gaining first-hand experiences with history. Many visitors developed relationships with particular plantations and people which manifested itself in repeat visits and positive word-of-mouth.

A breakthrough marketing effort occurred when the major plantations collaborated in developing a group ticket that could be purchased for one price and offered a savings for the visitor over individual ticket purchases. This strategy used the incentive of price to promote the idea of visiting the maximum number of sites. Development of the ticket, especially the pricing structure and the coordination of the bookkeeping involved, was time consuming. The impetus for the group ticket was a reflection of the plantations becoming more customer-oriented. Limited customer information, mostly provided through rudimentary research at admission desks and gift shops or first-hand conversations with visitors or information from tour guides, provided some customer-based information that indicated that visitors saw themselves coming to visit 'plantation country' rather than one particular site. Additionally, most visitors were choosing to go to more than one plantation, but often did not go to all four because buying four tickets was prohibitively expensive. Furthermore, buying individual tickets took time away from the tour of each site. So from the visitors' perspective, the group ticket made sense. Being visitor-driven allowed the individual properties to further realize their mission of sharing their history with more people and realizing increased revenues with which to maintain their sites. Visitation grew significantly.

The cooperative group ticket was accompanied by a trend towards more cooperative advertising efforts. It also accompanied a shift in direction as to which larger tourism centre the plantations aligned themselves with. As mentioned earlier, associations with Richmond, Williamsburg (Jamestown), and Hopewell had all been used to attract visitors to individual houses. Research at the admissions desks revealed that Williamsburg near Jamestown was by far the major destination from which visitors arrived at the plantations. Therefore, the plantations refocused their media budgets to focus more heavily on one market while maintaining a lesser presence in the other two markets.

References

Berkeley Plantation (2005). <www.berkeleyplantation.com/visit.html> (accessed 29 November 2006).

Brandenburger, A. M. and Nalebuff, B. J. (1996). Co-opetition. Doubleday, New York.

National Park Services (2006). James River Plantations. <www.cr.nps.gov/nr/travel/jamesriver> (accessed 29 November 2006). New York.

10

Major case study: Strategic partnerships between museums and corporate organizations—the marriage of the Museum of New Zealand Te Papa Tongarewa and TOWER

Suzette Major and Tamarisk Sutherland

Strategic partnerships between museums and corporate organizations provide an interesting example of the changing nature of the relationship between arts organizations and businesses. Museums, once seen as spaces of high culture removed from commercial interests, are now embracing business practices, such as marketing, to survive and thrive in the new economy. This case study examines a strategic collaboration between the Museum of New Zealand Te Papa Tongarewa and one of its founding corporate partners, TOWER. It considers where these organizations are situated on an evolutionary sponsorship cont-inuum (from one-off philanthropic transactions to long-term integrative collaborations), the benefits that have resulted from the arts/business partnership, and based on this evidence, speculates on how museums have developed towards an acceptance of marketing as a vital component of their arts business in the contemporary context of the creative industries.

Public museums in the early part of the twentieth century were regarded as temples of culture, set apart from wider society, where ritual acts of contemplation and learning took place in sacred, quiet spaces (Pointon, 1994; Duncan, 1995). It was argued that museums fulfilled a strong social role in educating society, as well as holding in perpetuity collection items for future generations. Revenue generation was not formerly a major part of the museum context because museums at this time received extensive support from the state (Hudson, 2004). In short, they did not yet need to become commercially enterprising and generate their own funding through such mechanisms as corporate sponsorship.

However, from the 1960s onwards, the roles of the museum expanded in response to social changes. This renewal and re-invention of the museum in the last 40 years has been the topic of much discussion and debate (Wittlin, 1970; Weil, 1990; Pointon, 1994; Skramstad, 1999; Anderson, 2004). By the end of the twentieth century, museums had entered the new era in which their financial survival had become a real concern for those in the sector, as they continued to experience a decrease in state funding (Karp, 1992). As such, museums have largely turned to business models that include marketing as a way to attract public and private support (Rentschler, 2002; Wallach, 2003).

Te Papa Tongarewa (Te Papa) came into existence during this new era of the commercialized museum. Opened in 1998, Te Papa is New Zealand's National Museum, situated on the edge of Wellington's waterfront in a controversial post-modern building. Since its inception, Te Papa has collaborated with numerous corporate sponsors, particularly in the mounting of large-scale exhibitions. This case study focuses on Te Papa's partnership with TOWER, with particular reference to one such exhibition: 'Henry Moore: A Journey Through Form' (staged in 2002).

'Henry Moore: A Journey Through Form' was displayed in the TOWER Gallery at Te Papa, from 23 February to 4 June 2002, as part of the New Zealand International Festival of the Arts. TOWER was the principal sponsor. The exhibition was conceived by Te Papa in partnership with The Henry Moore Foundation and was curated by Anita Feldman Bennet of The Henry Moore Foundation. It consisted of 15 sculptures by the world-renowned modernist sculptor Henry Moore. This was the first exhibition of Moore's work in New Zealand since an exhibition in 1956 at the Auckland Art Gallery. One sculpture 'Two Piece Reclining Figure: Points' (1969) was located in the plaza outside Te Papa and remaining works were displayed in the TOWER Gallery.

TOWER is a strong supporter of the arts in New Zealand. Along with its support of Te Papa and the TOWER Gallery, TOWER is associated with the TOWER New Zealand Youth Choir/TOWER Voices New Zealand, the New Zealand International Festival of the Arts, the Royal New Zealand Ballet and the Christchurch Arts Festival. TOWER says that it supports the arts because it is an integral part of New Zealand's identity and spirit, and beneficial to all people in New Zealand. According to TOWER the 'national well-being equals corpor-ate well-being' (TOWER Limited, 2006).

TOWER sees itself as a significant part of New Zealand, and this strong asso-ciation with New Zealand is a reason why, according to staff, that TOWER is associated with Te Papa (Fenton-Ellis, personal communication, 16 December 2005). TOWER has a long history in New Zealand, stretching back to the mid-nineteenth century. In 1869, the company was established as the Government Life Insurance Office. In 1987, it was renamed TOWER Corporation. TOWER'S business is focused on providing a comprehensive range of risk insurance and wealth management products to approximately 1 million customers in New Zealand, Australia and the Pacific Islands (TOWER Limited, 2006).

In 1998, TOWER became one of the founding partners of Te Papa, known as a 'corporate founding associate'. The partnership with Te Papa established the TOWER Gallery, a large exhibition space measuring over 800 square metres. The TOWER Gallery has been host to some diverse and highly regarded exhib-itions such as 'Gianni Versace: the re-invention of material', 'The Lord of the Rings Motion Picture Trilogy: The Exhibition' and 'Drawings from The Royal Collection'. TOWER was the principal sponsor of the major art exhibition 'Henry Moore: A Journey Through Form'. TOWER and Te Papa are continuing their relationship.

The success of the Te Papa–TOWER partnership highlights the changing face of the arts–business relationship (Scheff and Kotler, 1996; McNicholas, 2004). Once positioned in opposition, now museums and corporations can be close allies, working together for mutual gain. In this case, discussions with personnel from both sides suggest their relationship is given high regard, with each organization demonstrating a commitment beyond single exhibitions, such as the 'Henry Moore' exhibition, to the ongoing development of a mutu-ally beneficial, long-term partnership.

The extent to which Te Papa and TOWER have developed from a trad-itional transaction-type relationship to an integrated strategic collaboration is demonstrated by Group Sponsorship Manager at TOWER, K. Fenton-Ellis, who states:

> The relationship has developed to such a level that we very easily communicate whether it's by email or telephone, so it doesn't always need to have the formality about it. But we do ensure that we have formality at least once a year.
>
> (Fenton-Ellis, personal communication, 16 December 2005)

Fenton-Ellis further uses the analogy of a marriage to aptly describe the nature of the company's relationship with Te Papa:

> Will the relationship with a sponsorship organisation be a marriage? Well you look at a marriage: a marriage is something that you enter into with a great deal of hope, a great deal of enthusiasm, excitement and a dream for the future. Because marriage is all about the future, it's about that you want to spend time in your life with a certain person or organisation, and you enter with your eyes open, particularly when you are a mature organisation or mature person ... . Fundamentally you are there because you believe in the guiding and base-line philosophy, what drives the organisation, what drives the relationship? The values that you share, the dreams that you share and the aspirations that you share.
>
> (Fenton-Ellis, personal communication, 16 December 2005)

This degree of commitment to the arts–business partnership is evidence of what Austin (2000) calls the 'integrative stage' of strategic collaborations. Austin developed a collaboration continuum to strategically analyse cross-sector collaborations and highlighted how multifaceted relationships evolve over time, passing through a series of stages from philanthropic, to transactional, to an integrative-type partnership. The resources exchanged, benefits received, and ultimately the commitment to the relationship, suggests Te Papa and TOWER to be at an integrative long-term stage of strategic collaboration.

As with a marriage, such commitment brings high expectations, and this is certainly evident with the Te Papa–TOWER relationship. From TOWER'S point of view, Fenton-Ellis comments:

> We've been treated professionally, exceedingly well, and we have expectations. So when you've had that level of service, commitment to the relationship, you expect no less.
>
> (Fenton-Ellis, personal communication, 16 December 2005)

And from a museum perspective, Ellis agrees:

> It's also on a personal basis that brings a corporate into the family at Te Papa, so it offers an opportunity for us to have a friend along the road who is a partner and who is as interested in our ongoing success as we are, who has a high expectation, but we have continued to thrive to deliver on that. So a high expectation is a good thing.
>
> (Ellis, personal communication, 16 December 2005)

The relationship between TOWER and Te Papa has received much recognition and acknowledgment. In 1998, TOWER received the inaugural NBR Civil Sponsorship of the Arts Award (now known as the NBR Sponsorship of the Arts Award) for the portfolio of projects it was involved with at Te Papa.

TOWER won the special merit award with Te Papa for the 'Henry Moore' exhib-ition (Fenton-Ellis, personal communication, 16 December 2005).

The very fact that Te Papa would form such a long-term durable commitment with a corporate organization (and TOWER is only one of many) may have appeared abhorrent only a few decades ago. However, from Te Papa's perspective, the benefits of being associated with a corporate body are extensive and go beyond financial gain. As explained by Ellis:

> The fact that TOWER sponsors us says something about our brand. It says that we are trusted. It actually aligns some of the qualities of the TOWER brand with the Te Papa brand.
> (Ellis, personal communications, 16 December 2005)

The once-held perception that arts and business cannot work together seems to have all but disappeared. In the age of declining state funding, museums such as Te Papa can turn to corporate organizations to assist in their survival and success.

The bringing together of a business mindset with artistic ventures is also a mark of the changing face in the New Zealand arts environment in general (Volkerling, 2000a, b). Under 'creative industries' initiatives, arts and cultural activities in New Zealand are increasingly being considered in economic terms. Since 1999, the New Zealand Labour Government has taken the concept of creative industries to heart, and decided to target the creative industries (alongside Biotechnology and Information and Communications Technology) as a way of developing an 'innovative New Zealand' (Office of the Prime Minister, 2002). A result of creative industries initiatives is that arts and cultural activities are expected to be not only artistically rewarding, but also economically profitable. As a result, alongside the core function of public museums in New Zealand, are an increasing number of commercial ventures, such as gift stores, cafés, visitor-pays guided tours, exhibition audio guides, websites and specific temporary exhibitions as a means to generate funding. In short, the government's focus on the creative industries demands arts organizations be more business savvy and market orientated.

The Te Papa–TOWER strategic collaboration is an example of creative industries ideas at work. Their relationship brings together an arts and culture venture and a commercially driven organization. The success of this partnership, not only for managing to stage an internationally renowned exhibition, such as 'Henry Moore: A Journey Through Form', but also in terms of their ongoing collaboration, hints at how museums can meet the challenges of this new era. In response to declining state funding, as well as the need to be economically driven in light of creative industries initiatives, museums such as Te Papa are shifting their orientation to the market and the corporate world (Museum of New Zealand Te Papa Tongarewa, 2004, 2005). In this way, they are less a temple of culture and more a partner to society. By working with corporate organizations, museums can not only survive, but also thrive in today's marketplace.

References

Anderson, G. (2004). Introduction: reinventing the museum. *Reinventing the Museum: Historical and Contemporary Perspectives on the Paradigm Shift.* Altamira Press.

Austin, J. E. (2000). *The Collaboration Challenge.* John Wiley & Sons.

Duncan, C. (1995). *Civilising Rituals: Inside Public Art Museums.* Routledge.

Ellis, B. (2005). Personal communication, 16 December.

Fenton-Ellis, K. (2005) Personal communication, 16 December.

Hudson, K. (2004). The museum refuses to stand still. In *Museum Studies: An Anthology of Contexts* (B. Messias Carbonell, ed.), pp. 85–91, Blackwell Publishing Limited.

Karp, I. (1992). Introduction: museums and communities: the politics of public culture. In *Museums and Communities: The Politics of Public Culture* (I. Karp and S. Lavine, eds.), pp. 1–17, Smithsonian Institution Press.

McNicholas, B. (2004). Arts, culture and business: a relationship transformation, a nascent field. *International Journal of Arts Management,* 7(1), 57–69.

Museum of New Zealand Te Papa Tongarewa (2004). Statement of Intent 2004–2007. Museum of New Zealand Te Papa Tongarewa.

Museum of New Zealand Te Papa Tongarewa (2005). Te Papa Annual Report 1998–2005. Museum of New Zealand Te Papa Tongarewa.

Office of the Prime Minister (2002). Growing an Innovative New Zealand. Government document. New Zealand.

Pointon, M. (1994). *Art Apart: Art Institutions and Ideology Across England and North America.* Manchester University Press.

Rentschler, R. (2002). Museum and performing arts marketing: the age of discovery. *Journal of Arts Management, Law, and Society,* 32(1), 7–15.

Scheff, J. and Kotler, P. (1996). How the arts can prosper through strategic collaborations. *Harvard Business Review,* 74(1), 52–62.

Skramstad, H. (1999). An agenda for museums in the twenty-first century. In *Reinventing the Museum: Historical and Contemporary Perspectives on the Paradigm Shift* (G. Anderson, ed.) (2004), pp. 118–32, Altamira Press.

TOWER Limited (2006). Company Report 2006.

Wallach, A. (2003). Norman Rockwell at the Guggenheim. In *Art and Its Publics: Museum Studies at the Millennium* (A. McClellan, ed.), pp. 96–115, Blackwell Publishing Ltd.

Weil, S. E. (1990). Rethinking the museum: an emerging new paradigm. In *Reinventing the Museum: Historical and Contemporary Perspectives on the Paradigm Shift* (G. Anderson, ed.) (2004), pp. 74–79, Altamira Press.

Wittlin, A. (1970). A twelve point program for museum renewal. In *Reinventing the Museum: Historical and Contemporary Perspectives on the Paradigm Shift* (G. Anderson, ed.) (2004), pp. 44–60, Altamira Press.

Volkerling, M. (2000a). Heart of the Nation: A Cultural Strategy for Aotearoa New Zealand. Joint project with McDermott Miller, commissioned by the Minister for Culture and Heritage.

Volkerling, M. (2000b). From Cool Britannia to Hot Nation: Creative Industries Policies in Europe, Canada and New Zealand. Conference paper prepared for New Technologies, Arts and Politics Summer School on Cultural Policies. 24–26 August.

Index